FUJIFILM X100VI USER GUIDE

Complete Digital Photography Manual
for Beginners on How to Set-Up &
Master your New Mirrorless Camera
plus Tips & Tricks on Videography &
Connectivity

Ivan M. Hurt

TABLE OF CONTENTS

INTRODUCTION: X100VI FEATURES AND SPECS
.... 22

Camera Parts **22**

Top 22

The Back Controls.................................... 24

Front Features 27

Sides 28

Left Side: *29*

Right Side:.. *30*

Bottom **31**

Battery Compartment: 32

Additional Components: 32

DESIGN AND BUILD...**32**

X100VI's image quality advancements!...................**34**

Video Capabilities **35**

File Formats, Film Simulations **35**

Conclusion **36**

CHAPTER 1: GETTING STARTED 38

Attaching the Strap...**38**

Powering Up: Battery and Memory Card.................**40**

Adding Storage: The Memory Card **41**

Taking Out the Battery and Memory Card..............**42**

Important Information About Memory Cards........ 43

Charging the Battery...**44**

MONITORING Your Battery Charge........................ 45

Keeping Your Battery Healthy: Tips and Tricks 46

How to Power on the X100VI.................................**47**

First-time setup steps **48**

Customizing Your Experience: Language and Time Settings **50**

Connecting with your Smartphone.......................**51**

CHAPTER 2: EXPLORING THE X100VI CONTROLS **53**

Finding Your Perfect View: The X100VI's Viewfinder Window..**53**

Seeing Your Shots Clearly: The X100VI's LCD Monitor and Eye Sensor **55**

The LCD Monitor: Finding the Perfect Viewing Angle 56

The Eye Sensor: Your Smart Viewfinder Switcher.. 57

The Focus Stick: Your Targeting Tool **57**

The Shutter Speed Dial/Sensitivity Dial: Controlling Time and Light **59**

Fine-Tuning Your Photos: The X100VI's Exposure Compensation Dial **60**

Freezing the Moment: The X100VI's AEL/AFL Button 61

Seeing Clearly: Adjusting the Viewfinder Focus and Exploring Drive Modes 63
Fine-Tuning Your View (Optional): 63
Exploring the Drive Modes: 63

The X100VI's Command Dials 65
The Front Command Dial: A Multitasking Marvel .. 65
The Rear Command Dial: Partner in Focus 66

Keeping You Informed: The X100VI's Indicator Lamp 68

The Control Ring: Your Customizable Quick Access Tool 70

The MENU/OK button: Navigating the X100VI's Menus Like a Pro 71

Using the Touchscreen 73
the Touchscreen: Understanding the X100VI's Display Modes 74
Silencing Your Settings: Exploring Movie Optimized Control 76
The X100VI's Touch Function Gestures: Customize Your Shooting Experience 77
Mastering Playback with a Touch: The X100VI's Touchscreen Controls 79

The Q Button: Your Gateway to Quick Adjustments on the Fujifilm X100VI 80

X100VI Quick Menu for Movie: Taking Control of Your Videos................ 80

X100VI Quick Menu for Movie: Taking Control of Your Videos................ 82

How to Navigate & Customize the Quick Menu..... 84

Tailoring Your X100VI's Q Menu for Faster Shooting 87

Reprogramming the X100VI's Q Menu for RAW Shooters: Focus on Function 89

The X100VI's Q Menu: A JPEG Shooter's Workflow Companion 91

The Power of the Q Button: Refining JPEGs On-the-Go 92

Mastering the Fujifilm X100VI's Function Buttons: Customization for Efficiency 95

The Default Setup: 95

Customizing Function buttons for Your Workflow. 96

CHAPTER 3: IMAGE QUALITY SETTINGS 99

Image Size Setting: Choosing the Perfect Picture Size 99

Image Quality: Striking a Balance 100

RAW Recording: Going Deep..............................101

Select JPEG/HEIF: Choosing the Right Image Format 102

Film Simulations 103

Color Simulations 104

Black and White Simulations:................................ 105

Advanced Film Simulation Controls 106

MONOCHROMATIC COLOR: 106

GRAIN EFFECT: Adding Film Grain........................ 106

Color Chrome and Color Chrome FX Blue: 107

Smooth Skin Effect: Smoothing Skin Tones:......... 108

White Balance **108**

Custom White Balance.......................................**111**

Color Temperature **113**

Dynamic Range...**115**

D RANGE PRIORITY **117**

Tone Curve **118**

COLOR **119**

Sharpness...**119**

High ISO NR **120**

Clarity..**120**

Long Exposure NR (Noise Reduction) **120**

Color Space...**121**

Pixel Mapping: Fixing Stuck Pixels........................**121**

SELECT CUSTOM SETTING: Recalling Your Custom Presets **122**

EDIT/SAVE CUSTOM SETTING **124**

Building Your Custom Toolkit.............................. 124

Editing Existing Custom Settings 125

Updating your Custom Settings 127

Copying Custom Settings: Duplicating Your Expertise
.... 128

Deleting Custom Settings: Clearing the Decks 130

Renaming Custom Settings Banks: Personalize Your
Workflow... 131

Auto Update Custom Setting: Keeping Your Presets
Fresh.. 132

CHAPTER 4: MASTERING FOCUS: A GUIDE TO AF/MF SETTINGS... 134

Focus Area **136**

AF Mode..**137**

ZONE CUSTOM SETTING......................................**137**

AF-C Custom Settings..**137**

Focus Tracking **140**

Decoding Tracking Sensitivity............................... 140

Speed Tracking Sensitivity: Reacting to Changes in
Speed 142

Zone Area Switching: Prioritizing Focus Within a Zone
.... 143

Pre-Configured Focus Tracking Options (SETS 1-5)
.... 144

Set 6: Customizing Your Focus Tracking............... 146

STORE AF MODE BY ORIENTATION: **147**

AF POINT DISPLAY: **148**

WRAP FOCUS POINT: 149

NUMBER OF FOCUS POINTS: 149

PRE-AF: 150

Mastering Portraiture: Face/Eye Detection Settings
....152

Subject Detection Settings 154

Focus Control with AF+MF 156

Manual Focus with MF Assist..................................158

INTERLOCK MF ASSIST & FOCUS RING...................159

FOCUS CHECK 160

INTERLOCK SPOT AE & FOCUS AREA 160

INSTANT AF SETTING 161

DEPTH-OF-FIELD SCALE 162

RELEASE/FOCUS PRIORITY 162

AF+MF Override: 163

AF Range Limiter: Sharper Focus, Faster AF...........164

TOUCH SCREEN MODE 165

Touch Controls for Focus Zoom on X100VI 167

Corrected AF Frame 169

CHAPTER 5: SHOOTING SETTINGS 171

Sports Finder Mode 171

Pre-Shot Photography..172

Self-Timer: Taking Selfies and Perfecting Timing ... 173

Save Self-Timer Setting 174

Self-Timer Lamp..174

Interval Timer Shooting: Unveiling the Magic of Timelapses..175
Important Considerations for Interval Timer Shooting 176

AE BKT Setting 178

Film Simulation Bracketing (Film Simulation BKT): 179

Photometry: BECOMING A MASTER of Metering ..180

Shutter Types: Capturing Quietly and Achieving Blazing Speeds 183

Flicker Reduction 185

FLICKERLESS S.S. SETTING: Fine-Tuning for Flicker-Free Photos 187

IS MODE: 187

ISO Auto Setting 188

Conversion Lens Options..189

Neutral Density Filter (ND Filter)..........................190

Wireless Communication 190

CHAPTER 6: FLASH SETTING: STILL PHOTOGRAPHY..192

Flash Function Setting..192

Flash Settings...194
   1. Flash Control Mode:...................................... 195
   2. Flash Compensation/Output:......................... 195
   3. Flash Mode (TTL):... 196
   4. Sync (H/1ST CURTAIN or I/2ND CURTAIN): 196

Red Eye Removal 197

TTL Lock: Achieving Consistent Flash.....................198

LED Light Setting..200

COMMANDER SETTING...200

CH Setting..201

Built-in Flash...201

CHAPTER 7: PLAYBACK MENU: MANAGING AND
EDITING YOUR PHOTOS 203

RAW Conversion: In-Camera RAW Conversion Made
Easy...203
   RAW Conversion Settings Explained 205

HEIF TO JPEG/TIFF CONVERSION...........................207

ERASE (Deleting Images) 208
   Deletion Process (FRAME)................................... 208
   SELECTED FRAMES 209
   ALL FRAMES 209

CROP 210

RESIZE..211

Protect: Safeguarding Your Photos 212

Image Rotate: Keeping Your Photos Straight.........213

Voice Memos: Capturing Memories with Your Voice 215

Shining Stars on Your Photos: Using the Rating System on the Fujifilm X100VI 217

Wirelessly Sharing Photos with Your Smartphone. 218
    Filtering Images for Smartphone Transfer 219

Customizing Transfer Button...................................220

Slide Show 222

Photobook Assist: Crafting Photobooks with Ease 222

Creating Print Orders for DPOF Printing (DPOF) 224

Printing Photos Directly to Fujifilm instax SHARE Printers..226

DISP ASPECT (for HDMI Output)............................227

CHAPTER 8: NETWORK AND USB SETTINGS... 229

Connecting Your X100VI to Your Smartphone via Bluetooth 229

AIRPLANE MODE...233

instax PRINTER CONNECTION SETTING 233

Uploading Your Photos RIGHT UP to the Cloud with Frame.io Camera to Cloud 233

Connection Mode: Connecting Your X100VI to External Devices via USB 236

Power Up or Talk It Up: Managing USB Connections with Power Supply/Comm Setting 238

CHAPTER 9: CUSTOMIZING YOUR CAMERA MENUS 240

Which Menus can you Customize 240
The Q Menu: Your On-the-Go Settings Hub 241
My Menu: Your Personalized Control Center 242

Steps to Customize the MY MENU 243
Keeping Your "My Menu" UpDATED 246

Customizing the Q Menu 246

CHAPTER 10: THE SECRET SAUCE OF PHOTOGRAPHY: UNDERSTANDING THE EXPOSURE TRIANGLE 249

Shutter Speed: The Timekeeper of Light 249

Aperture: The Size of the Light Gate 249

ISO: The Sensor's Sensitivity to Light 250

Understanding Exposure Modes 251

Program AE (P Mode): Letting the Camera Take the Wheel 251
Program Shift in P Mode: Fine-Tuning the Auto .. 253

Shutter-Priority AE (S Mode): Taking Control of Motion **254**
Important Tips for Using S Mode: 256

Long Exposures: Your Creativity, Your Style **257**
Time (T) Mode: Long Exposures Made Easy......... 258
Bulb (B) Mode: Ultimate Control 259
Remote Release: Hands-Free Long Exposures 260

Aperture-Priority AE (A Mode): Taking Control of Field DEPTH **262**
Understanding Aperture in A Mode:................... 263

Manual Exposure (M Mode): Taking Full Control .. **264**
Manual Mode: Mastering or Mystery? 265
M Mode: Quality Over Quantity 267

ISO: Adjusting Light Sensitivity............................ **270**

Exposure Triangle & Stop System......................... **271**

Capturing the IDEAL Moment: Mastering Exposure for Action Photos **272**

Metering Modes for Action: LOCATING THE IDEAL Focus **274**
Multi Metering: Your Speedy All-Rounder 275
Center-Weighted Metering: Prioritizing the Center
.... 276
Spot Metering: Focusing on Your Subject 276
Average Metering: A Simple Option 276
SELECTING the PERFECT Metering Mode:............ 277
Link Spot Metering with AF Points 277

Automatic ISO: Helping TO Focus on the Action 278

Default Sensitivity: 279

Max. Sensitivity: 280

Min. Shutter Speed: Controlling Motion Blur in Auto ISO 280

Boost Mode: Supercharge Your Action Photography (if applicable).. 281

CHAPTER 11: DRIVE MODES 283

Burst Mode / Continuous Shooting Mode 284

Use Burst Mode Wisely.. 287

Activating Burst Mode on Your Fujifilm X100VI..... 288

Step 1: Turn on Burst Mode 288

Step 2: Choosing the PERFECT Focus Mode 289

Step 3: Choosing the APPROPRIATE Camera Settings 292

Step 4: Taking the Burst 293

Shutter Types vs Burst Mode 293

Burst Mode Tips 296

HDR Photography: Capturing Scenes with Rich Detail 299

Understanding Dynamic Range 302

Method 1: Adjusting the Scene for Better Capture 302

Method 2: Expanding Your Camera's Dynamic Range 303

Understanding How Dynamic Range Works on Your Fujifilm Camera 304

Unlocking Extra Detail: RAW Files 306

Classic Option: Filters for Landscape Photography 307

Understanding Dynamic Range vs. HDR in Photography 308

Dynamic Range Settings Explained 311

High Dynamic Range (HDR) Settings 312

Choosing Between Dynamic Range and HDR 315

RAW Files and HDR: IMPORTANT INFORMATION YOU SHOULD KNOW 316

Panoramic Photography **318**

What is Panoramic Photography? 318

Taking Panoramas: 318

Tips for Flawless Panoramas: 319

AREAS OF CONSIDERATION When Shooting 320

Adding Artistic Effects with Advanced Filters **321**

Using Advanced Filters 321

Exploring the Built-in Filters 322

Partial Color Filters for Creative Black and White with a Pop 322

CHAPTER 12: UNVEILING THE ESSENTIALS: YOUR FUJIFILM X100VI ACCESSORY KIT **324**

LENS ADD-ONS **325**

Broadening Your Horizons: The Fujifilm TCL-X100II Tele Conversion Lens.. 325

Maintaining Image Quality: *326*

Aesthetics and Convenience: *326*

Performance and Usability *326*

Considering the Downsides: Optical Viewfinder and Alternatives *327*

Recap: TCL-X100II's Strengths and Weaknesses *328*

Expanding Your Horizons: The Fujifilm WCL-X100II Wide Conversion Lens **329**

Maintaining Image Quality: *329*

Practical Considerations: *330*

My Overall Take: *330*

Protectors Filters (PRF-49 / PRF-49S) **330**
Lens Hood (LH-X100): **331**
The Unsung Hero: AR-X100 Adapter Ring **331**

Illuminating Possibilities: External Flashes for Fujifilm X100VI **332**

Fujifilm EF-X500: **332**
Choosing the Right Flash: **333**
The Fujifilm EF-X20 Flash: Compact Powerhouse **333**

Exposure Setting Dial: *334*

Switch for wide panel adjustment: *335*

Mounting Lock Releasing Button: *335*

Wireless Slave Flash Selector: *335*

Fujifilm EF-X60 Flash: Power and Flexibility in a Compact Package **336**

Exposure Control: *337*

High-Speed Sync (FP Mode): *337*

Wireless Flash Freedom: *338*

Optical Wireless Mode: *338*

The Fujifilm EF-42 Flash: A Classic Option for X100 Cameras 340

Versatility and Power: *340*

User-Friendly Controls: *340*

Automatic Convenience: *341*

Manual Flash Control: *341*

Additional Features: *342*

Technical Specifications: *342*

Compared to Newer Flashes: *343*

Fujifilm Wireless Commander EF-W1 343

Radio-controlled wireless communication system: *344*

Versatile Flash Control: *344*

Enhanced Usability: *344*

NAS Compatibility: *345*

Fine-Tuning Flash Output: *345*

Enhance Your Video & Photography with the Fujifilm TG-BT1 Tripod Grip 346

Improved Video Stability: 346

Wireless Convenience (with Bluetooth-compatible X-series cameras): 347

Overall Versatility: 347

Compatibility: 347

Effortless Directional Control: 348

Built for Tough Conditions: 348

Comfort and Convenience: 348

Dual Functionality: 349

Fujifilm Grip Belt GB-001: Simple Yet Effective Camera Hold 349

Enhanced Grip and Security 349

Compatibility 350

Simple and Lightweight Solution......................... 350

Fujifilm NP-W126S Li-ion Battery: Powering Your X-Series Camera 351

Fujifilm Battery Charger BC-W126S: Keeping Your X-Series Cameras Powered Up 352

Fujifilm Leather Case LC-X100V: Premium Protection and Style for Your X100V 353

Protective Elegance 353

Functional Design 353

Overall Value: 354

Camera Case Importance: 354

Beyond Protection: 354

Fujifilm MIC-ST1 Stereo Microphone: Enhancing Your X-series Video Audio 355

Clearer Audio for Your Videos: 355

Compact and User-Friendly Design: 355

Fujifilm RR-100 Remote Release: Capture Sharper Images with Stable Shutter Release 356

Combating Camera Shake: 356

Fujifilm Software Ecosystem **358**

Official Fujifilm Software 359

FUJIFILM X App *359*

FUJIFILM X Acquire *359*

FUJIFILM X RAW STUDIO *359*

Third-Party Software Options 359

Capture One *359*

RAW FILE CONVERTER EX enhanced by SILKYPIX technology *360*

Choosing the Right Software 360

CHAPTER 13: KEEPING YOUR FUJIFILM X100VI RUNNING SMOOTHLY: A TROUBLESHOOTING GUIDE **361**

Power and Battery **361**

Language Barrier? Switching to English **366**

Shooting Issues **366**

Playback Troubles **371**

Connection Conundrums **373**

Wireless Transfer Woes **376**

Miscellaneous Issues **377**

INDEX **379**

BIBLIOGRAPHY **389**

INTRODUCTION: X100VI FEATURES AND SPECS

Ever craved a camera that seamlessly blends classic design with cutting-edge image quality and portability? The Fujifilm X100 series has consistently been dream camera for photographers worldwide, and its popularity is evident by the lengthy waiting lists. Now, the highly anticipated X100VI has arrived! Let's dive in and explore whether this latest iteration lives up to the series' remarkable reputation.

CAMERA PARTS

TOP

The top of your Fujifilm X100VI offers a streamlined layout designed for intuitive control and creative freedom. Let's break down each component and explore how it empowers your photography:

1. Strap eyelet
2. Focal plane mark
3. Hot shoe

4. Sensitivity Dial
5. Shutter Speed Dial
6. Exposure compensation dial
7. Fn1 button
8. On/Off switch
9. Shutter button
10. Microphone

1) Strap Eyelet: This secure loop allows you to attach a neck strap or wrist strap for comfortable carrying and added stability while shooting.
2) Focal Plane Mark: This subtle mark on the top plate indicates the sensor's position within the camera. Understanding this helps you accurately visualize where your image will be captured in relation to external elements like filters or lens hoods.
3) Hot Shoe: This versatile mount expands your lighting options. You can attach an external flash unit for additional illumination in low-light situations, or explore creative possibilities with strobe lights or wireless triggers.
4) Sensitivity Dial (ISO): This dial allows you to adjust the camera's sensitivity to light. Higher ISOs are ideal for capturing fast-moving subjects or low-light scenes, but can introduce grain into your image. Conversely, lower ISOs excel in bright conditions, producing cleaner images. Experimenting with ISO lets you achieve the perfect balance between light sensitivity and image quality.
5) Shutter Speed Dial: This controls how long your camera's shutter remains open, capturing light onto the sensor. Faster shutter speeds freeze motion, ideal for capturing action shots or crisp details. Slower shutter

speeds light enter more, perfect for capturing flowing water, night scenes, or creative light trails.

6) Exposure Compensation Dial: This dial lets you fine-tune the camera's automatic exposure settings. Positive values brighten your image, while negative values darken it. This control offers on-the-fly adjustments to achieve the exact brightness you envision, especially in challenging lighting conditions.

7) Fn1 Button (Function Button): This customizable button allows you to assign a frequently used function for quick access. Options might include white balance presets, focus peaking, or film simulation modes. Having your preferred function at your fingertips streamlines your workflow and keeps you focused on capturing the moment.

8) On/Off Switch: This switch powers your camera on and off. A simple yet essential control, it allows you to conserve battery life when not actively shooting.

9) Shutter Button: This is the heart of your photographic journey. Pressing this button down activates the camera's shutter, capturing a single image. Softly engaging the shutter button before a full press allows you to focus before taking the shot, ensuring sharp results.

10) Microphone: This built-in microphone captures audio during video recording. You can also use an external microphone attached via the camera's hot shoe for enhanced audio quality.

THE BACK CONTROLS

The rear of your Fujifilm X100VI provides intuitive controls for composing, reviewing, and navigating your photographic journey. Let's unlock the potential of each component:

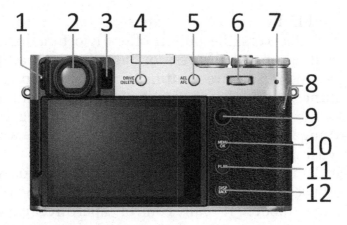

1. Diopter adjustment control
2. Viewfinder window (corrected duplicate)
3. Eye sensor
4. DRIVE/DELETE button
5. AEL (exposure lock) / AFL (focus lock) button
6. Rear command dial
7. Indicator lamp
8. Q (quick menu) button
9. Focus stick (focus lever)
10. MENU/OK button
11. DISP (display) / BACK button
12. PLAY (playback) button

1) Diopter Adjustment Control: This dial allows you to fine-tune the viewfinder's clarity to perfectly match your eyesight. A clear viewfinder is crucial for precise image composition and focusing.
2) Eye Sensor (corrected – not a duplicate): This sensor detects when you bring your eye close to the viewfinder, automatically switching the camera from the rear LCD screen to the viewfinder for a more immersive shooting experience.

3) AEL/AFL Button (Auto Exposure Lock/Auto Focus Lock): This versatile button offers two functionalities depending on a half-press or full press. A half-press locks the exposure settings, ensuring consistent brightness throughout a burst of images. A full press locks the focus on a specific subject, enabling you to rearrange the composition of your shot without refocusing.

4) Rear Command Dial: This dial provides a secondary way to adjust various camera settings, depending on the selected mode. It can control aperture, exposure compensation, or white balance, offering a quick and convenient way to fine-tune your image creation.

5) Indicator Lamp: This small light blinks or illuminates to provide visual feedback on camera status, such as self-timer activation, low battery, or successful focus lock.

6) Q (Quick Menu) Button: This button provides instant access to frequently used shooting settings. It's a customizable menu, allowing you to tailor it to your specific preferences and shooting style.

7) Focus Stick (Focus Lever): This multi-directional joystick allows you to quickly select and shift the focus point around the frame, ideal for off-center compositions or tracking moving subjects.

8) MENU/OK Button: This button grants access to the camera's main menu, where you can explore and adjust a wider range of settings. Pressing the middle of the button confirms your selections within the menu.

9) DISP (Display) / BACK Button: The DISP button cycles through various display options on the rear LCD screen, allowing you to view essential shooting information or a clean image preview. The BACK button navigates back within menus or cancels selections.

10)PLAY (Playback) Button: This button switches the camera to playback mode, allowing you to review captured images and videos.

FRONT FEATURES

The anterior side of your Fujifilm X100VI houses key elements for capturing the world around you. Let's delve into each component and understand its role in your photographic journey:

1. Front Command Dial
2. Fn2 button
3. Viewfinder selector
4. AF-assist illuminator / Self-timer lamp
5. Flash
6. Lens
7. Viewfinder Window

1) Viewfinder Selector Dial: This dial allows you to switch between the optical viewfinder and the electronic viewfinder (EVF) depending on your preference. The optical viewfinder provides a classic shooting experience, while the EVF offers a real-time view of the image with camera settings applied.
2) Lens: The heart of your X100VI, this high-quality lens captures light and focuses it onto the camera's sensor,

creating the foundation of your image. Explore different apertures and focal lengths to achieve creative effects and focus on your desired subjects.

3) Fn2 Button (Function Button): Similar to the Fn1 button on top, this customizable button allows you to assign a frequently used function for quick access. This strategic placement provides easy access while holding the camera for shooting.

4) AF-assist Illuminator / Self-timer Lamp: This small light serves two purposes. In low-light conditions, it briefly illuminates the scene to assist the camera's autofocus system in achieving precise focus. It also blinks as a self-timer reminder when activated.

5) Flash: This built-in flash provides additional lighting when needed, especially in low-light situations. Redirect the flash towards the ceiling or wall for softer lighting effects, or use it directly for dramatic impact.

SIDES

The sides of your Fujifilm X100VI offer additional controls and connections for enhanced functionality. Let's explore each side and its components:

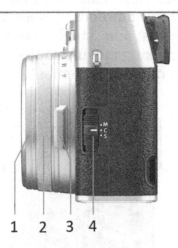

1 2 3 4

1. Front ring
2. Control/Focus ring
3. Aperture ring
4. Focus mode selector

1) Focus Ring: Rotating this ring manually adjusts the focus distance on your subject. This allows for precise control over where you want the image to be sharp.

2) Control Dial (or Rear Control Dial): This dial, also accessible from the back, provides a secondary way to adjust various camera settings depending on the selected mode. It can be a convenient way to fine-tune aperture, exposure compensation, or white balance while holding the camera to your eye.

3) Aperture Ring: This ring controls the size of the lens opening, allowing more or less light to enter the camera. Larger apertures (lower f-numbers) blur the background for a blurred background, while smaller apertures (higher f-numbers) create sharper images throughout the frame.

4) Focus Mode Selector: This dial allows you to choose between different autofocus modes. Options might include autofocus for single subjects, continuous autofocus for tracking moving subjects, or manual focus for full mastery of focus placement.

Right Side:

1. Microphone/remote release connector
2. USB connector (Type-C)
3. HDMI Micro connector (Type D)

1) Microphone/Remote Release Connector: This versatile port allows you to attach an auxiliary microphone for enhanced audio recording during video shooting. Additionally, you can connect a remote shutter release cable for triggering the camera shutter without making physical contact with the camera itself, ideal for minimizing camera shake.
2) USB Connector (Type-C): This port serves multiple purposes. You can use it to transfer captured images and videos to your computer, charge the camera's internal

battery, or connect the camera to a compatible external power source.

3) HDMI Micro Connector (Type D): This port allows you to connect your X100VI to an external monitor or high-definition television for viewing your images and videos on a larger screen.

BOTTOM

The bottom of your Fujifilm X100VI houses essential components that power your camera and provide stability:

1. Cable channel cover for DC coupler
2. Battery-chamber cover latch
3. Battery-chamber cover
4. Tripod mount
5. Speaker

1. Battery latch
2. Memory card slot

3. Battery chamber

BATTERY COMPARTMENT:

1) Battery Latch: This lever secures the battery compartment cover, keeping the power source safely housed within the camera.
2) Battery Chamber: This compartment holds the rechargeable lithium-ion battery that powers your X100VI. Ensure you have a charged battery for uninterrupted shooting sessions.
3) Battery-Chamber Cover Latch: This lever opens the battery compartment cover, allowing you to access the battery and memory card.

ADDITIONAL COMPONENTS:

1) Tripod Mount: This threaded socket allows you to securely attach the camera to a tripod for stable shooting, ideal for long exposures, self-portraits, or videography.
2) Speaker: This built-in speaker allows you to playback recorded audio during video review or hear camera sounds like shutter clicks or beeps.

Note:
The cable channel cover for the DC coupler is not typically a component used during everyday photography. This cover protects a port used for connecting an optional AC power adapter for extended shooting sessions where a battery might not be sufficient.

DESIGN AND BUILD

The X100VI stays true to the series' beloved heritage. It retains the classic, rangefinder-inspired design that photographers adore. While the lens barrel might be a touch longer and the weight slightly increased, these differences are barely noticeable during use. Fujifilm has prioritized both form and function, delivering a camera that's as comfortable and familiar as ever. The robust, weather-resistant body ensures durability for wherever your photographic journey takes you, and the compact size lets you capture fleeting moments on the go without feeling weighed down. This balance between classic design and modern performance is a major win For photographers who give precedence to both style and substance.

Photographer's idea:
While some photographers might prefer a larger grip for extended use, the X100VI's size is ideal for street photography and travel, where discretion and portability are key. However, if you find yourself needing a bit more stability, consider adding a small camera hand grip for enhanced comfort during long shooting sessions.

The X100VI retains the winning formula that photographers have come to love: the super-sharp 23mm f/2 fixed lens, the versatile hybrid optical/electronic viewfinder (OVF/EVF), the handy built-in neutral density (ND) filter, and the all-weather construction – all ensuring you're Equipped for any photographic scenarios scenario. Some photographers might be curious about the battery choice. The X100VI utilizes the NP-W126S battery, opting for size consistency with the previous model and compatibility with existing X100 series accessories. While the newer NP-W235 battery offers increased power, Fujifilm prioritized maintaining the camera's compact design. This decision ensures a familiar form factor and an effortless switch for X100 users, but it's understandable if some power-hungry photographers crave a longer battery life.

X100VI'S IMAGE QUALITY ADVANCEMENTS!

The most significant upgrade is the powerful new 40.2MP X-Trans CMOS 5 sensor, a remarkable leap from the 26MP sensor in its predecessor. This translates to stunning detail in your photos, allowing you to crop and enlarge photographs without sacrificing quality – perfect for capturing those fleeting moments with precision. The improved ISO range, starting at ISO 125, lets you shoot confidently in various lighting conditions, while the maximum electronic shutter speed of 1/180,000 sec offers exceptional flexibility for creative effects, like freezing super-fast motion. While these ultra-fast shutter speeds might be niche for everyday use, they cater to photographers who specialize in capturing action at its peak. The more common 1/4,000 sec mechanical shutter speed remains for those who prefer a familiar and reliable option.

The X100VI boasts a real game-changer – In-Body Image Stabilization (IBIS)! This innovative technology lets you capture sharper images in low-light situations, even at slower shutter speeds. IBIS essentially compensates for camera shake, ensuring crisp photos even when you're shooting handheld. Fujifilm claims the IBIS provides as much as 6 stops of stabilization, and while we weren't able to precisely verify that number, real-world usage suggests impressive results. We were able to capture sharp photos at speeds as slow as 1/16th of a second, and in some well-lit environments, even 1/4th of a second delivered usable images! This constitutes an important improvement for photographers who frequently photograph under low illumination, opening doors to creative possibilities and sharper results. If low-light photography is your forte, or you simply want more versatility in various lighting, the X100VI's IBIS is a major upgrade.

VIDEO CAPABILITIES

The X100VI isn't just for photos anymore! It boasts significant improvements in video capabilities, making it a compelling option for photographers who also dabble in videography. While previous X100 cameras primarily focused on stills, the X100VI offers impressive options like 4K recording at 60 frames per second (fps) and even higher resolution 6.2K recording at 30 fps. These specs might not be groundbreaking compared to dedicated video cameras, but when combined with the powerful IBIS, the X100VI becomes extremely appealing for "hybrid shooters." These are photographers who value portability but also need to capture high-quality video for various projects. In today's video-driven world, the X100VI's versatility is a major asset.

The X100VI is a joy to use for short video clips, opening doors for creative projects that previous X100 cameras might not have been ideal for. While dedicated videographers may find the standard 35mm focal length restrictive, some users might discover this perspective perfectly suited for their documentary-style projects. The combination of 4K/60fps and 6.2K/30fps recording options, along with the X100VI's superb image quality and in-body image stabilization (IBIS), makes it a highly capable hybrid camera for photographers who also aim to record high-quality video on the go.

FILE FORMATS, FILM SIMULATIONS

Fujifilm's renowned Film Simulations are back and better than ever! The X100VI boasts a total of 20 built-in film simulations, including the new Reala Ace. These simulations replicate the essence of classic film stocks, allowing you to achieve a variety of creative styles straight out of the camera. Whether you're an experienced photographer or newly starting, experimenting with these simulations is a fun way to add unique character to your photos.

And to make your life easier, the X100VI now supports the HEIF file format. This format offers superior compression compared to traditional JPGs, meaning you can store more photographs without sacrificing quality – a welcome improvement for photographers who generate a lot of content. With a combination of stunning image quality, diverse Film Simulations, and efficient file formats, the X100VI empowers you to capture and share exceptional photos with ease.

CONCLUSION

So, is the Fujifilm X100VI a worthy successor? The answer is a resounding yes! Whether you're a seasoned professional or an aspiring photographer, the X100VI offers the tools and capabilities to elevate your storytelling through captivating images. It builds upon the beloved design and image quality of the X100 series, while introducing significant improvements in performance, video capabilities, and versatility. The X100VI's compact size makes it an ideal companion for photographers on the go, yet its technical specifications rival much larger cameras. But beyond specs, the X100VI provides a unique user experience that's hard to describe – a true "photographer's camera" that fosters a connection with the creative process. In essence, the X100VI empowers you to capture not just images, but emotions and stories that will resonate with you and your viewers.

As a long-time X100 series user, I can confidently say that the X100VI fulfills every wish I've had for the future of the line. Don't get me wrong, more megapixels are always tempting, but the X100VI's 40MP sensor is more than enough for most photographers. While additional video features might be appealing to some, the X100VI provides a compelling balance between stills and video capabilities without sacrificing its signature compact design. These are minor considerations when you look at the bigger picture – the X100VI represents the culmination of years of refinement, making it a truly mature and complete camera system.

The X100VI is a culmination of innovation, design excellence, and a deep understanding of what photographers truly crave. It's a camera that begs to be taken out and used, ready to capture the world around you in stunning detail and timeless style.

CHAPTER 1: GETTING STARTED

Now that you're familiar with the Fujifilm X100VI's anatomy (refer to the previous chapter for a refresher on parts and functions), it's time to power it up! This chapter will guide you through the essential first steps of prepping your camera for action. We'll cover attaching a strap for comfortable carrying, inserting a battery and memory card for capturing those precious moments, and setting the date, time, and language for proper organization. Finally, we'll explore connecting your X100VI to the Fujifilm XApp for a seamless shooting and sharing experience. Let's dive into getting your camera ready to roll!

ATTACHING THE STRAP

Your Fujifilm X100VI comes with a handy strap for carrying your camera comfortably. Let's get it attached following these steps!

1. **Protecting Your Camera:** Before attaching the strap, take a moment to find the **eyelets** on your camera. These are small metal rings, usually on the sides. The included **protective covers** (small black rings) help prevent the strap from scratching the camera's finish. Simply slip a cover onto each eyelet, with the black side facing the camera.
2. **Opening the Clip:** The strap clips have a clever locking mechanism. Locate the small **clip attaching tool** (usually a thin piece of plastic) that came with your camera. It aids you in opening the clip safely. Find the **strap clip** itself (the metal piece that attaches to the eyelet). Using the tool, gently pry open the clip following the illustration in your manual.

Tip: Hold the clip steady with one hand while using the tool with the other.

3. **Attaching the Clip:** Now that the clip is open, it's time to connect it to the eyelet. Slide the open end of the clip over the eyelet. With the tool still holding the clip open, carefully remove the tool while keeping the clip in place with your other hand. The clip should snap shut around the eyelet. Repeat this process for the other clip and eyelet.

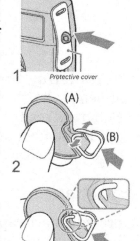

4. **Keeping the Tool Handy:** The tool for attaching clips might seem small, but it's important! You'll need it again to remove the strap. So keep it in a secured location, like a camera bag pocket.

Ready to Attach the Strap? Great! Once you've attached both clips to the eyelets, we can move on to the next step: connecting the actual strap itself.

5. **Attaching the Strap:** Once you've attached both clips to the eyelets, we can connect the actual strap. Feed the **strap through one of the protective covers** and then through the attached clip. Finally, **fasten the buckle** according to the illustration in your manual. **Remember:** Double-check the strap to ensure it is fastened to prevent accidental drops.

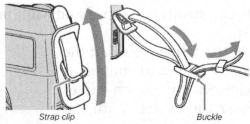
Strap clip   Buckle

6. **Completing the Setup:** That's it! You've successfully attached the strap to your Fujifilm X100VI. Now your camera is ready to be carried comfortably wherever you go. Remember to repeat the procedure for the other eyelet to ensure balanced carrying.

POWERING UP: BATTERY AND MEMORY CARD

Before you start capturing stunning photos, let's get your Fujifilm X100VI powered up! Here's how to place the battery and memory card:

1. **Finding the Battery Compartment:** Locate the cover of the battery compartment located underneath your camera. It usually has a small latch or switch.

2. **Opening the Door:** Slide the latch or switch according to the markings to gently open the cover of the compartment. Remember, it's best to power off your camera before doing this.

Important Reminders:

- **Power Down First:** Always power off your camera prior to opening the battery compartment. This helps protect your images and memory card.

- **Be Gentle:** The compartment cover is there to keep your battery safe, so don't use excessive force when opening it.
3. **Inserting the Battery:** Observe your battery and find the labeled markings for correct orientation. The battery should slide in easily without any force. Make sure it's securely latched in place before closing the compartment.

ADDING STORAGE: THE MEMORY CARD

Having now inserted the battery, let's add some storage for your photos! The Fujifilm X100VI uses an SD memory card (available separately).

1. **Locate the Slot for the Memory Card:** Usually sits right next to the battery compartment.
2. **Prepare Your Card:** Grab your SD memory card and make sure it's oriented correctly. The card usually has a little indent or hole on one corner. This notch should face the same direction as the notch on the slot.
3. **Insert Gently:** Holding the card by its edges, slide it into the slot following the indicated direction. You should feel a slight resistance, and then the card should click into place. **Important:** Don't force the card in – if it's not going smoothly, double-check the orientation.
4. **Closing Up Shop:** Once the card is secure, close the memory card slot cover. The cover should latch shut easily. If it doesn't, make sure the battery is properly inserted as well.

Safety Reminders:
- **Power Down:** As with the battery, it's always a good idea to power off the camera prior to opening the slot for memory card.

- **Don't Force It:** A slight push is all that is needed to insert the card. If you feel resistance, check the orientation and avoid using force.

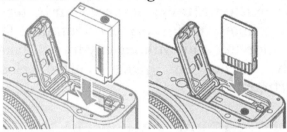

TAKING OUT THE BATTERY AND MEMORY CARD

When you're finished capturing stunning photos, here's how to easily take out the battery and memory card from your Fujifilm X100VI:

Power Down and Open Up:
1. **Turn it Off:** Always ensure the camera is powered down before opening the compartment for the battery. This helps protect your precious photos.
2. **Open the Door:** Find the cover for the battery compartment, usually beneath the camera. Slide the latch or switch according to the markings to gently open it.

Taking Out the Battery:
1. **Find the Latch:** Look for the battery latch inside the compartment.
2. **Press and Slide:** Gently slide the camera's battery out after pressing the slide to the side.

Important Note: The battery may get warm in hot environments. Be careful when handling it in such situations.

Taking the Memory Card Out:

1. **Press and Release:** Locate the slot, typically next to the battery compartment. Press the memory card gently until it clicks and releases slightly.
2. **Slide it Out:** With a slow and steady motion, slide the card out of the slot by hand. Be mindful of not letting it fall by removing your finger slowly.

Hot Card Alert:

If you see a thermometer icon on the camera's screen, it means the memory card might be hot. In that case, wait a few moments to allow it cool before removing it.

IMPORTANT INFORMATION ABOUT MEMORY CARDS

Here are some key things to remember about memory cards for your Fujifilm X100VI:

- **Safety First:** Memory cards are small and pose a choking hazard. Keep them out of reach of children. If a child ingests a card, promptly get medical help.
- **Adapter Use:** If you're using an adapter for a miniSD or microSD card, be sure it's the correct size to avoid getting stuck in the camera's slot. If the card doesn't eject normally, don't force it. See a qualified service center for assistance.
- **Keep it Clean:** Avoid sticking labels or other objects. Peeling them off can damage the camera.
- **Compatibility:** Some memory cards might cause movie recording to stop unexpectedly. It's always best to check your camera's manual for recommended card types. The following are the types of memory cards you can use with your X100VI: SD, SDHC, SDXC, UHS-1.
- **Formatting:** When you format a new memory card, a special folder gets created to store your photos. Here are some important things to remember about this folder:
  - Don't change its name or delete it.

- Don't remove, rename, or edit image files directly on the card using a gadget, such as a PC.
- Use the camera for deleting unwanted pictures.
- To edit or rename photos, copy them to your computer first, then rename or edit the duplicates, rather than the originals on the card. This helps avoid any playback issues on the camera.

CHARGING THE BATTERY

The included NP-W126S battery must be recharged before you can start capturing photos with your Fujifilm X100VI. Here's how to do it:

Getting Ready to Charge:
- **Turn it Off:** Always ensure the camera is switched off before connecting it to a charging source.
- **Know Your Options:** You can charge the battery using either a USB cable or a separate battery charger (available separately).

Charging via USB:
1. **Connect the Cable:** Directly connect your camera to the USB port of your computer with a USB cable. Steer clear of USB hubs or keyboard connections.
2. **Computer Requirements:** For USB charging to work, your computer needs to be compatible with the camera. This means it should have a USB interface and operating system certified by the manufacturer, and it should be turned on during charging.
3. **Charging Time:** A full charge via USB can take around 5 hours, depending on the power production of your computer's USB port.

Important Notes:
- **Sleep Mode Interruption:** If your computer goes into sleep mode while charging, the charging process

will stop. To resume, wake up your computer and disconnect and reconnect the USB cable.

- **Compatibility Notice:** USB charging might not work with all computers due to variations in model, settings, and power output.

Using a Separate Charger (Optional):

For a faster charging option, you can purchase a separate BC-W126S battery charger (not provided alongside the camera). This charger plugs into a household AC power outlet for a more convenient charging experience.

Battery Care Tips:

- While charging times are mentioned, remember that extreme temperatures can affect how long it takes to fully charge the battery.
- For optimal battery life, it's recommended to use genuine Fujifilm batteries and chargers.

MONITORING YOUR BATTERY CHARGE

The Fujifilm X100VI has a handy indicator lamp that lets you know the status of your battery as it charges:

- **Light On:** This means your battery is currently charging.
- **Light Off:** Congratulations! The battery is completely charged and prepared for use.
- **Light Blinking:** Uh oh! A blinking light indicates an error during charging. Refer to your camera's manual for troubleshooting steps in this case.

Important Safety Reminders:

- **Specific Cable:** The provided USB cable is designed for your camera. It's best to use it only with the camera to avoid potential malfunctions in other devices.
- **Keep it Clean:** Avoid sticking labels or objects onto the battery. This could make it difficult or not feasible to take out the battery much later.

- **Battery Safety:** For safety reasons, never short-circuit the battery terminals and always use genuine Fujifilm batteries crafted to fit your camera. Don't tamper with the battery's casing or labels either.

KEEPING YOUR BATTERY HEALTHY: TIPS AND TRICKS

Here are some additional pointers for optimizing your Fujifilm X100VI battery life:

- **Regular Charging:** Unlike some batteries, the X100VI's battery loses charge slowly when inactive. To ensure a full charge when you need it, it's a good idea to charge the battery a day or two before you plan to use the camera extensively.
- **Replacing Old Batteries:** Batteries have a limited lifespan, and after a while, they won't hold a charge as well. If you find that your battery isn't charging fully or doesn't last optimally, it might be time for a replacement.
- **Clean Terminals:** Dirty battery terminals can affect how well the battery charges. Make a habit of occasionally wiping off dust from the connections using a dry material.
- **Temperature Matters:** Extreme temperatures, hot or cold, can hamper the charging process. If possible, try to charge your battery in moderate temperatures for optimal performance.
- **Bluetooth and Battery Life:** Using Bluetooth functions like connecting to your smartphone has the potential to deplete your battery more quickly. Consider switching it off to preserve power.
- **Camera On During Charging:** If you accidentally turn on the camera while it's connected to a USB charger, the charging process will stop, and the USB connection will power the camera instead. This will

actually drain the battery slowly. It's best to turn it off while charging.

- **USB Power Indicator:** The camera will show a "power supply" icon while it's being powered by a USB connection. This is helpful to know if the camera is charging or just using the USB for power.

HOW TO POWER ON THE X100VI

Getting started with your Fujifilm X100VI is easy! Here's how to power it on and off:

- **Find the Switch:** Locate the **ON/OFF switch** on your camera. It's usually a small switch on the top or side of the camera body.
- **Power Up:** To turn on your camera, simply tap the switch to the **ON** position.
- **Power Down:** When you're finished capturing stunning photos, slide the switch back to **OFF**.

Keeping Your View Clear:

By the way, keeping the viewfinder and lens clean is essential for capturing crisp, clear photos. Make sure to remove fingerprints or smudges with a gentle lens cleaning cloth before shooting.

Waking Up from a Nap:

If your camera powers off automatically due to inactivity (a feature you can customize in the settings menu), you can easily wake it back up in two ways:

- **Half-Press the Shutter Button:** Just give the shutter button (the button you press to take photos) a gentle half-press, to activate it.

- **The On/Off Switch:** Alternatively, you can use the **ON/OFF switch** again. Slide it to **OFF** for a moment, then back to **ON**.

FIRST-TIME SETUP STEPS

Let's get your device ready to capture amazing photos by following these first-time setup steps:

1. **Power On!** Slide the **ON/OFF switch** to power on your camera.
2. **Pick Your Language:** The camera will greet you with a language selection screen. Use the navigation controls (buttons or dials) to highlight your preferred language and press the **MENU/OK** button to confirm.
3. **Time Zone Traveler:** Next, you'll be asked to set your time zone. Use the focus lever (a small joystick-like control) to navigate and select the time zone. You can also select whether to enable daylight saving time (DST) using the same control. Once you're happy with your selections, highlight **SET** and tap **MENU/OK** to confirm.

In a Hurry? You can simply press the **DISP/BACK** button to skip setting the time zone. You can always come back and adjust these settings later in the camera's menu.

4. **Setting the Clock:** The final step in this initial setup is setting the camera's clock.

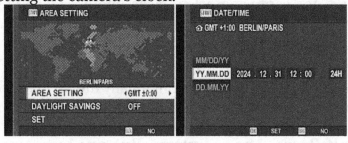

5. **Let's Get Rolling:** Once you've set your time zone (or skipped that step for now), press the **MENU/OK** button to proceed to the next step.

6. **Connect with Your Smartphone (Optional):** The camera might show a QR code on the screen. This code can be scanned using your smartphone's camera app to access a webpage for downloading the Fujifilm smartphone app. This app enables the transfer of images to your phone or even control the camera remotely. Downloading the app is entirely optional. It is a handy tool for sharing photos on the go.

Tip: If you decide to download the app, you can find more information about its features and functionalities in the app's own user guide.

7. **Formatting Your Memory Card (Important!):** Before you start capturing photos, it's essential to get your memory card formatted. Formatting prepares the card to work properly with your camera and organizes it for storing your photos.

Here's how to get it done:

- Use the navigation controls (buttons or dials) to find the **MENU** button. Press it to access the camera's settings menu.

- Look for the **(SET UP)** tab then navigate to it.

- Within the **SET UP** tab, find the option labeled **USER SETTING** and select it.

- Inside the **USER SETTING** menu, scroll down to find **FORMAT**. Highlight it and press the **MENU/OK** button.

A confirmation message will pop up. In order to continue formatting, highlight **OK** and press **MENU/OK** one last time.

Important Reminders:

- Formatting removes all information, so make sure you've backed up any important files before proceeding.
- It's recommended to format regularly, especially after using it within a computer or other gadget. This helps ensure optimal performance and prevents potential compatibility issues.

CUSTOMIZING YOUR EXPERIENCE: LANGUAGE AND TIME SETTINGS

The Fujifilm X100VI allows you to personalize your experience by letting you choose your preferred language and set the correct time and date whenever it's needed. Here's how:

Changing the Language:

1. **Finding the Language Menu:** To open the camera's settings, tap the **MENU** button. Navigate to the 🔧 **(SET UP)** tab using the control buttons.

2. **Exploring Options:** Within the **SET UP** tab, select **USER SETTING**. This submenu contains various camera settings, including language.

3. **Picking Your Language:** Scroll down to find the 🔲🈁**LANG** option and highlight it. A list of available languages will appear. Use the controls to choose your desired language and press **MENU/OK** to confirm.

Setting the Date and Time:

1. **Accessing Date/Time Settings:** Similar to changing the language, press **MENU** to open the settings menu and tap the ![icon] (**SET UP**) tab.
2. **Setting the Clock:** Within the **SET UP** menu, select **USER SETTING**. Scroll down to find **DATE/TIME** and highlight it.
3. **Adjusting Time and Date:** Use the focus lever (the small joystick-like control) to navigate between the minute, hour, day, month, and year options. Once you've highlighted a specific field, utilize the buttons (up and down) to adjust the value. Finally, tap **MENU/OK** to confirm the clock setting.

Reminders and Tips:

- If you remove the battery for a lengthy period, the camera clock will reset to default, and you'll see the language selection screen again after switching on the camera.
- Skipping Steps: The camera might prompt you to confirm skipping certain setup steps during the first-time setup process. Choosing **NO** will ensure you go through all the steps again on turning on the camera some other time. However, selecting **YES** helps you revisit these settings later if needed.

CONNECTING WITH YOUR SMARTPHONE

X100VI can connect to your smartphone via Bluetooth®. This helps you transfer photos to your phone or even control the camera remotely using the Fujifilm app. Here's how to get connected:

1. Pairing Up:

- Activate the camera to make sure Bluetooth is enabled on your smartphone.
- Two methods exist for initiating pairing on the camera:

- ○ **Shooting Mode:** If you're currently in shooting mode, simply press the 🅱 **(Bluetooth button)**.
- ○ **Playback Mode:** Alternatively, if you're in playback mode reviewing your photos, hold down the **DISP/BACK** button. This will also bring up the Bluetooth pairing menu.

2. Navigating the Camera Menu:
- Once you've pressed the Bluetooth button or held the DISP/BACK button, you'll see the Bluetooth menu on the camera screen.
- Use the navigation controls (buttons or dials) to highlight **Bluetooth** and press the **MENU/OK** button to confirm.

3. Pairing Confirmation:
- In the Bluetooth menu, select **PAIRING** and press **MENU/OK** again. This initiates the pairing process between your smartphone and camera.

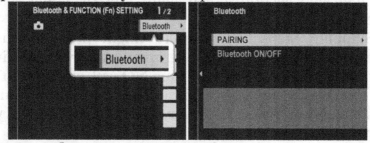

4. Smartphone App Connection:
- Open the Fujifilm application. The app should prompt you to complete the Bluetooth pairing process with the camera. Follow the instructions on your smartphone screen to finalize the pairing.

5. Connection Established:
Once pairing is successful, your camera and smartphone will automatically connect via Bluetooth.

CHAPTER 2: EXPLORING THE X100VI CONTROLS

FINDING YOUR PERFECT VIEW: THE X100VI'S VIEWFINDER WINDOW

The Fujifilm X100VI offers two amazing ways to see your shot: both the optical (OVF) and electronic (EVF) viewfinders. They each have their strengths, so let's explore how to use them and choose the one that suits you best.

The Classic View: Optical Viewfinder (OVF)

- **A classic look (OVF):** This viewfinder offers a more traditional experience, similar to what you might see on a film camera. You'll see the world through the lens, with bright framing lines to guide your composition. Photographers love the simplicity and natural feel of the OVF. **Pro Tip:** Since the OVF shows a slightly wider view than the final photo, you may adjust your framing slightly for critical shots.

- **Sharp and Clear:** The OVF delivers a bright, high-resolution view of your subject, perfect for capturing fleeting expressions or fast-paced action.

- **See Beyond the Frame:** The OVF shows a slightly wider view than the final photo, giving you a little extra wiggle room for composing your shot. **Pro Tip:** Be mindful of parallax, the slight shift that can occur between the OVF and the final image, especially when focusing close-up.

A Digital Companion: Electronic Viewfinder (EVF)

- **A digital view (EVF):** Imagine a tiny high-tech screen showing you exactly what the camera sensor "sees." This is the EVF. It lets you preview your shot with all your camera settings applied, like shutter speed, aperture, as well as film simulations! This is a great choice for precise framing and checking exposure on the fly.
- **You receive what is displayed:** The EVF displays a real-time preview of your image exactly as the camera sensor will capture it, complete with your chosen settings like aperture, shutter speed, and film simulations. This is a fantastic tool for ensuring precise composition and exposure.
- **A World of Information:** The EVF can also show you helpful information like focus peaking (highlighting sharp areas) and field depth preview, letting you see how much of your scene will be focused.

Switching Views:

The handy viewfinder selector switch lets you toggle between these viewfinders with a simple pull. Pull it **anticlockwise** to switch to the **EVF** and **clockwise** for the **OVF**. The camera will also automatically switch to the EVF when you're recording videos.

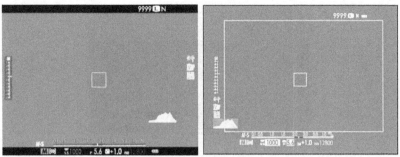

EVF (left - anticlockwise), OVF (right - clockwise)

Optimal Combination of Benefits: Electronic Rangefinder (ERF)

The X100VI has a neat trick up its sleeve for the OVF – a tiny electronic rangefinder (ERF) window! The ERF combines the classic feel of the OVF with the focus assist of the EVF. When activated (by pulling the selector clockwise while in OVF mode), it displays a split-image to help you achieve precise manual focus. This is especially helpful for photographers who enjoy the classic feel of manual focusing. **Note:** The ERF only works when you have the autofocus mode set to 'Single Point'.

So, which viewfinder is right for you? It all depends on your preference! The EVF offers a what-you-see-is-what-you-get preview, while the OVF provides a more natural, immersive experience.

SEEING YOUR SHOTS CLEARLY: THE X100VI'S LCD MONITOR AND EYE SENSOR

The X100VI's tilting LCD monitor is a fantastic tool for composing your shots, reviewing your work, and navigating the camera's menus. Here's a more detailed examination of its features:

THE LCD MONITOR: FINDING THE PERFECT VIEWING ANGLE

The LCD monitor cleverly tilts, giving you more flexibility in how you hold the camera. This can be a lifesaver while taking pictures from strange positions, like low to the ground or high overhead. **Just a heads-up:** Be gentle when tilting and avoid touching the wires behind the monitor. Also, keep your digits or items out of the way to prevent any accidental damage or pinching.

Taking Control with a Touch:

The Liquid Crystal Display is also a touchscreen, letting you interact with the camera in a whole new way. Here are some cool things you can do with a touch:

- **Shoot with a Tap:** Compose your shot and simply touch the screen where you want to focus and capture the image!
- **Focus on Point:** Want to focus on a specific subject? Just tap it on the screen!
- **Menu Magic:** Navigate through the camera's menus and adjust settings with a tap.
- **Movie Maestro:** When shooting videos, the touchscreen offers optimized controls for a smooth filming experience.
- **Playback Perfection:** Review your photos and videos with ease, zooming in and swiping through your creations with a touch.

The X100VI has a clever eye sensor that automatically switches between the viewfinder and the LCD monitor. Here's how it works:

- **Seeing Through Your Eye:** When you raise the camera over your eyes, the sensor detects it and switches to the viewfinder for a classic shooting experience.
- **Smart Sensor:** Remember that the sensor might react to other objects that look like your eye, or have a strong light source focused on it.
- **Tilted for Touch:** The eye sensor won't work if the LCD screen is slanted for touch control. This is to prevent accidental switching while you're using the touchscreen features.

Turning it Off: If you prefer to manually switch between the viewfinder and LCD monitor, you can disable the eye sensor in the camera's menu settings under "🔧 SCREEN SET-UP" > "VIEW MODE SETTING."

So, whether you prefer the classic viewfinder experience or the convenience of the tilting touchscreen, the X100VI offers the perfect way to see your world and capture stunning photos.

THE FOCUS STICK: YOUR TARGETING TOOL

This is a miniature joystick on the back of your camera. Follow this guide to utilize it:

- **Point and Shoot:** Tilt the stick in any direction to move the focus area around the frame. This lets you choose exactly where you want your camera to focus. Perfect for portraits where you want sharp eyes, or landscapes where you want a specific element in focus.

- **Menu Navigation:** The focus stick isn't just for focusing! You can access the camera's menu items and adjust settings with a quick press or tilt.

Customizing Your Focus Stick (Optional):

Want to personalize your focus stick experience? Hold down the center button and you can choose its function. You can also access more detailed settings through the menu (🔧 BUTTON/DIAL SETTING > FOCUS LEVER SETTING). Feel free to experiment and find what works best for you!

Pro Tip: Focus Wrapping

The X100VI offers a neat option called "Wrap Focus Point." This setting determines what happens when you reach the edge of the screen with the focus point. By default, it might stop, but with **"Wrap Focus Point"** enabled, it will jump to the opposite side of the screen, letting you quickly switch focus points. You can adjust this setting in the 🔲 AF/MF SETTING menu.

THE SHUTTER SPEED DIAL/SENSITIVITY DIAL: CONTROLLING TIME AND LIGHT

This handy dial does double duty! Rotate it normally to adjust the shutter speed, a crucial setting that determines the duration of camera's sensor light exposure. Slower shutter speeds allow more illumination, blurring motion for creative effects. Faster shutter speeds freeze action in its tracks.

Taking it Up a Notch: Adjusting ISO (Sensitivity)

Want to capture photos in dim light without blur? Lift the dial slightly and rotate it to adjust ISO, or sensitivity. Higher ISO enables you take images in darker environments, but can introduce some grain. Experiment and find the right balance for your shooting situation.

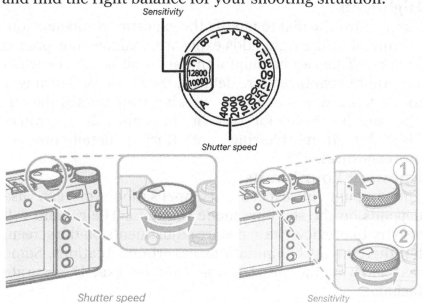

Shutter speed

Sensitivity

FINE-TUNING YOUR PHOTOS: THE X100VI'S EXPOSURE COMPENSATION DIAL

The X100VI's exposure compensation dial is a powerful tool that lets you take even greater control over the brightness of your photos. Here's how it works:

Turning Up the Brightness or Bringing Down the Highlights:

Simply turn the dial to modify the exposure compensation. Turning it to the right adds exposure, making your photos brighter. This can be helpful in darker situations or when you want to capture more detail in the shadows. Turning it to the left reduces exposure, making your photos darker. This can be useful for very bright scenes or to protect highlights from blowing out (losing detail due to overexposure).

Knowing Your Limits:

The amount of exposure compensation you can use depends on the shooting mode you're in. The camera will also try to preview the exposure adjustments on the screen, but there might be limitations in certain situations, Some reasons why the preview may not be exactly accurate include:

- If you set the amount of exposure compensation > ±3 EV
- If the D Range Priority setting is set to Strong or Weak

- If Dynamic Range is set to 200% or 400%

A Peek Through the Viewfinder:
Don't worry if the on-screen preview isn't perfect. You can always get a more accurate idea of the exposure by partially depressing the shutter button. This will give you a preview through the viewfinder or on the LCD monitor.

Unlocking More Control (Optional):
The X100VI offers an extra layer of customization. By turning the exposure compensation dial to "C," you can utilize the front command dial for even finer control over exposure compensation, with a wider range of adjustments between -5 EV and +5 EV. You can also choose what the front command dial controls by pressing its center button.

FREEZING THE MOMENT: THE X100VI'S AEL/AFL BUTTON

Imagine you've found the perfect composition, but the lighting is tricky, or your subject is moving. The X100VI's AEL/AFL button (Auto Exposure/Auto Focus Lock) comes to the rescue! Here's how this handy button helps you capture fleeting moments with perfect focus and exposure.

Locking in the Light and Focus:
1. **Frame Your Shot:** Compose your photo and position your subject within the focus area.
2. **Half Press, Lock In:** With the shutter button halfway pressed, the camera locks both focus and exposure. This

means the focus point and brightness stay locked, even if you recompose your shot or the lighting changes slightly. This is perfect for capturing moving subjects or scenes with uneven lighting.

3. **Capture the Moment:** Once you've locked focus and exposure, just press the shutter release downwards to take the photo.

Important Note: This function with the shutter button only works if you have it enabled in the camera's menu settings under 🔧 BUTTON/DIAL SETTING > SHUTTER AF, SHUTTER AE. Make sure it's set to "ON" to take advantage of this powerful feature.

Beyond Lock and Hold:
While the default setting locks focus and exposure when you hold the AEL/AFL button, you can assign other functions to it! Dive into the camera's menu (🔧 BUTTON/DIAL SETTING > FUNCTION (Fn) SETTING) to explore your options. You can choose to have it control features like white balance or ISO, giving you quick access to these settings.

Spreading the Love: Assigning Lock to Other Buttons:
The AEL/AFL button isn't alone in the locking game. You can assign focus lock or exposure lock to additional function keys. This lets you customize your shooting experience and put important functions within easy reach. Imagine locking focus with one button and adjusting exposure with another for ultimate control!

Separate but Equal: Independent Focus and Exposure Lock

Want even more control? By assigning focus lock and exposure lock to separate buttons, you can lock them independently. This provides ultimate flexibility, especially for situations where lighting or focus might change rapidly.

SEEING CLEARLY: ADJUSTING THE VIEWFINDER FOCUS AND EXPLORING DRIVE MODES

The X100VI offers even more features to enhance your shooting experience. Now let's examine how to modify the viewfinder focus for a crisp view and explore the creative possibilities of the drive modes.

FINE-TUNING YOUR VIEW (OPTIONAL):

If you wear glasses, you may have to modify the viewfinder focus for optimal clarity. Here's how:

1. Locate the diopter adjustment control, usually a small lever near the viewfinder.

2. Gently rotate the control till the data is clearly displayed and in focus.
3. Once adjusted, you're good to go!

EXPLORING THE DRIVE MODES:

The X100VI boasts a variety of drive modes, letting you capture single photos or bursts of images depending on your needs. To access these modes, simply press the DRIVE/DELETE button. Here are some well-known options:

- **Still Image:** This is your classic single-shot mode, perfect for capturing decisive moments.
- **CH (Continuous High Speed Burst):** For fast-paced action, this mode fires off a quick series of images, ideal for capturing fleeting moments like a child's laughter or a bird in flight.
- **CL (Continuous Low Speed Burst):** Want a slower burst rate? This mode is a good choice for situations where you want to capture a sequence of events but don't need the lightning-fast speed of CH mode.
- **BKT (Bracket):** This mode takes multiple photos with different exposure settings, giving you greater adaptability when shooting in tricky lighting areas. You can utilize bracket exposure, white balance, or even both!
- **HDR (High Dynamic Range):** This mode combines multiple exposures into a single image, capturing a wider range of tones and detail, perfect for scenes with high contrast between highlights and shadows.
- **Multiple Exposure:** Feeling creative? This mode lets you overlap multiple exposures in a single image for a unique and artistic effect.
- **Movie:** Of course, the X100VI isn't just for stills! Switch to movie mode to capture stunning high-resolution videos.
- **Adv. (Advanced) Mode:** This mode unlocks a variety of specialized shooting options for photographers who want even more creative control.

THE X100VI'S COMMAND DIALS

The X100VI features two command dials, strategically placed for quick and convenient adjustments. These dials allow you to fine-tune your photos and navigate the camera with ease. Let's delve into what each dial can do:

THE FRONT COMMAND DIAL: A MULTITASKING MARVEL

The Front Command dial can be used to adjust settings, navigate menus, and even review your photos! Here's a breakdown of its functions:

- **Spinning Through Settings:** Simply turn the dial to adjust aperture, exposure compensation, or ISO (depending on your settings). This lets you make quick changes on the fly without having to fumble through menus.
- **Menu Navigation:** Need to navigate the camera's menus? You can also utilize the front command dial to scroll through menus and select options, making it a breeze to find the setting you need.
- **Photo Playback:** During playback, turn the dial to review your captured images, zooming in to check focus or swiping through your portfolio of photos.

Double Duty with a Press (Optional):
By pressing the Front Command Dial directly inward, you can cycle through different functions assigned to the rotation of the dial. This lets you quickly change what you'll use the dial for and put even more control at your fingertips.

Pro Tip: Customize Your Command Dial (Optional):

Head over to the camera's menu (BUTTON/DIAL SETTING > COMMAND DIAL SETTING) to choose what function the dial controls when rotated. You can even set the direction of rotation (clockwise or counterclockwise) to match your preference.

THE REAR COMMAND DIAL: PARTNER IN FOCUS

It works hand-in-hand with the front dial, primarily focusing on adjusting shutter speed. Rotate it to control how long the camera's sensor is illuminated, allowing you to capture sharp action shots or create beautiful blurs for artistic effect.

Menu Maneuvering:
Just like the front dial, the rear dial lets you navigate the camera's menus. Rotate it to highlight different menu items and options, simplifying the process of finding the setting you need.

Shifting the Program (Optional):
In some shooting modes, the rear dial allows you to "shift the program," which means changing the blend of aperture and shutter speed while maintaining the same overall exposure. This is a handy way in modifying your photos without going into full manual mode.

Taking Control of Shutter Speed:

The rear dial shines excels in terms of adjusting shutter speed. Rotate it to control how long the camera's sensor is illuminated. Faster shutter speeds freeze action, while slower speeds blur motion for creative effects.

Quick Menu Magic:
The rear dial can also be used within the quick menu. This menu helps you navigate commonly used configurations, and the rear dial lets you quickly adjust them without diving deep into the main menu.

Focusing on What Matters:
The rear dial plays a role in focusing as well. You can use it to adjust the size of the focus frame, choosing a larger area for easier focusing on still subjects or a smaller point for precise focusing on specific details.

Playback Perfection:
During photo playback, the rear dial lets you zoom in and out on your captured images. Whether you want to check for sharp focus on a specific area or get a thorough examination of the overall composition, the rear dial is your zoom control. It even works differently depending on whether you're viewing a single image or multiple images at once (multi-frame playback).

A Customizable Button (Optional):
Just like the front dial, the rear dial has a hidden talent! On clicking it directly inward, you can activate a role allocated to the "DIAL" function button. This lets you personalize your shooting experience and put even more control at your fingertips.

Focus Exploration (Optional):
If you've assigned the "FOCUS CHECK" function to a button, pressing the rear dial lets you magnify the area of active focus for even improved precision for focus

confirmation. This is especially helpful for critical focus situations.

Pro Tip: Customize Your Command Dials (Optional):
Remember, you can customize the functions of both command dials to match your shooting style. Head over to the (BUTTON/DIAL SETTING > COMMAND DIAL SETTING) menu to choose what functions each dial controls when rotated. You can even set the rotation direction (clockwise or counterclockwise) for a more natural feel.

KEEPING YOU INFORMED: THE X100VI'S INDICATOR LAMP

The X100VI's indicator lamp is your little status update light, keeping you informed about the camera's current state. Let's decipher its different colors and blinks:

Green Glow: Focus Confirmed
A steady green light means you've got focus locked in! This is a good indicator that the person or object you are photographing is clear and ready to be captured.

Green Blinks: Take the Shot (But Be Aware)
A green light that blinks shows when to capture a photo, but there might be a slight hitch. This can be the case when the camera is warning you about a reduced shutter speed, which can cause blur if your camera or subject moves. Proceed with caution but know you can still capture the image.

Green and Orange Blinks: Capturing Memories (Busy Camera)

A combination of green and orange blinks means the camera is busy recording pictures. While it's working its magic, you can capture additional photos, but there might be a short wait between shots. This is also the indicator you see during the uploading of photos to your smartphone or tablet (but only if you've selected photos for upload).

Solid Orange: Hold On, Almost Done

A steady orange light shows the camera is currently recording pictures, and it needs a moment to finish processing the image before you can take another one. Be patient, the wait won't be long!

Orange Blinks: Flash Needs a Recharge

If you see the orange light blinking, it means the flash is charging up and won't be active for another shot. This is temporary, and the flash will be ready again soon.

Red Blinks: Uh Oh, Something's Not Right

A red light that blinks is a warning sign. This might indicate a lens error or a problem with the memory card. Consult your camera's manual for troubleshooting steps.

A Few Extra Notes:

- The indicator lamp turns off on using the viewfinder, so you won't see it while looking through the optical viewfinder.
- You can customize the behavior of the indicator lamp during movie recording in the camera's menu.
- The lamp might also blink green during interval timer photography when the display is off.

THE CONTROL RING: YOUR CUSTOMIZABLE QUICK ACCESS TOOL

The X100VI's control ring is a fantastic feature that puts a variety of functions at your fingertips, allowing you swiftly modify the settings while shooting. Here's how it works:

Taking Control with a Twist:
By turning the control ring, you can access various camera functions depending on how you've customized it.

Customizing Your Control Ring (Optional):
You can choose which function you wish to modify through hitting the control ring choices button (Fn2) or diving into the camera's menu. Here are your options:

- **STANDARD:** This setting lets the control ring function change based on the mode you're in. For example, in aperture priority mode (A), it might adjust aperture, while in film simulation mode, it might cycle through different film simulations.

- **WHITE BALANCE:** Quickly adjust white balance to conform to the lighting, ensuring accurate color reproduction in your photos.

- **FILM SIMULATION:** Capture photos with different creative looks to cycle through various film simulation modes offered by the X100VI.

- **DIGITAL TELE-CONV.:** Boost your effective focal length electronically for a closer view of your subject without needing an additional telephoto lens.

Focusing Manually (Optional):

Regardless of the function assigned, the ring will always be used for manual focus. This lets you precisely control where the camera focuses.

Finding the Perfect Fit:
Experiment with different control ring settings to find what works best for you. You can change it on the fly depending on the shooting situation. Prefer to explore different film simulations? That's a great option too!

THE MENU/OK BUTTON: NAVIGATING THE X100VI'S MENUS LIKE A PRO

The X100VI's menus offer a vast array of settings to customize your shooting experience. This guide will show you how to navigate these menus with ease.

Opening the Door to Settings:
To access the menus, simply press the MENU/OK button. This will display the relevant menu depending on whether you're in still photography, movie recording, or playback mode.

Understanding the Menu Structure:
The menus are categorized by tabs, to facilitate finding the setting you need. Think of them like sections in a book.

Highlighting Your Tab:

1. With the menus displayed, tap the focus lever or stick to the left. This will highlight the tab for the current menu you're in.
2. Now, use the focus stick up or down in order to access tabs until you find the one containing the setting you want to adjust.

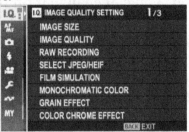

Diving Deeper:
Once you've found the right tab, push the right focus stick. This will move the cursor into the menu itself, where the individual settings and options can be seen.

Command Dials for Smooth Scrolling:
- Use the front command dial to quickly select different menu tabs or scroll through pages within a menu.
- The rear command dial lets you highlight specific menu items within the current menu tab.

Finding the Perfect Setting:
With the menu item highlighted, you can usually adjust the setting using the focus stick or the command dials. Consult your camera's handbook for detailed guidelines on changing individual settings.

A Few Extra Tips:
- The camera might display different menus according to the mode you're in.
- Some menu items might have sub-menus for even more specific adjustments.

USING THE TOUCHSCREEN

The X100VI's touchscreen adds another layer of convenience and control to your shooting experience. Let's explore how to enable touch features and utilize them for both shooting and playback.

Turning on the Magic Touch (Optional):
Touch functionality isn't enabled by default. To activate it, head over to the camera's menu (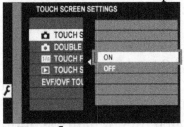BUTTON/DIAL SETTING > TOUCH SCREEN SETTING) and select "ON" for the "TOUCH SCREEN SETTING" option.

Shooting with a Touch:
Once touch is enabled, you can interact with the camera's display in various ways:

- **Focus and Shoot:** Tap the desired focal point for the camera. This is a great way to quickly establish the focal point, especially for off-center compositions. Half-press the shutter button in order to capture the image.
- **Focus Lock:** Lock the focus by long pressing the screen on a specific point. It is helpful in circumstances when the subject might move slightly, and you want to guarantee the focus stays locked.
- **Focus Area Selection (EVF):** Even when using the electronic viewfinder (EVF), leveraging the touchscreen is possible. Go to the menu and select the region that will respond to your touch for focus selection.
- **Face/Subject Detection (Optional):** If you've enabled face or subject detection in the camera's

settings (AF/MF SETTING menu), the touchscreen can be utilized to choose the specific face or subject you want the camera to target. This is helpful for situations with multiple faces or objects in the frame.

Touch for Playback Perfection:

The touchscreen also shines during playback:

- **Swiping:** Swipe your finger across the screen to navigate through your captured images.
- **Pinching:** To enlarge or reduce a specific area of the image, pinch your thumb and index finger together on the screen.
- **Double Tap:** Double-tap the screen in order to enlarge the area where you tapped. This is a quick way to check focus or examine details.
- **Dragging:** While zoomed in, you can move your finger across to view different sections of the picture.

A Few Extra Notes:

- Remember, touch functionality is optional, and you can always turn it off if you prefer traditional button controls.
- The touchscreen might not work perfectly in all situations, especially with wet fingers or gloves.

THE TOUCHSCREEN: UNDERSTANDING THE X100VI'S DISPLAY MODES

The X100VI's LCD monitor offers various touchscreen modes, allowing you to customize your shooting experience. Let's break down what each mode means and guidelines for usage:

Tapping into Different Functions:

By tapping the touchscreen mode indicator on the display, you can cycle through different modes, each offering unique functionalities. Here's a closer look:

- **TOUCH SHOOTING:** This mode is all about simplicity. Just tap the focus area, and the camera will do the rest. Half-press the shutter button to capture the image. In burst mode, your camera will keep taking pictures provided that you hold your finger on the screen.

- **AF (Autofocus):** This mode provides more control over focusing. When in single autofocus mode (S - AF-S), tapping the screen sets the focus on that point. The focus will stay locked till you press the "AF OFF" icon on the screen. In continuous autofocus mode (C - AF-C), tapping the screen initiates focus to continuously adjust focus as the subject moves, you can tap "AF OFF" to lock focus at that point. **Note:** In manual focus mode (MF), tapping the screen will temporarily switch to autofocus, but you can then manually fine-tune the focus via the focus ring.

- **AREA:** This mode lets you choose a specific point for focus or zooming. Simply tap the desired area to move the focus frame (or zoom area) to that point.

- **OFF:** If you prefer traditional button controls or don't want to accidentally activate the touchscreen, you can turn it off using this mode.

Choosing the Right Mode:
The best touchscreen mode based on the way you shoot and your preference. Here's a quick guide:

- **For quick and easy shooting:** Use TOUCH SHOOTING.
- **For more control over focus locking:** Use AF mode.
- **For precise focus or zoom point selection:** Use AREA mode.
- **To disable touchscreen functionality:** Use OFF mode.

The X100VI's "Movie Optimized Control" feature is a game-changer for videographers. It enables you adjust settings quietly while recording, preventing unwanted camera sounds from getting detected via the microphone. You should be aware of the following:

Activating the Silent Treatment:

Two approaches are available for activating Movie Optimized Control:

1. Head over to the camera's menu (🎥 MOVIE SETTING > MOVIE OPTIMIZED CONTROL) and select "ON."
2. Tap the movie-optimized mode button (if available on your X100VI model).

Focus on Filming, Not Clicking:

Once Movie Optimized Control is activated, the camera disables the physical dials for:

*   Aperture
*   Shutter Speed
*   ISO
*   Exposure Compensation

This prevents any clicking or turning sounds from these dials from being recorded in your videos. Don't worry, you can still adjust these settings! The camera employs these methods for silent adjustments:

*   **Command Dials:** Use the front and rear command dials to adjust settings like ISO, shutter speed, and aperture electronically. These dials rotate silently, ensuring quiet operation.
*   **Touchscreen (Optional):** Adjusting certain settings like exposure compensation or focus is possible if your X100VI model has a touchscreen.

Additional Movie Magic:
Movie Optimized Control also provides access to other filming-related settings through the touchscreen or menu:

- **Internal/External Mic Level:** Adjust the recording level of the built-in or an external microphone for optimal audio quality. (External mic level adjustment is accessible when a mic is connected)
- **Wind Filter:** Reduce wind noise for clearer audio, especially useful when shooting outdoors.
- **Headphone Volume:** Control the volume level of your headphones if you're monitoring audio while recording.
- **Film Simulation:** Apply different creative looks to your videos with various film simulation modes.
- **White Balance:** Ensure accurate color reproduction in your videos by adjusting the white balance.
- **IS Mode/IS Mode Boost:** Choose from different image stabilization options to minimize camera shake and create smoother footage.

Disabling the Silence (Optional):
To access the physical dials again, simply tap the movie-optimized mode button (if available) or disable Movie Optimized Control in the camera's menu.

Key Takeaways:
Movie Optimized Control is a powerful tool for videographers, allowing you to adjust settings silently and capture high-quality audio in your videos.

THE X100VI'S TOUCH FUNCTION GESTURES: CUSTOMIZE YOUR SHOOTING EXPERIENCE

The X100VI's touchscreen offers flick gestures that are adaptable to quickly access frequently used functions, similar to pressing function buttons. Let's explore this feature in detail.

Flick and Access:

Imagine making swipes in different directions. These swipes, called "flick gestures," can be assigned various functions. For example, a flick up could display the histogram, while a flick left could change the film simulation mode.

Turning it On:
By default, touch gestures are disabled. To activate them, navigate to the camera menu > 🔧BUTTON/DIAL SETTING and select "ON" for the "T-Fn (TOUCH FUNCTION)" option.

Default Flick Gesture Roles:
The camera comes with pre-assigned functions for each flick gesture:

- **T-Fn1 (Flick Up):** Displays the histogram, a graph showing the tonal distribution of your image.
- **T-Fn2 (Flick Left):** Allows you to cycle through different film simulation modes, which apply various creative looks to your photos.
- **T-Fn3 (Flick Right):** Lets you adjust white balance to ensure accurate color reproduction in your photos.
- **T-Fn4 (Flick Down):** Activates the electronic level, a virtual horizon indicator that helps you keep your camera straight.

Assigning Your Own Roles:
The beauty of touch gestures lies in their customizability. Head over to the camera menu to assign various roles to each gesture. Follow these steps:

- **Choose from a variety of functions:** The camera offers a variety of functions you can assign to the gestures, such as ISO adjustment, focus mode selection, or activating self-timer.
- **Disable gestures (Optional):** If you don't prefer using flick gestures, you can choose "NONE" to disable them entirely.

Important Note:

Assigning functions via touch gestures is unavailable when using optical viewfinder (OVF). Flick gestures only work on activating the LCD display.

Benefits of Customization:

By assigning your most-used functions to the flick gestures, you can gain quicker access to them while shooting. This streamlines your workflow and helps you concentrate on capturing the moment.

MASTERING PLAYBACK WITH A TOUCH: THE X100VI'S TOUCHSCREEN CONTROLS

The X100VI's touchscreen shines during playback mode, helping to navigate through your photos and zoom in on details with ease. Below is an overview of these touch controls:

Turning on the Magic Touch (Optional):

To activate it, if touch functionality for playback isn't enabled by default, navigate to the camera menu > 🔧 BUTTON/DIAL SETTING and select "ON" for the "TOUCH SCREEN SETTING" option.

1. **Navigating Images:** Simply swipe your finger across the screen to move through your captured photos. Swipe left to view the next image and right for the previous one.

2. **Zooming In:** For a thorough examination of specific areas of your image, touch the screen with two fingers then widen the distance between them (pinch-out gesture). This will magnify the area where your fingers touched.

3. **Zooming Out:** In order to refocus, touch the screen with two fingers and pinch them together (pinch-in gesture).

4. **Double Tap for Details:** Double-tap the screen to zoom in to that point. This is a great way to check focus accuracy or examine details.
5. **Dragging for Exploration:** While zoomed in on an image, you can swipe on the display to view various areas of the photo. This lets you explore the entire image at a magnified level.

A Few Notes:
- Remember, touch functionality is optional, and you can always use the traditional playback buttons if you prefer.
- The touchscreen might not work perfectly in all situations, especially with wet fingers or gloves.

THE Q BUTTON: YOUR GATEWAY TO QUICK ADJUSTMENTS ON THE FUJIFILM X100VI

The X100VI's **Q (Quick) Button** is your shortcut to essential shooting settings. With a single press, you can access a menu which helps you adjust various options without diving deep into the camera's main menus.

Activating the Quick Menu:
Simply press the **Q button** located on back of your camera. This will display the Quick Menu within the LCD display.

X100VI QUICK MENU FOR MOVIE: TAKING CONTROL OF YOUR VIDEOS

The list of options displayed in the Q menu will vary depending on what you're doing currently: Stills, Videos or

Playback. The list of items displayed when shooting stills typically include:

1. **SELECT CUSTOM SETTING (Optional):** If you've created custom shooting banks, you can access them here for quick application of saved settings. Otherwise, the current shooting mode will be displayed.

2. **AF Mode (Autofocus Mode):** Choose between different autofocus modes for optimal focus control in various shooting scenarios.

3. **Dynamic Range:** Adjust the camera's dynamic range to record specifics in dark and bright areas.

4. **White Balance:** Ensure accurate color reproduction under different lighting conditions.

5. **High ISO NR (Noise Reduction):** Reduce noise in images captured at high ISO settings.

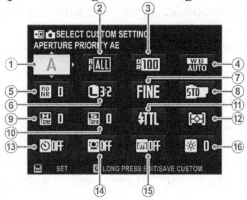

6. **Image Size**

7. **Image Quality:** Select the desired resolution and compression level for your photos.

8. **Film Simulation:** Apply various creative color profiles to your images to get a distinctive appearance.

9. **Highlight Tone**

10. **Shadow Tone:** Adjust the brightness of highlights and shadows in your photos.

11. **Flash Function Setting:** Control the flash mode (on, off, etc.)

12. **Photometry:** Select the metering mode to determine how the camera measures light for exposure.
13. **Self-Timer:** Set a timer for delayed shutter release, helpful for capturing selfies or group photos.
14. **Face/Eye Detection:** Enable or disable face and eye detection for autofocus and exposure prioritization.
15. **Subject Detection:** (Optional on some models) Choose the type of subject the camera prioritizes for focus.
16. **EVF/LCD Brightness:** Adjust the luminosity of the EVF or LCD monitor for better visibility.

Customizing the Quick Menu (Optional):
Hold the **Q button** just a brief moment to access the Quick Menu edit options. Here, you can:
- Rearrange the order of the options for a personalized layout.
- Choose which options appear for rapid access to the settings you use most often.

Keep it Quick and Easy:
The Q Button and Quick Menu are designed to streamline your expertise with shooting. By having these essential settings readily available, you can spend less time navigating menus and more time capturing stunning photos.

X100VI QUICK MENU FOR MOVIE: TAKING CONTROL OF YOUR VIDEOS
The X100VI's Q (Quick) Button becomes even more useful when switching to movie mode. Below is an overview of the movie-specific options you can access and adjust quickly:

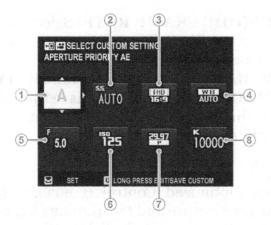

1. **SELECT CUSTOM SETTING (Optional):** Similar to the option for Stills.

2. **S.S. (MOVIE OPTIMIZED CONTROL):** Turn on/off movie optimized controls for silent adjustments during filming (explained in previous section).

3. **MOVIE MODE RESOLUTION/ASPECT RATIO:** Choose the desired resolution and aspect ratio for your video recordings. This can affect file size and video quality.

4. **WHITE BALANCE:** Ensure accurate color reproduction in your videos under various lighting conditions.

5. **APERTURE (MOVIE OPTIMIZED CONTROL):** Adjust the aperture (when Movie Optimized Control is on, use the command dials for silent adjustments). The light output reaching the sensor is regulated by the aperture.

6. **ISO (MOVIE OPTIMIZED CONTROL):** Control how sensitive the camera is to illumination (when Movie Optimized Control is on, use the command dials for silent adjustments). Higher ISO allows filming in low light but can introduce noise.

7. **MOVIE MODE FRAME RATE:** Select the frame rate of your movies. This affects the smoothness of motion and slow-motion capabilities.
8. **WHITE BALANCE COLOR TEMP. (WHEN L SELECTED):** If White Balance is set to "L" (Kelvin), you can fine-tune the color temperature for more precise white balance control.

Remember:
When Movie Optimized Control is enabled (option 2), adjustments for aperture and ISO (options 5 & 6) are made silently using the command dials. Other options are modifiable by tapping the touchscreen or using the focus stick.

Quick Access for Smoother Filming:
The Q Button with its movie-specific options allows you to make crucial adjustments to your video settings without interrupting your filming flow. This is particularly helpful when lighting conditions change or you wish to quickly modify a setting for creative effect.

HOW TO NAVIGATE & CUSTOMIZE THE QUICK MENU
The Q Button on your X100VI is a powerful tool for swiftly accessing and adjusting essential shooting settings. This section offers a step by step process for using the Quick Menu for both viewing and changing settings, along with customization options.

Accessing the Quick Menu:
1. Tap the **Q button**. The Quick Menu will appear on your LCD screen.

Navigating the Menu:
2. Use the **focus stick** to highlight the setting you want to adjust.

3. Rotate the **rear command dial** to modify the value of the highlighted setting.

Quick Access to Custom Settings (Optional):

- Long press the **Q button** as the Quick Menu appears. This lets you jump to the "EDIT/SAVE CUSTOM SETTING" menu for stills or video. Here, you can create and manage custom shooting profiles containing your preferred settings.

Exiting the Quick Menu:

4. Once you've made your adjustments, simply tap the **Q button** again to exit the Quick Menu and return to shooting mode.

Touchscreen Navigation (Optional):

Your X100VI has touchscreen functionality. If enabled, you can use touch controls to navigate the Quick Menu by tapping on the desired setting or swiping to navigate the options.

Customizing the Q Button (Optional):

The Q Button can be even more versatile! Through the camera menu, it's possible to:

- **Assign a function button to the Q button's place:** This enables you to use a function button for the Quick Menu instead of the dedicated Q Button.
- **Assign a different function to the Q Button:** Select from various camera functions to be triggered by the Q Button press, such as ISO adjustment or focus mode selection.

Scaling Up or Down: Choosing the Right Number of Slots (Newer Models):

- Unlike older Fujifilm models that have a fixed 16 slots, newer models allow you select the number of settings displayed in the Q Menu.

- You can select from 4, 8, 12, or 16 slots depending on your needs and how cluttered you prefer the menu to be.
- To adjust the number of slots, head over to the camera menu (🔧 BUTTON/DIAL SETTING > EDIT/SAVE QUICK MENU) for stills or video mode.

Seeing Through the Settings (Optional):
- By default, the Q Menu has a black background. However, you can opt for a transparent background.
- This transparent background is particularly beneficial for JPEG shooters, as it allows you to see the live preview of your image update as you adjust settings in the Q Menu. This provides a visual reference for the impact of your changes.
- To switch between backgrounds, navigate to the camera menu (either 🔧 SCREEN SETTING or 🔧 BUTTON/DIAL SETTING) and locate the "Q Menu Background" option.

Creating Your Personalized Menu (For All Models):
- Regardless of the number of slots you choose, you can program each individual slot in the Q Menu to display the specific setting you use most often.
  - This way, you can prioritize the settings you need quick access to and minimize time spent navigating through the menu.
  - To customize the Q Menu items, access the "EDIT/SAVE QUICK MENU" menu (as described in the previous tip) and choose the slot you want to edit. A list of available settings will be displayed, allowing you to pick one to appear in that specific slot.

Disabling the Q Button (Optional):

If you prefer not to use the Q Button, you can disable it entirely. Navigate to the camera menu and select "NONE."
Remember:
- The specific Quick Menu options might differ depending on the shooting mode (photo or movie).

TAILORING YOUR X100VI'S Q MENU FOR FASTER SHOOTING

The X100VI's Q Menu is a powerful tool for quickly accessing and adjusting shooting settings. This guide personalizes the Q Menu to display the settings you use most often, making your shooting experience more efficient.

1. Long press the **Q button** while in shooting mode. This will display the current Q Menu.
2. The camera automatically displays the Movie and Photo Q Menus when in movie and photo modes.
2. Use the **focus stick** for navigating through the Q Menu options.
3. Once you've highlighted your desired setting, press the **MENU/OK button**.

Alternative Edit Method (Optional):
You can also edit the Q Menu through the camera's main menu. Navigate to (🔧BUTTON/DIAL SETTING > EDIT/SAVE QUICK MENU) for stills or videos.

From Style to Function:
While the default Q Menu focuses heavily on customizing the style of JPEG photos, you can adapt it to your workflow:
- **RAW Photographers:** Remove styling options entirely and replace them with settings you use frequently, like exposure compensation, white balance, or autofocus mode.

- **JPEG Photographers:** Rearrange the styling options (Grain effect, film simulation, etc.) for a more efficient workflow.

Available Options:

The Q Menu can't accommodate every setting, but it offers an assortment of commonly adjusted functions, including:
- Image size and quality
- Film simulation
- White balance
- Focus mode
- ISO
- Aperture (when Movie Optimized Control is off)
- Exposure compensation
- And many more!

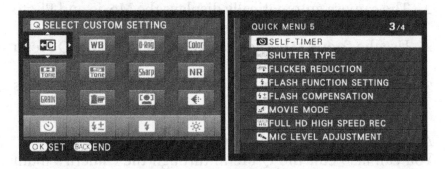

Remember:
- Consult your camera's manual for a complete list of available Q Menu settings.

Benefits of a Customized Q Menu:
- Gain quicker access to the most common settings that you use.
- Streamline your shooting workflow.
- Prioritize settings relevant to your shooting style (RAW vs JPEG).

RAW photography offers the ultimate control over image editing in post-processing software. Since in-camera image adjustments like Film Simulation aren't as crucial for RAW shooters, the Q Menu can be repurposed to prioritize settings that directly impact focusing and image capture. Here are some pointers:

Focus First:

As a RAW shooter, precise focusing is essential. Consider dedicating the uppermost row of the Q Menu to focus-related options, allowing for quick adjustments during shooting:

- **Continuous Focus Tracking Mode:** Switch between various autofocus tracking modes (single point, continuous, etc.) to optimize focus for different shooting scenarios (e.g., static subjects vs. moving subjects).
- **MF Assist Mode:** Enable or disable focus peaking or magnified view for manual focus assist, ensuring critical sharpness.
- **Face/Eye Detection:** Turn on/off face and eye detection autofocus for capturing portraits or prioritizing specific subjects within the frame.

Fine-Tuning the Preview:

- **Electronic Shutter:** Include Electronic Shutter in the Q Menu for quick switching. This can minimize shutter shock in some situations, potentially improving image sharpness.
- **White Balance:** Having White Balance readily accessible allows for on-the-go adjustments to obtain precise color representation in the RAW preview.

Balancing Information and Distraction:

- **Highlight & Shadow Tone and Dynamic Range (Optional):** Consider keeping these settings in the main menu for reference. While not crucial for RAW capture, they can provide a general idea of the image's dynamic range and potential shadow/highlight recovery capabilities in post-processing software.
- **Film Simulation (Optional):** Move Film Simulation to a less prominent location or even the main menu. Since it won't affect your RAW file, it can be employed occasionally for a quick monochrome preview (e.g., Black & White) to aid composition or exposure decisions.

Decluttering for Focus:
- **"None" Option:** Don't hesitate to utilize the "None" option for slots you don't find helpful. This minimizes distractions and keeps the Q Menu focused on the settings you most commonly use.

Remember:
The specific focus options available might vary slightly depending on your X100VI model. Consult your camera's manual for a complete list.

Benefits of a Focus-Centric Q Menu:
By placing these focus options at your fingertips, you can:
- Achieve faster and more precise focus adjustments.
- Adapt your autofocus strategy to different shooting situations.
- Maintain control over critical focus points, especially under difficult lighting circumstances.
- **Freeing Up Function Buttons:** Some of these features could be included to free up valuable custom buttons for frequently used items you might prefer to have immediate access to without accessing the Q Menu.

THE X100VI'S Q MENU: A JPEG SHOOTER'S WORKFLOW COMPANION

The X100VI's Q Menu can be a valuable tool for JPEG photographers who rely on in-camera image processing. This guide explores customizing the Q Menu to optimize your job processes and quickly achieve the desired look for your JPEGs straight out of the camera.

Aligning with Your Process:

Imagine yourself outdoors, camera in hand, ready to capture a scene. The ideal Q Menu setup should mirror your natural shooting workflow, allowing for quick adjustments based on the scene at hand.

Example Workflow (Next Section):

We'll explore a sample workflow in the next part, but the general idea is to:

1. **Identify a Base:** Start by selecting a relevant Custom Setting if you've created them beforehand. These presets can provide a foundation for different shooting scenarios (e.g., landscape, portrait).

2. **Refine Based on the Scene:** Once you have a starting point, use the Q Menu to fine-tune settings specific to the scene you're capturing. This might involve adjustments to:
   ◊ Film Simulation (achieve a specific color profile)
   ◊ White Balance (ensure accurate color reproduction)
   ◊ Grain Effect (add or remove film-like texture)
   ◊ Image Size & Quality (adjust resolution and compression)
   ◊ Other settings relevant to your creative vision

Remember:

This is merely a general example, and the specific order and settings you prioritize will be based on your individual shooting style and preferences.

The Advantages of a Simplified Q Menu:
- Achieving your desired results quickly and efficiently.
- Spending less time navigating menus and more time capturing the scene.
- Fine-tuning your JPEGs in-camera for a finished look without extensive post-processing.

THE POWER OF THE Q BUTTON: REFINING JPEGS ON-THE-GO

The X100VI's Q Button truly shines for JPEG photographers. While creating custom settings with preferred film simulations and other adjustments is valuable, the ability to adjust the parameters in real-time is what makes it a powerful tool. This guide explores how a photographer might use the Q Menu to achieve stunning JPEGs straight out of the camera.

A Case Study: Capturing Death Valley's Beauty:
The example below takes us to visit the Death Valley, where the photographer (whom we'll call Maxwell) aimed to capture the landscape's unique colors without extensive post-processing. Here's how the Q Menu played a crucial role:

Step 1: Selecting the Right Base (Custom Setting):
1. Maxwell encountered a landscape dominated by browns and yellows. Knowing that Velvia, a popular film simulation, wouldn't render these colors optimally, he opted for a "Travel" custom setting which employs Astia as its foundation. This provided a starting point with a different color profile.

The Power of Custom Settings:
Creating custom settings beforehand allows you to save preferred configurations for various shooting scenarios (portraits, landscapes, etc.). When you encounter a similar scene, simply recalling the relevant custom setting provides a solid base to build upon.

Step 2: Fine-Tuning with White Balance (WB):
2. Since accurate color is crucial for pleasing JPEGs, the Auto White Balance of the camera wasn't ideal. The yellow tones in the scene caused the camera to cool down the colors excessively. Here's how the Q Menu helped achieve the desired look:
    ○ **Kelvin White Balance:** Switching the temperature to 5600K (suitable for warm golden hour light) and using Kelvin White balance, Maxwell adjusted the overall color temperature to better match the warm tones of the scene.
    ○ **White Balance Shift (Optional):** A slight adjustment of +1 Magenta further refined the color reproduction, likely adding some warmth and counteracting any remaining coolness.

Verifying the Results:
In order to compare the colors, our photographer had to transition from the EVF to the actual scene. This back-and-forth verification ensures that the adjustments in the Q Menu are achieving the desired effect.

Step 3: Enhancing Color Vibrancy (Optional):
3. Having established a perfect starter with White Balance adjustments, Maxwell noticed the scene's colors were particularly vivid. Since their "Travel" custom setting possesses a zero (neutral saturation) color value, he used the Q Menu to increase the Color value to +2. This

boosted the color saturation without making it appear overly intense, highlighting the scene's natural vibrancy.

Fine-Tuning Color:
The Q Menu allows quick adjustments to Color, allowing you to increase or decrease color saturation to align with your artistic vision or the characteristics of the scene.

Step 4: Adding Depth with Contrast Control:
4. Maxwell felt the image lacked contrast, hindering the layering effect of the hills. His "Travel" custom setting had a +1 Shadow tone and a -1 Highlight tone. Here's how they used the Q Menu to address this:
    o **Highlight Tone:** Increased to +2 to preserve more detail in the brighter areas (highlights), potentially revealing more texture and definition in the sky.
    o **Shadow Tone:** Increased to +2 to recover more detail in the darker regions (shadows), likely enhancing the separation between the different layers of hills.

Seeing the Final Result:
By alternating the EVF and the actual scene, Maxwell confirmed that the adjustments to Color, Shadow tone, and Highlight Tone in the Q Menu achieved the desired look - a photo with vivid colors and depth.

The Efficiency of the Q Menu:

The photographer emphasizes that these Q Menu adjustments only took few seconds. This highlights a key advantage - it allows for swift fine-tuning of settings directly in the shooting process, saving valuable time compared to navigating through deeper menu structures.

Conclusion:
By combining custom settings as a foundation and then using the Q Menu for on-the-go adjustments, JPEG shooters can leverage the X100VI to produce astounding outcomes straight out of the camera. This method maximizes the camera's capabilities for capturing images with the desired color, saturation, and contrast, allowing photographers save time editing and more time creating.

MASTERING THE FUJIFILM X100VI'S FUNCTION BUTTONS: CUSTOMIZATION FOR EFFICIENCY

The Fujifilm X100VI comprises six function buttons (Fn buttons), two strategically placed on the front and four on the rear, designed to grant you rapid access to regularly utilized settings. This guide explores the default configuration and customization options for these buttons.

THE DEFAULT SETUP:

1. **Back/Top Camera Function Buttons:**

   a. **Button 1 (AEL/AFL):** Locks exposure (AE Lock) and/or focus (AF Lock) for recomposing shots, allowing you to adjust framing without affecting the locked settings.

b. **Center of Rear Command Dial:** Activates Focus Check, providing an enlarged perspective for precise focusing confirmation.

c. **Button 3 (Q):** Accesses the Quick Menu, a versatile menu displaying frequently adjusted shooting settings.

d. **Button 4 (Fn1):** Toggles Face Detection on/off, ideal for portraiture where the camera prioritizes focusing on faces.

2. **Front-of-Camera Function Buttons:**

a. **Button 1 (Fn2):** Handles the role that has been allocated to the camera's control ring. Depending on your configuration, it can adjust ISO, shutter speed, aperture, or other settings.

b. **Viewfinder Selector (rotate and hold):** Activates the ND filter (Neutral Density filter), helpful for reducing the quantity of light reaching the camera, for using wider apertures or slower shutter speeds in bright conditions.

CUSTOMIZING FUNCTION BUTTONS FOR YOUR WORKFLOW

While the default configuration offers a suitable place to start, you can personalize the function buttons using the camera's menu:

1. Navigate to 🔧 **BUTTON/DIAL SETTING > FUNCTION (Fn) SETTING**.
2. Select the desired function button (Fn1, Fn2, etc.).
3. Select your desired setting to assign from a vast range of options, including:
   a. Image Size & Quality
   b. Film Simulation
   c. White Balance
   d. Focus Mode
   e. Exposure Compensation
   f. AF-C Custom Settings
   g. Subject Detection
   h. ISO Auto Setting
   i. Movie Recording Options
   j. Preview Options (Depth of Field, Exposure, etc.)
   k. Many More (Consult camera manual for full list)
4. Alternatively, you could select "NONE" to disable a function button entirely if you don't find it useful.

Benefits of a Customized Setup:
By assigning functions you use frequently to the Fn buttons, you can:
1. **Increase Efficiency:** Gain instant access to crucial settings, minimizing time spent navigating menus.
2. **Streamline Workflow:** Organize controls to match your shooting style for a smoother experience.
3. **Personalize Control:** Adapt the camera's functionality to your preferences.

Important Considerations:
1. **Function Limitations:** Some options (like MOVIE RECORDING RELEASE) are unavailable when using the optical viewfinder.
2. **Viewfinder Selector:** This button cannot be reprogrammed.

3. **Disabling Buttons:** Use "NONE" to deactivate a button if you don't find it useful.

Remember:
1. Refer to your camera's manual for a complete list of assignable functions.
2. Try out the different configurations to discover the setup that enhances your shooting experience.

CHAPTER 3: IMAGE QUALITY SETTINGS

The Fujifilm X100VI boasts a powerful image engine, and the Image Quality settings menu lets you fine-tune how your photos are captured and saved. Don't worry if it seems like a lot at first – we'll break it down step-by-step!

Accessing the Settings:

1. With your camera in photo mode, press the **MENU/OK** button.
2. Look for the tab labeled **I.Q. (IMAGE QUALITY SETTING)** and select it.

Understanding the Options:

The options you see will depend on whether you're taking photos or videos. Here's a breakdown of major settings and their modalities:

IMAGE SIZE SETTING: CHOOSING THE PERFECT PICTURE SIZE

This setting on your Fujifilm X100VI determines how big and detailed your photos will be. Think of it like choosing a canvas size for a painting. A larger canvas holds more detail, but a smaller one is easier to manage. Here's a breakdown to help you decide:

Options: You'll see three options: Large, Medium, and Small. Each offers different aspect ratio and size choices (like 3:2 or 16:9). The image's shape is referred to as its aspect ratio; like a wider rectangle (16:9) or a square (1:1).

Choosing Your Size:

- **Large (L):** This is the highest resolution, perfect for capturing maximum detail for printing large photos or cropping later. It takes up the most storage capacity within your memory card, though.

- **Medium (M):** A decent trade-off between file size and quality. Great for most everyday shooting and sharing.
- **Small (S):** Ideal for situations where you need to save space, like emailing photos or posting them online. The detail won't be as high, but they'll still look great!

Special Modes: The Sports Finder mode and 1.29x Crop mode in burst shooting offer a different set of medium-sized options. These are optimized for capturing fast-moving subjects.

A Handy Tip: This setting stays put even when you turn off the camera or switch shooting modes. This means you only need to adjust it when you want a different size for your photos.

Remember: There's no one-size-fits-all answer. Choose the ideal image size, considering how you plan to use and share your photos.

IMAGE QUALITY: STRIKING A BALANCE

This setting on your X100VI lets you find the perfect balance between image quality and file size. Consider it as choosing the quality setting on a downloaded video – higher quality means a sharper image but a larger file. Below is an overview of the options:

Understanding the Options:
- **FINE:** This offers the best quality images, ideal for capturing all the detail you can. It also creates the largest files.
- **NORMAL:** A perfect trade-off between file size and quality. Great for everyday shooting and sharing.
- **RAW:** This captures the most data from the camera's sensor, giving you the most flexibility for editing later on a computer. However, RAW files are much larger than JPEGs.

Double Duty with RAW+JPEG:

- **FINE+RAW** and **NORMAL+RAW:** These options let you record both a RAW file and a JPEG file simultaneously. The JPEG is a compressed file you can easily share, while the RAW file gives you maximum editing potential.

Function Button Bonus: You can assign RAW recording to a function button to enhance switching on the fly. This is handy for switching between RAW and JPEG quickly without diving into menus.

Choosing Your Quality:

- **For most situations:** "FINE" or "NORMAL" JPEG will be a great choice.
- **For maximum editing flexibility:** Choose RAW, especially for important photos or ones you plan to edit heavily.
- **Need both flexibility and sharability?** Use FINE+RAW or NORMAL+RAW.

Pro-Tip: Begin with a higher quality setting if you're unsure, as you can always reduce the file size later if needed.

RAW RECORDING: GOING DEEP

RAW recording on your X100VI is for photographers looking to properly manage their images. RAW files capture all the data from the camera's sensor, giving you maximum flexibility for editing later on a computer. However, RAW files are much larger than compressed JPEGs. This setting helps to choose the compression level for your RAW files.

Understanding Compression:

- **UNCOMPRESSED:** This creates the highest quality RAW files, but they are also the largest. Choose this if you need the absolute most data for editing.

- **LOSSLESS COMPRESSED:** This compression reduces file size without sacrificing image quality. It's a great equilibrium between storage space and quality.
- **COMPRESSED:** This offers the smallest file size, probably with a slight decrease in image quality. Use this if storage space is a major concern.

Who Should Use Which Setting?
- **Most Users:** "LOSSLESS COMPRESSED" is a great default choice. It balances quality and file size well.
- **Professionals or Those Editing Heavily:** "UNCOMPRESSED" might be preferred for maximum editing flexibility, especially for critical photos. Just stay abreast of the larger file sizes.
- **Travelers or Those with Limited Storage:** "COMPRESSED" can be a good option to save space, but remember that there may be a slight quality trade-off.

SELECT JPEG/HEIF: CHOOSING THE RIGHT IMAGE FORMAT

The X100VI lets you choose between JPEG and HEIF for saving your photos. Here's a breakdown to help you decide your ideal format:
- **JPEG:** This is the widely used and supported format. Almost any device can open and view JPEG photos. It's a good choice for sharing and for compatibility.
- **HEIF:** This is a newer format that offers superior compression, meaning you can store more photos on your memory card. However, HEIF is inferior to JPEG in terms of support. Some devices and software may be unable to open HEIF photos without additional steps.

Below are some more things to consider:

- **Clarity Setting:** If you usually use the Clarity feature for adding a touch of edge sharpness, you'll need to stick with JPEG, as HEIF doesn't support it.
- **Color Space:** HEIF uses a different color space (sRGB) by default than JPEG. This might not be a major concern for everyday use, but some professional photographers might prefer the options offered by JPEG's color space.
- **Sharing and Compatibility:** If you plan on sharing your photos widely or using them with older devices, JPEG is the safer bet due to its universal compatibility.

Choosing Your Format:
- **For most users:** JPEG is a great all-around choice for compatibility and ease of sharing.
- **For those who want to conserve space:** HEIF can be a good option if you're comfortable with potentially needing to convert files for wider compatibility.

FILM SIMULATIONS

One of the joys of owning a Fujifilm camera is the incredible choice of Film Simulations. These replicate the appearance and atmosphere of vintage film stocks, adding instant character and nostalgia to your digital photos. Part 1 of this guide will explore the first nine simulations, helping you choose the best for your creative vision.

Simulating Classic Film: Film Simulations are like creative filters, but they go beyond simple color adjustments. They capture specific film stocks, including their grain, color response, and tonality.

Choosing Your Palette: Think of each Film Simulation as a different color palette. Consider the mood you wish to create and the subject you're photographing when making your selection.

- **STD PROVIA/STANDARD:** This is a versatile option, ideal for many subjects. It produces natural-looking colors.

- **V Velvia/VIVID:** If you love bold, saturated colors, Velvia is your pick. It's perfect for landscapes, nature shots, and anything that pops with color.

- **S ASTIA/SOFT:** This simulation creates a softer, more subdued look. It is perfect for portraits or a more muted aesthetic.

- **Cc CLASSIC CHROME:** Similar to Astia, Classic Chrome offers a softer feel with slightly enhanced shadows, creating a calming effect.

- **C REALA ACE:** This newcomer to the X100VI lineup ensures accurate color reproduction with a slightly "harder" tonality, making it appropriate for a range of scenes.

- **NH PRO Neg. Hi:** For portraits with a touch more contrast, PRO Neg. Hi is a good option. It enhances colors slightly for a more vibrant look.

- **NS PRO Neg. Std:** It delivers portraits with soft color gradations and natural-looking skin tones.

- **NC CLASSIC Neg.:** Want to add some punch to your photos? Classic Neg. offers richer colors and a "harder" tonality for a more dramatic look.

- **NN NOSTALGIC Neg.:** This simulation adds a warm amber tint to highlights and deepens shadows, creating a vintage, printed-photo aesthetic.

- **E** **ETERNA/CINEMA:** This simulation creates a soft, cinematic look with rich shadows, ideal for achieving a film-like aesthetic.

- **Eb** **ETERNA BLEACH BYPASS:** It offers a desaturated, high-contrast appearance which functions effectively for both stills and videos.

BLACK AND WHITE SIMULATIONS:

- **A** **ACROS:** For stunning black and white photos, ACROS delivers rich detail and sharpness. It also offers color filter options (Yellow, Red, Green) that affect how different colors are rendered in grayscale.

  - **Ay** **ACROS+Ye FILTER:** This adds a touch of contrast and makes the sky darker for a classic black and white look.

  - **Ar** **ACROS+R FILTER:** This filter creates a more dramatic effect with higher contrast and darker skies.

  - **Ag** **ACROS+G FILTER:** This is perfect for portraits, as it helps render skin tones more pleasingly.

- **B** **MONOCHROME:** Similar to ACROS, Monochrome offers black and white shooting with color filter options (Yellow, Red, Green) to influence grayscale rendering. The filter effects are identical to those offered with ACROS.

- **SEPIA** **SEPIA:** This simulation adds a warm, nostalgic sepia tone to your photos.

Creative Combinations:

Film simulations can be paired with other settings like Tone and Sharpness to further refine your creative vision. The next section deals with some of these!

ADVANCED FILM SIMULATION CONTROLS

Now that you've explored the world of Fujifilm Film Simulations, let's dive deeper into some advanced controls that helps to personalize your look.

MONOCHROMATIC COLOR:

The X100VI lets you add a touch of color to your black and white photos through the **MONOCHROMATIC COLOR** setting. This is available for both ACROS and MONOCHROME Film Simulations. Consider it as adding a subtle color tint. The color can be modified on two axes:

- **WARM-COOL:** This lets you shift the overall color temperature. Move towards "Warm" for a reddish tint or "Cool" for a bluish tint.
- **G (Green) - M (Magenta):** This axis allows for more precise color adjustments. For example, shifting towards "M" (Magenta) might add a subtle purple hue to your black and white image.

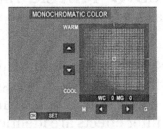

GRAIN EFFECT: ADDING FILM GRAIN

The **GRAIN EFFECT** setting lets you add a realistic film grain effect, further enhancing the classic film look. Here's how to control it:

- **ROUGHNESS:** This determines how coarse or smooth the grain appears. Choose "STRONG" for a more noticeable, vintage-style grain or "WEAK" for a subtler effect. "OFF" disables the grain effect entirely.
- **SIZE:** "LARGE" creates a more pronounced grain, while "SMALL" gives a finer, smoother look.

COLOR CHROME AND COLOR CHROME FX BLUE:

These settings are designed to boost the color saturation for specific color ranges.
- **Color Chrome Effect:** This targets highly saturated colors like greens, yellows, and reds, making them even more vibrant.
- **Color Chrome FX Blue:** This one focuses specifically on blues, increasing their tonal range for richer, deeper blues.

How to Apply Them:
- **Strength:** Both effects come in three strengths: "Strong," "Weak," and "Off." Choose "Strong" for a dramatic effect or "Weak" for a more subtle enhancement. "Off" disables the effect entirely.

Who Should Use Them?
- **Selective Color Boost:** These effects are great for circumstances where you desire certain colors to stand out, like emphasizing the blue of a clear sky.

A Word of Caution:
- **Overdoing It:** Exercise caution not to exceed limits with these settings, as they can make colors look unnatural and oversaturated. Use them with a light touch for maximum outcomes.

SMOOTH SKIN EFFECT: SMOOTHING SKIN TONES:

Purpose: The Smooth Skin Effect helps soften blemishes and imperfections on skin, aiming to create a smoother complexion in portraits.

How it Works: This effect works by slightly blurring areas with skin tones.

Strength: Similar to the color effects, Smooth Skin Effect comes in "Strong," "Weak," and "Off" options. Choose the strength that's well suited for you.

Who Should Use It? It is helpful for portrait photography, especially to achieve a more polished look. Moreover, beware of not overdoing it, as it can create an overly artificial look.

WHITE BALANCE

This is a crucial setting on your X100VI that ensures colors in your photos appear natural. Imagine taking a picture of a white shirt under different lighting conditions – it might look yellowish under incandescent bulbs or slightly blueish under fluorescent lights. White balance corrects for this, making the white shirt appear truly white regardless of the light source.

Understanding the Options:
The X100VI offers several white balance options:

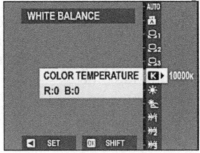

108

- **Automatic Modes:**
  - ◦ **WB W AUTO WHITE PRIORITY:** This prioritizes whiter whites, useful under incandescent bulbs where things might appear too yellow otherwise.
  - ◦ **AUTO:** This is a general automatic mode that works in most situations.
  - ◦ **WB A AUTO AMBIENCE PRIORITY:** This prioritizes warmer whites, ideal for keeping a cozy feel in photos taken under incandescent bulbs.

- **Custom White Balance:** A maximum of three unique white balance customs (1CUSTOM 1, 2CUSTOM 2, CUSTOM 3) can be made by taking a picture of a white object under the specific lighting you'll be shooting in. The camera will then use that information to achieve perfect white balance for those conditions.

- **K Color Temperature:** This allows you to manually set the white balance based on the color temperature of the illumination. Here are some common options:
  - ◦ **DAYLIGHT:** For outdoor shots in natural sunlight.
  - ◦ **SHADE:** For subjects under the shade outdoors.
  - ◦ **FLUORESCENT LIGHT options:** Choose between different types of fluorescent lighting (daylight, warm white, cool white).
  - ◦ **INCANDESCENT:** For indoor lighting with incandescent bulbs.
  - ◦ **UNDERWATER:** Reduces the blue cast common in underwater photography.

Selecting the Appropriate Setting:

- **Most Situations:** "AUTO" or "AMBIENCE PRIORITY" (depending on the desired warmth) will be a perfect starter.
- **Precise Control:** Use Color Temperature or Custom White Balance for critical shots or specific lighting conditions.

Pro-Tip: If you have any doubts concerning the illumination, you can always try random shots and adjust the white balance later.

Moving Beyond Auto:

- While "AUTO" is convenient, it might not always produce perfect results, especially under specific lighting conditions or close-up portraits. In these cases, consider:
  - **Custom White Balance:** This lets you create a white balance setting tailored to the exact lighting you're shooting in.
  - **Matching the Light Source:** Select a white balance option (Daylight, Fluorescent, etc.) that closely resembles the actual lighting to obtain a precise starting point.

Flash and White Balance:

- **Auto Magic:** Only the "AUTO," "WHITE PRIORITY," "AMBIENCE PRIORITY," and "UNDERWATER" modes modify white balance for the flash. If you use other white balance choices, you'll need to deactivate the flash to ensure proper color reproduction.

Fine-Tuning for Perfection:

- Pressing the "MENU/OK" button lets you further refine the balance via the focus stick on choosing a white balance option. This is helpful for achieving the most precise color accuracy.

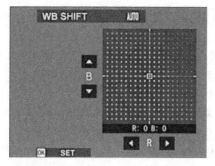

Exiting and Limitations:

- You can exit the white balance menu without fine-tuning by pressing "DISP/BACK" after selecting an option.
- While fine-tuning, remember you can't shift the focus stick to the side. Use the up, down, left, and right movements to make adjustments.

CUSTOM WHITE BALANCE

This is an effective instrument on your X100VI that enables you achieve perfect color accuracy under any lighting condition. This guide will explain the modalities effectively.

What is Custom White Balance?

On taking a shot, the camera tries to automatically determine the white balance depending on the source of illumination. However, automatic settings aren't always perfect. Custom WB lets you take control and ensure colors appear natural in your photos, especially under peculiar lighting circumstances.

Using Custom White Balance:

1. **Choose a Custom Slot:** The X100VI offers three custom WB slots (CUSTOM 1, CUSTOM 2, CUSTOM 3).
2. **Find a White (or Colored) Object:** Ideally, use a white object like a piece of paper or a white wall. Colored

objects could be utilized, but they will add a color cast to your photos.

3. **Frame the Target:** On your camera screen, you'll see a target for white balance. Line up your white (or colored) object so it fills the frame.

4. **Capture the Reference:** Completely press the shutter button to capture the reference image.

5. **Check the Results:** A message displays on the camera:
   - **"COMPLETED!"** This means the white balance was measured successfully. Press "MENU/OK" to confirm and use this custom WB setting.
   - **"UNDER"** The image was too dark. Increase exposure compensation and give it another shot.
   - **"OVER"** The image was too bright. Decrease exposure compensation then repeat it.

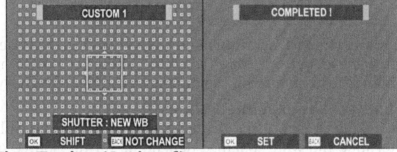

Fine-Tuning (Optional):

After capturing the reference, you can further refine the white balance via the focus stick. This helps in achieving the most precise color accuracy. Should you choose not to fine-tune, press "DISP/BACK" to exit.

Tips for Success:

- Use a clean, neutral-colored object for the most accurate results.
- Ensure the reference object fills the frame and is evenly lit.

- If using colored objects, be aware they will add a color cast to your photos.

COLOR TEMPERATURE

Understanding color temperature is key to achieving perfect white balance with your Fujifilm X100VI. This guide will explain this concept for your creative advantage.

What is Color Temperature?
Imagine a blacksmith heating a metal rod. As the temperature rises, the color it glows changes from red (low temp) to yellow (medium temp) to white (high temp). Color temperature works similarly, but instead of heat, it measures light's color. It's expressed in Kelvins (K).

- **Sunlight:** Has a color temperature around 5500K and appears white to our eyes.
- **Lower Temperatures:** Light sources like incandescent bulbs have a lower color temperature (around 2800K) and appear warmer, with a yellowish or reddish cast.
- **Higher Temperatures:** Fluorescent lights often have a greater color temperature (around 6500K) and appear cooler, with a bluish tinge.

Why Does it Matter?
Our brains adjust to different lighting conditions, so a white shirt under sunlight appears white to us. But the camera captures the actual color of the light source. This is where white balance comes in. By adjusting white balance to align with the light's color temperature, you ensure your photos appear natural.

Creative Control:

While achieving natural-looking colors is essential, color temperature is creatively suitable. You can:

- **Make Pictures Warmer:** Use a lower color temperature setting to add a warm, cozy feel to your photos.
- **Make Pictures Cooler:** Use a higher color temperature setting to create a crisp, clean look.
- **Drastic Effects:** For artistic expression, you can deliberately select a color temperature far from reality to make a special color cast.

Setting the Color Temperature:

1. **Access the Menu:** Press the "MENU/OK" button.
2. **Navigate to Image Quality Settings:** Look for the "IMAGE QUALITY SETTING" tab and select it using the navigation controls.
3. **Find White Balance Menu:** Locate the option labeled "WHITE BALANCE SETTINGS" and highlight it.
4. Tap the MENU/OK button.
5. **Choose the "K" Option:** Look for the option labeled with a "K" symbol. This represents the color temperature setting.
6. **Adjusting the Temperature:** Use the focus stick to move up or down and change the color temperature value. It can also be modified in 10K increments via rotation of the rear command dial.

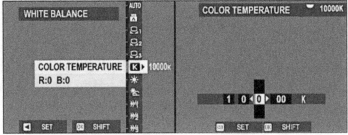

7. **Valid Range:** The X100VI helps to set a color temperature between 2500K (very warm) and 10000K (very cool).
8. **Fine-Tuning (Optional):** After choosing a temperature, you can further refine it via the focus stick. It helps in achieving the most precise white balance.
9. **Confirming Your Choice:** Tap "MENU/OK" to verify your choice and apply the chosen color temperature. The selected temperature will now be displayed on your camera screen.

10. **Exiting Without Fine-Tuning:** Should you decide not to fine-tune, simply press the "DISP/BACK" button after selecting a color temperature.

Choosing the Right Temperature:
- **Match the Light Source:** For natural-looking colors, select a color temperature that closely resembles the actual lighting in your scene.
- **Creative Control:** Experiment with different temperatures to create a specific mood or artistic effect.

DYNAMIC RANGE

Dynamic Range (DR) is a critical concept in photography, referring to the camera's ability to record specifics in the brightest highlights and darkest shadows of a scene. The X100VI offers a powerful Dynamic Range setting which helps you to optimize image quality in various lighting conditions.

Understanding Dynamic Range:
Imagine a scene under a brilliant sky and dark foreground shadows. A camera having a limited DR might capture the sky perfectly but lose details in the shadows, making them appear black and lacking detail. Conversely, a camera having a high DR can capture both the bright sky and the details in the shadows, resulting in a more natural-looking image.

The X100VI's Dynamic Range Options:
Your X100VI lets you choose from several Dynamic Range settings:

- **AUTO:** This is the optimal choice. By default, the camera chooses either 100% or 200% DR based on the scene and shooting conditions. You'll see the selected shutter speed and aperture displayed on partially pressing the shutter button.

- **DR100** **100%:** This setting is suitable for most situations. It offers a good balance between highlight and shadow detail but might struggle in high-contrast scenes like sunsets or backlit subjects. This setting can also be useful if you prefer a bit more contrast in your photos.

- **DR200** **200%:** This expands the dynamic range, aiming to preserve details in both highlights and shadows. This is ideal for high-contrast scenes or moments that you would want to photograph maximum detail across the entire image. However, be aware that at higher ISO sensitivities, using 200% DR may introduce a grainy effect called "mottling" in the image.

- **DR400** **400%:** It is the most extreme DR setting, offering the greatest ability to capture details in shadows and highlights. However, it's also the most vulnerable to causing mottling, especially at higher ISOs. Use this setting cautiously in situations where capturing maximum detail in both highlights and shadows is crucial.

Selecting the Appropriate Environment:

- **Most Situations:** "AUTO" or "100%" are good starting points for everyday shooting.
- **High-Contrast Scenes:** Use "200%" or "400%" for scenes with bright highlights and dark shadows, but be mindful of potential mottling.

D RANGE PRIORITY

The Fujifilm X100VI's D RANGE PRIORITY setting builds upon the Dynamic Range (DR) concept we discussed earlier. While DR affects the overall range of tones captured, D RANGE PRIORITY specifically focuses on maintaining details in shadows and highlights for a more natural look in high-contrast scenes.

Understanding D RANGE PRIORITY:

Imagine a landscape photo under a brilliant sky and dark foreground rocks. Without D RANGE PRIORITY, the sky might be blown out (pure white with no detail) and the rocks might appear too dark. D RANGE PRIORITY helps retain details in both areas, resulting in a more balanced and natural-looking image.

D RANGE PRIORITY Options:

The X100VI offers several D RANGE PRIORITY options:

- **AUTO:** This lets the camera automatically adjust contrast based on the lighting conditions. A perfect starter for most situations.
- **STRONG:** This applies a significant reduction in contrast, ideal for scenes with extreme contrast like

sunsets or backlit subjects. Use with caution, because it could make the image appear flat if used in moderately lit scenes.

- **WEAK:** This applies a subtle reduction in contrast, suitable for settings with a somewhat strong contrast to retain some contrast for a defined look.
- **OFF:** Disables D RANGE PRIORITY. Use this for full control over contrast through other settings like TONE CURVE or manual adjustments.

Availability and Considerations:
- **ISO Sensitivity:** "WEAK" is available across the complete range of ISO (250-12800), while "STRONG" is only available at higher ISOs (500-12800).
- **Manual Adjustments:** When D RANGE PRIORITY is set to anything other than "OFF," it will adjust TONE CURVE and DYNAMIC RANGE settings. If you want manual control over these settings, choose "OFF."

Selecting the Appropriate Environment:
- **Most Situations:** "AUTO" is a perfect starter.
- **High Contrast:** Use "STRONG" or "WEAK" depending on the scene's intensity.
- **Manual Control:** Use "OFF" to adjust contrast manually.

TONE CURVE

This is a powerful tool that helps to modify the tonal range of your photos, essentially affecting the distribution of highlights, shadows, and midtones. Imagine a graph where tonal values are plotted along the horizontal axis, while brightness is plotted on the vertical axis. A linear line represents a flat image, while curves could be utilized for brightening highlights, darken shadows, or create a more dramatic contrast.

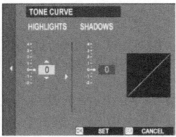

- **HIGHLIGHTS (-2 to +4):** Use positive values to brighten highlights and make them appear harsher. Use negative values to darken highlights and make them softer.
- **SHADOWS (-2 to +4):** Use positive values to lighten shadows and reveal more detail. Use negative values to darken shadows for a more dramatic effect.

COLOR

This adjusts the overall color density of your photo. Positive values increase color saturation, while negative values make colors less saturated.

SHARPNESS

The Sharpness setting controls how crisp and defined the outlines in your photos appear.

- **Positive values (+1 to +4):** Sharpen the image, making edges appear more defined. Be careful to not sharpen it too much since it results in a harsh, unnatural look.
- **Negative values (-1 to -4):** Soften the image, making edges appear smoother. This helps in reducing the appearance of noise or creating a more artistic effect.

HIGH ISO NR

Digital cameras introduce noise (grain) at higher ISO sensitivities. High ISO NR helps reduce this noise but can also affect image detail.

- **Positive values (+1 to +4):** Increase noise reduction, smoothing out the image but potentially softening details.
- **Negative values (-1 to -4):** Decrease noise reduction, preserving details but potentially showing more noise.

CLARITY

This setting enhances the definition of edges and midtone details in your image without significantly altering highlights or shadows.

- **Positive values (+1 to +5):** Increase image definition, making details appear sharper and more pronounced. Use higher values cautiously, as excessive clarity can create an artificial or halos around edges.
- **Negative values (-1 to -5):** Soften the image, making details appear smoother. It's ideal for portraits or landscapes to get a more delicate look.
- **0:** Maintains the default level of clarity.

LONG EXPOSURE NR (NOISE REDUCTION)

This setting specifically targets noise reduction for long exposure photos (typically those with shutter speeds slower than 30 seconds).

- **ON:** Reduces noise (mottling) that can appear in long exposure images. This comes at the cost of slightly longer save times.
- **OFF:** Disables long exposure NR. Use this if noise reduction isn't a concern and you prefer the fastest save times.

COLOR SPACE

This setting determines the range of colors your camera can capture and record.

- **sRGB:** The recommended setting for most situations. It offers a good balance between compatibility and color accuracy for web, social media, and everyday printing.
- **Adobe RGB:** A wider color gamut suitable for professional printing where a broader range of colors is necessary. However, not all devices can display the full Adobe RGB spectrum, so compatibility might be an issue.

PIXEL MAPPING: FIXING STUCK PIXELS

Digital cameras are complex electronic devices, and sometimes, individual pixels can malfunction, causing them to appear constantly bright or discolored in your photos. This is where Pixel Mapping comes in – a handy feature on your X100VI that can potentially fix these issues.

What is Pixel Mapping?

Imagine a million tiny dots (pixels) forming the picture on your camera sensor. Occasionally, a pixel can get stuck, causing it to display a single color (usually bright) all the time. Pixel Mapping is a process that attempts to identify and fix these stuck pixels by manipulating electrical charges on the sensor.

When to Use Pixel Mapping:

If you notice small, bright spots consistently appearing in your photos or movies, you might have stuck pixels. This can happen due to dust, heat, or normal wear and tear. In such cases, Pixel Mapping is worth a try.

Using Pixel Mapping on Your X100VI:

1. **Access the Menu:** Press the "MENU/OK" button while in shooting mode.

2. **Navigate to Image Quality Settings:** Look for the "IMAGE QUALITY SETTING" tab and select it using the navigation controls.
3. **Find Pixel Mapping:** Locate the option labeled "PIXEL MAPPING" and highlight it.
4. **Initiate the Process:** Tap "MENU/OK" once more to start Pixel Mapping.

Important Considerations:
- **Success Not Guaranteed:** While Pixel Mapping can be effective, it doesn't guarantee success. Sometimes, stuck pixels might be permanent hardware issues.
- **Battery Level:** Completely charge the battery before attempting Pixel Mapping, as the procedure could be time consuming.
- **Camera Temperature:** Pixel Mapping might not be available if too much heat is present in the camera's interior. Let it cool down before trying again.
- **Processing Time:** Allow several tens of seconds for Pixel Mapping to complete.

After Pixel Mapping:
- Take a test shot after the process is finished to see if the bright spots have disappeared.
- If the issue persists, consult your camera manual or contact Fujifilm support to seek help.

SELECT CUSTOM SETTING: RECALLING YOUR CUSTOM PRESETS

The Fujifilm X100VI allows you to save frequently used shooting configurations as custom settings for quick recall. This guide explains how to access and use these saved presets.

What are Custom Settings?
Imagine you have a favorite white balance, film simulation setting, and dynamic range combination for street

photography. The entire configuration can be saved as a custom setting, allowing you to instantly switch to those settings whenever you're out capturing street scenes.

The "SELECT CUSTOM SETTING" Option:

This menu option lets you recall the seven configured customs (CUSTOM 1 through CUSTOM 7) you've previously saved using the "EDIT/SAVE CUSTOM SETTING" function (explained earlier).

Here's how it is used:

1. **Access the Menu:** Press the "MENU/OK" button while in shooting mode.
2. **Navigate to Shooting Menu:** Find and tap the "Shooting Menu" tab using the navigation controls.
3. **Find "SELECT CUSTOM SETTING":** Scroll through the menu options and find "SELECT CUSTOM SETTING." Highlight it.
4. **Choose Your Preset:** An inventory of your custom settings banks (CUSTOM 1 to CUSTOM 7) will pop up. Use the navigation controls to choose the preset you want to recall.
5. **Apply the Settings:** The camera will instantly load all the settings saved in that particular custom bank, including film simulation, dynamic range, white balance, and other configurations you defined.

"NOTHING SELECTED" Option:

Should you choose not to recall any saved settings and choose to utilize the current camera configuration, simply highlight "NOTHING SELECTED" on the list.

Benefits of Custom Settings:

- **Quick Recall:** Saves time by instantly switching to your preferred shooting configurations.
- **Consistency:** Ensures consistent results by applying your preferred settings only a click away.
- **Experimentation:** Helps to create and test different shooting styles easily.

EDIT/SAVE CUSTOM SETTING

Imagine having instant access to your favorite shooting setups – a specific film simulation for portraits, a dynamic range configuration for landscapes, or a strong contrast black and white mode for street photography. The Fujifilm X100VI's "EDIT/SAVE CUSTOM SETTING" feature helps achieve just that! This guide will explain how to make and save your personalized shooting configurations.

BUILDING YOUR CUSTOM TOOLKIT

This section focuses on creating new custom settings banks on your X100VI.

Why Use Custom Settings?

Custom settings are like pre-sets that store all your preferred shooting configurations in one place. You can:

- **Switch Quickly:** Instantly alternates various shooting styles without manually adjusting numerous settings.
- **Maintain Consistency:** Ensure consistent results by applying your preferred settings with a single click.
- **Experiment with Ease:** Create and test different shooting styles without having to remember complex settings adjustments.

Saving Your First Custom Setting:

1. **Access the Menu:** Press the "MENU/OK" button while in shooting mode.
2. **Navigate to Image Quality Settings:** Locate the " **IQ** IMAGE QUALITY SETTING" tab and select it using the navigation controls.
3. **Find "EDIT/SAVE CUSTOM SETTING"** Scroll through the options and find "EDIT/SAVE CUSTOM SETTING." Highlight it and press "MENU/OK."
4. **Choose a Bank:** You'll see an inventory of custom setting banks labeled "CREATE NEW C1" through

"CREATE NEW C7." These represent empty slots for saving your new settings. Use the navigation controls to choose the preferred bank (C1 to C7) for your custom preset.

5. **Confirm Saving:** A dialog box for confirmation will appear requesting confirmation to save the current settings. Highlight "OK" and press "MENU/OK" to proceed.

EDITING EXISTING CUSTOM SETTINGS

This segment provides instructions on editing and saving your desired shooting configurations within a custom setting bank on your X100VI.

1. **Access the Menu:** Press the "MENU/OK" button while in shooting mode.

2. **Navigate to Image Quality Settings:** Locate the 🔲 "IMAGE QUALITY SETTING" tab and select it using the navigation controls.

3. **Find "EDIT/SAVE CUSTOM SETTING"** Scroll through the options and find "EDIT/SAVE CUSTOM SETTING." Highlight it and press "MENU/OK."

Alternatively, for Movie Settings: For creating a custom setting specifically for movie recording, navigate to the "MOVIE SETTING" menu and select "EDIT/SAVE CUSTOM SETTING" there.

4. **Choose the Bank:** An inventory of your custom setting banks (CUSTOM 1 to CUSTOM 7) will pop up. Use the navigation controls to select the bank for editing.

5. **Access Editing Menu:** Highlight "EDIT/CHECK" and press "MENU/OK."

Customizing Your Settings:

An inventory of shooting menu items you can customize within this bank will be displayed via the camera. These might include:

- Film Simulation
- White Balance
- Dynamic Range
- D RANGE Priority
- Tone Curve
- Sharpness
- Noise Reduction (ISO and Long Exposure)
- And many more!

6. **Edit Individual Settings:** Use the navigation controls to highlight a specific setting you wish to modify within your custom bank. Press "MENU/OK" to access that setting's adjustment menu.

7. **Make Adjustments:** Modify the setting to your preference using the navigation controls and dials.

8. **Save Changes:** Once you've adjusted the setting, press "MENU/OK" to save the changes then revert to the inventory of shooting menu items within your custom bank.

9. **Repeat for Other Settings:** Continue highlighting and adjusting other settings to add in your custom configuration.

Remember: You can customize as many settings as you want within a single custom bank. This helps you create highly personalized shooting presets for various situations.

After Editing:

Once you've finished customizing all the desired settings, you can exit the editing menu and your custom bank will be saved with your preferred configuration. Now, you can easily recall this entire setup anytime you want using the "SELECT CUSTOM SETTING" function explained earlier.

UPDATING YOUR CUSTOM SETTINGS

The Fujifilm X100VI offers a convenient feature called "Auto Update Custom Setting" that helps you manage your custom settings efficiently. This section explains its modalities, including saving your changes manually on disabling Auto Update.

Auto Update Custom Setting:

By default, the X100VI automatically saves modifications to individual settings within a custom bank. This ensures your custom settings always reflect the latest adjustments you've made.

Disabling Auto Update:

There might be cases where you would love to try experimenting with various settings within a custom bank without permanently saving those changes. For this purpose, you can disable Auto Update in the following menus:

- **Photo Menu:** Navigate to "IMAGE QUALITY SETTING" and then "AUTO UPDATE CUSTOM SETTING." Select "DISABLE" if you want to turn off automatic saving for photo-related custom settings.

- **Movie Menu:** Go to "MOVIE SETTING" and select "AUTO UPDATE CUSTOM SETTING." Choose "DISABLE" to disable automatic saving for movie-specific custom settings.

Saving Changes Manually (On disabling Auto Update):

On disabling Auto Update, any adjustments you make to individual settings within a custom bank won't be saved automatically. However, you can save them manually:

- **Saving Specific Items:** After editing settings, highlight the specific items you wish to save in the list and press the "Q" button. This saves only the selected adjustments.

- **Saving All Changes:** To save all the changes you made within the custom bank, return to Step 3 of the editing process (outlined in the earlier section) and select "SAVE THE CHANGES."
- **Discarding Changes:** In case you decide not to keep your edits, you can select "RESET THE CHANGES" to revert the custom bank to its previous state.

Copying Edited Items:

Here's a helpful tip: If you disable Auto Update and edit an item within a custom bank, a red dot pops up next to that item on the list. This indicates that the changes haven't been saved yet. However, if you copy such an item (marked with a red dot) to another custom bank, the copied item will retain the unsaved changes.

COPYING CUSTOM SETTINGS: DUPLICATING YOUR EXPERTISE

The Fujifilm X100VI allows you to copy custom settings between banks, conserving time. This guide explains how to efficiently duplicate your personalized shooting configurations.

Why Copy Custom Settings?

Imagine you have a custom setting (let's call it "Street Photography") that you like but want to modify slightly for a different scenario, like "Night Street Photography." Copying the existing settings and then making a few adjustments within the copy is a much faster approach than creating a new custom setting from scratch.

Copying Custom Settings:

1. **Access the Menu:** Press the "MENU/OK" button while in shooting mode.
2. **Navigate to Image Quality Settings:** Locate and choose the "IMAGE QUALITY SETTING" using the navigation controls.

Alternatively, for Movie Settings: To copy settings specifically for movie recording, navigate to the "MOVIE SETTING" menu and select "EDIT/SAVE CUSTOM SETTING" there.

3. **Choose the Source Bank:** You'll see a list of your custom setting banks (CUSTOM 1 to CUSTOM 7). Highlight the bank containing the settings you want to copy (the source bank). Press "MENU/OK" to select it.

4. **Initiate Copying:** Highlight "COPY" and press "MENU/OK."

5. **Select the Destination Bank:** A new list will appear showing the available custom setting banks again. This time, you're choosing the destination bank for copying the settings. Highlight the desired bank (C1 to C7) and press "MENU/OK."

6. **Confirm Overwriting:** A confirmation dialog pops up on the camera, informing you that any existing settings in the destination bank will be overwritten. Highlight "OK" and press "MENU/OK" to proceed with copying.

Copying Completed:

The selected settings from the source bank shall be copied to the destination bank, effectively creating a duplicate. Any previous configurations in the destination bank will be replaced.

Benefits of Copying:

- **Efficiency**: Copying custom settings is ideal for streamlining your workflow and create variations of your favorite shooting configurations. It adapts your camera to different shooting scenarios without starting from scratch each time.
- **Save Time:** Quickly create new custom settings based on existing configurations.
- **Maintain Consistency:** Ensure a perfect starter for variations of a shooting style.

- **Experimentation:** Modify copied settings without affecting the original custom bank.

DELETING CUSTOM SETTINGS: CLEARING THE DECKS

One day may arrive when you no longer need a particular custom setting or want to free up a custom bank for a new configuration. The Fujifilm X100VI allows you to easily delete unwanted custom settings.

Why Delete Custom Settings?

- **Free Up Space:** If you have too many custom settings, deleting unused ones can free up banks for new configurations.
- **Start Fresh:** Perhaps you've refined your style of shooting and your old custom settings are no longer relevant. Deleting them helps to create new presets that better reflect your current preferences.

Deleting Custom Settings:

1. **Access the Menu:** Press the "MENU/OK" button while in shooting mode.
2. **Navigate to Image Quality Settings:** Locate the "IMAGE QUALITY SETTING" tab and select it using the navigation controls.

Alternatively, for Movie Settings: To delete settings specifically for movie recording, navigate to the "MOVIE SETTING" menu then choose "EDIT/SAVE CUSTOM SETTING" there.

3. **Choose the Bank to Delete:** You'll see a list of your custom setting banks (CUSTOM 1 to CUSTOM 7). Highlight the bank containing the settings for deletion. Press "MENU/OK" to select it.
   4. **Initiate Deletion:** Highlight "ERASE" and press "MENU/OK."
   5. **Confirm Deletion:** A confirmation dialog pops up, requesting confirmation for the deletion. Highlight "OK" and press "MENU/OK" to proceed.

Settings Deleted:
Once confirmed, any custom settings saved to the chosen bank will be permanently deleted. The bank will become empty and set for a new custom configuration.

RENAMING CUSTOM SETTINGS BANKS: PERSONALIZE YOUR WORKFLOW

The Fujifilm X100VI allows you to assign custom names to your setting banks, making them easier to identify and manage. This guide explains how to add descriptive and meaningful names to your custom settings.

Why Rename Custom Settings?
By default, custom setting banks are named "CUSTOM 1" through "CUSTOM 7." While this works initially, renaming them with descriptive titles can significantly improve your workflow.

- **Clarity and Recognition:** Imagine having custom settings named "Landscape" or "Portrait" instead of generic numbers. Descriptive names simplify recognizing the purpose of each bank at a glance.
- **Organization:** As you create more custom settings, renaming them helps you categorize and organize them based on shooting style (e.g., "Street B&W," "Night Portraits"), making them quicker to find.

Renaming Your Custom Banks:
1. **Access the Menu:** Press the "MENU/OK" button while in shooting mode.
2. **Navigate to Image Quality Settings:** Locate and choose the "IMAGE QUALITY SETTING" using the navigation controls.

Alternatively, for Movie Settings: To rename settings specifically for movie recording, proceed to the "MOVIE SETTING" menu and select "EDIT/SAVE CUSTOM SETTING" there.

3. **Choose the Bank to Rename:** An inventory of your custom setting banks pops up. Highlight the bank you want to give a new name and press "MENU/OK" to select it.
4. **Initiate Renaming:** Highlight "EDIT CUSTOM NAME" and press "MENU/OK."
5. **Create Your New Name:** The camera allows you input a different name for the custom settings bank using the on-screen keyboard. Use descriptive terms that reflect the objective of the settings within that bank (e.g., "Macro Focus," "Vivid Street").
6. **Store the Modified Name:** Once you've entered a desired name, highlight "SET" and press "MENU/OK".

Descriptive Names Matter:
Taking a moment to rename your custom settings banks can significantly improve your overall shooting experience. With clear and descriptive names, finding the right settings becomes effortless, allowing you to focus on obtaining the ideal picture.

Remember: Renaming your custom settings banks is a simple but highly beneficial step. Do it for all your frequently used presets to create a well-organized and efficient shooting system on your Fujifilm X100VI.

AUTO UPDATE CUSTOM SETTING: KEEPING YOUR PRESETS FRESH

The Fujifilm X100VI offers a convenient feature called "Auto Update Custom Setting" that helps you manage your custom shooting configurations efficiently. This guide explains the modalities and effects on your presets.

What is Auto Update Custom Setting?
Imagine you've created a custom setting for street photography with a specific film simulation and white balance combination. With Auto Update enabled, any adjustments you make to these settings within that custom

bank (e.g., slightly tweaking the film simulation grain) will be automatically saved. This ensures your custom settings are always up-to-date with the latest changes you've made.

The Two Options:

The X100VI helps you select between two behaviors for Auto Update:

- **ENABLE:** Any modifications you make to individual settings within a custom bank are automatically saved, keeping your presets constantly updated.

- **DISABLE:** With this option selected, changes to settings within a custom bank won't be saved automatically. This gives you greater command of your presets and allows you try out adjustments without permanently altering your saved configuration. However, you'll need to manually save any desired changes (explained in a separate guide).

Choosing the Right Option:

The ideal choice is based on your workflow:

- **Enable (Default):** Ideal if you prefer your custom settings to always reflect the latest adjustments you've made. This is a good choice if you're confident on your configurations and want a streamlined workflow.

- **Disable:** Suitable for trying out various configurations within a custom bank without accidentally overwriting your original preset. This gives you more control over saving specific changes.

CHAPTER 4: MASTERING FOCUS: A GUIDE TO AF/MF SETTINGS

The Fujifilm X100VI offers a comprehensive set of autofocus (AF) and manual focus (MF) settings, enabling you to adjust how your camera achieves sharp images. This guide explores these settings and their functionalities.

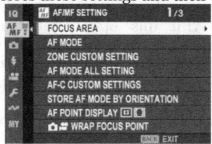

Accessing AF/MF Settings:
1. **Press MENU/OK:** Press the "MENU/OK" button in the photo shooting display.
2. **Navigate to AF/MF Settings:** Find the **AF/MF SETTING** tab (marked with a **AF/MF** icon) and select it using the navigation controls.

Understanding the Options: (Availability might differ based on the shooting mode)

1) **FOCUS AREA:** Choose the specific focus area. Options might include single points, zones, or wide-area coverage.

2) **AF MODE:** Select the autofocus mode (AF-S for single autofocus, AF-C for continuous autofocus).

3) **ZONE CUSTOM SETTING:** Tailor the actions of specific focus zones within the frame.

4) **AF MODE ALL SETTING:** Adjust general autofocus settings applicable to all AF modes.

5) **AF-C CUSTOM SETTINGS:** Fine-tune how the camera tracks moving subjects in continuous autofocus mode.

6) **STORE AF MODE BY ORIENTATION:** Save the chosen AF mode for different camera orientations (portrait vs. landscape).

7) **AF POINT DISPLAY:** Enable or disable the on-screen display of autofocus points.

8) **WRAP FOCUS POINT:** Set whether the focus point automatically jumps over the opposite side of the frame when reaching an edge.

9) **NUMBER OF FOCUS POINTS:** Select how many autofocus points are available for selection.

10) **PRE-AF:** Maintain continuous autofocus despite half pressing the shutter button (may drain battery faster).

11) **AF ILLUMINATOR:** Activate a light to assist focusing in low-light conditions.

12) **FACE/EYE DETECTION SETTING:** Configure how eyes and faces are identified and focused on by the camera.

13) **SUBJECT DETECTION SETTING:** Specify the subject type (e.g., humans, animals) for improved autofocus performance.

14) **AF+MF:** Combine autofocus with manual focus adjustments for fine-tuning.

15) **MF ASSIST:** Utilize visual aids (focus peaking or split image) to achieve precise manual focus.

16) **INTERLOCK MF ASSIST & FOCUS RING:** Link the focus ring function to activating MF assist tools.

17) **FOCUS CHECK:** Enlarge the central area of the frame to verify focus accuracy.

18) **INTERLOCK SPOT AE & FOCUS AREA:** Link the metering point to the chosen focus area.

19) **INSTANT AF SETTING:** Adjust the responsiveness of autofocus on half-pressing the shutter button.

20) **DEPTH-OF-FIELD SCALE:** Display a scale in the viewfinder to estimate depth of field based on focus distance.
21) **RELEASE/FOCUS PRIORITY:** Select if the camera prioritizes taking the picture (release) or achieving focus first.
22) **AF RANGE LIMITER:** Restrict the autofocus range to improve focusing speed for close-up shots.
23) **TOUCH SCREEN MODE:** Configure autofocus behavior when using the touchscreen for selecting focus points.
24) **CORRECTED AF FRAME:** Enable adjustments for minor focus calibration if needed.

FOCUS AREA

This setting determines where the camera will prioritize focusing, affecting both autofocus (AF) and manual focus (MF) modes. The X100VI offers various options, including single points, zones, and wide-area coverage. Below is an overview of some common Focus Area options:

- **Single Point:** Ideal for precise focus on a specific subject positioned inside the frame.
- **Zone:** The frame sectioned, allowing you to choose a broader area for autofocus to prioritize.
- **Wide Area:** By default, the camera chooses focus points throughout the frame.

Choosing the Right Focus Area:
The best Focus Area choice depends on your shooting situation:

- **Portraits:** Use a single point on the subject's eyes.
- **Landscapes:** Wide-area autofocus might be suitable for capturing overall sharpness.
- **Action:** Zone focusing can be helpful for tracking moving subjects within a specific area.

AF MODE

This setting modifies the automatic focus of the camera. The X100VI offers two main AF modes:

- **AF-S (Single Autofocus):** Focuses once on half-pressing the shutter button, and locks focus until the button is fully pressed or focus is remeasured.
- **AF-C (Continuous Autofocus):** Continuously adjusts focus provided that the shutter button is half-pressed, ideal for tracking moving subjects.

AF Mode All Setting:

This enables you personalize the initial focus point selection for the "ALL" Focus Area option, which covers the entire frame. You can configure this independently for both AF-S and AF-C modes.

ZONE CUSTOM SETTING

This powerful feature enables you create custom focus zones within the frame specifically for the "ZONE" Focus Area. You can create and save three custom zones (ZONE CUSTOM 1, ZONE CUSTOM 2, ZONE CUSTOM 3) varying in size and positions tailored to your shooting preferences.

Benefits of Zone Customization:

- **Precise Focus Control:** Zone focusing provides more control within a specific area of focus.
- **Focus Peaking:** Combine Zone Customization with focus peaking (a visual aid in MF mode) for even more precise manual focusing within your designated zone.

AF-C CUSTOM SETTINGS

Capturing sharp images of moving subjects requires a camera that can effectively track their focus. The Fujifilm X100VI's AF-C Custom Settings offer a powerful solution, allowing you to optimize autofocus for various scenarios.

What are AF-C Custom Settings?

These settings are specifically designed for the AF-C (Continuous Autofocus) mode. They determine how the camera tracks and prioritizes focus on subjects in motion. The X100VI provides pre-configured settings (Sets 1-5) for different subject types, along with the custom settings (Set 6).

Understanding Sets 1-5:

- **SET 1: MULTI PURPOSE** (Default): This is a versatile option suitable for an array of moving subjects with predictable motion. It offers a good balance between tracking accuracy and responsiveness.
- **SET 2: IGNORE OBSTACLES & CONTINUE TRACKING THE SUBJECT:** Choose this setting when your subject might be temporarily obscured by other objects in the frame. The camera will prioritize maintaining focus on the originally selected subject even if it's briefly hidden. This is ideal for situations like photographing athletes running behind fences or birds flying through branches.
- **SET 3: ACCELERATING/DECELERATING SUBJECTS:** This setting is designed for subjects whose speed is constantly changing, such as cars racing or animals running erratically. The camera anticipates these changes and adjusts focus accordingly to maintain lock on the subject.

138

- **SET 4: FOR QUICKLY APPEARING SUBJECT:** This setting prioritizes quickly acquiring focus on subjects that enter the frame abruptly. Choose this for fast-paced action photography where subjects might appear unexpectedly, like capturing athletes emerging from starting blocks or street performers suddenly entering the scene.
- **SET 5: FOR CHAOTIC MOVING & ACCEL./DECEL. SUBJECT:** This is designed for the most unpredictable subjects with rapid changes in speed, direction, and movement depth (front-to-back and left-to-right). Think of erratically flying birds, energetic pets, or athletes performing complex maneuvers. This setting attempts to anticipate these erratic movements and maintain focus lock.

SET 6: CUSTOM - Unleashing Your Focus Control:
Set 6 helps to make your custom focus tracking behavior by adjusting three sub-settings:

- **TRACKING SENSITIVITY:** Governs how quickly the camera reacts to changes in the subject's movement. Higher sensitivity means faster focus adjustments but might be prone to hunting (focus constantly shifting back and forth) in low-contrast environments.
- **SPEED TRACKING SENSITIVITY:** Specifically targets the sensitivity towards a subject's speed changes. Adjusting this alongside Tracking Sensitivity allows for more granular control over focus tracking behavior.
- **ZONE AREA SWITCHING:** Influences how readily the camera switches focus between different focus zones within the frame. A lower setting prioritizes keeping focus on the initially selected subject, while a higher setting allows for faster focus shifts if the subject moves out of the zone.

Selecting the Appropriate Setting:

139

The best AF-C Custom Setting depends on the specific movement of your subject:

- **Predictable Motion:** Use Set 1 (Multi-Purpose) for most situations.
- **Temporary Obscuration:** Choose Set 2 (Ignore Obstacles) if your subject may be briefly hidden.
- **Erratic Movement:** Select Set 3 (Accelerating / Decelerating Subject) for subjects with constantly changing speeds.
- **Sudden Appearances:** Use Set 4 for subjects abruptly entering the frame.
- **Highly Erratic Movement:** Choose Set 5 for subjects with unpredictable changes in speed, direction, and depth.
- If you find a particular setting close to ideal but needs slight adjustments, use Set 6 to customize the Zone area Switching, Tracking Sensitivity, and Speed Tracking Sensitivity to accomplish the intended focus tracking behavior.

FOCUS TRACKING

The Fujifilm X100VI's AF-C Custom Settings empower you to fine-tune focus tracking for capturing sharp images of moving subjects. Let's delve deeper into the first parameter within these settings - Tracking Sensitivity – to comprehend its effects on focus behavior.

DECODING TRACKING SENSITIVITY

What is Tracking Sensitivity?
Imagine you are filming runners. Tracking Sensitivity dictates the duration for which the camera prioritizes focusing on the runner (your subject) before potentially switching focus to another object that enters the frame (like a bird flying across the background). A higher Tracking

Sensitivity value makes the camera more "sticky" with the initial subject, while a lower value makes it more responsive to potential new subjects stepping into the focus area.

Understanding the Options:
The Tracking Sensitivity is adjustable from 0 to 4 on the X100VI. Below is an overview of what each value generally means:

- **0 (Lowest):** The camera reacts very quickly to changes within the focus area. Even slight movements of your subject might trigger a focus shift. This can be beneficial for capturing fast-paced action or rapidly switching focus between subjects, but there's a higher chance of unintended focus changes.

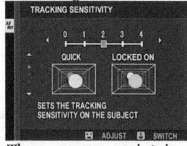

- **1-2 (Low):** The camera maintains a harmonious combination of keeping focus and reacting to potential new subjects entering the frame. This is a versatile starting point for many situations.
- **3 (High):** The camera prioritizes staying focused on the initial subject for a longer duration. This is ideal to ensure focus remains locked on your subject even if there's some background movement. However, it might be less responsive for quick focus switch to another subject.
- **4 (Highest):** The camera shows the most persistence in maintaining focus on the initial subject. This setting is suitable for absolutely prioritizing focus lock on a specific subject, even if there are significant distractions

in the background. However, it becomes less adaptable to changing focus needs.

Selecting the Appropriate Setting:
The ideal Tracking Sensitivity depends on your shooting scenario:

- **Fast-paced action with potential focus switching:** Use a lower value (0-1).
- **Balanced focus tracking for various situations:** Start with a mid-range value (1-2).
- **Prioritizing focus lock on a specific subject:** Select a higher value (3-4).

SPEED TRACKING SENSITIVITY: REACTING TO CHANGES IN SPEED

While Tracking Sensitivity determines how readily the camera switches focus based on subject presence within the frame, Speed Tracking Sensitivity focuses specifically on a subject's velocity changes. Here's what this means:

- **Imagine tracking a car accelerating around a racetrack.** A higher Speed Tracking Sensitivity value makes the camera more responsive to the car's increasing speed, adjusting focus accordingly to maintain lock. A lower value might struggle to stay current with such rapid acceleration.

Understanding the Options:
Speed Tracking Sensitivity also ranges from 0 to 2 on the X100VI:

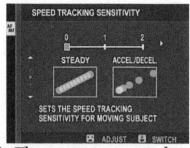

- **0 (Lowest):** The camera reacts less aggressively to changes in subject speed. This can prove advantageous while focusing on subjects with predictable or slow changes in velocity.
- **1-2 (Higher):** The camera prioritizes adapting focus based on the subject's acceleration or deceleration. This is ideal for tracking fast-moving subjects with frequent speed variations.

Selecting the Appropriate Setting: Consider your subject's movement pattern:

- **Predictable speed:** Use a lower value (0).
- **Frequent speed changes:** Select a higher value (1-2).

Remember: Experimenting with both Tracking Sensitivity and Speed Tracking Sensitivity allows for a nuanced approach to focus tracking, adapting to your subject's behavior and desired focus behavior.

ZONE AREA SWITCHING: PRIORITIZING FOCUS WITHIN A ZONE

In this mode, the frame is divided into sections. Zone Area Switching determines how the camera prioritizes focus within that zone:

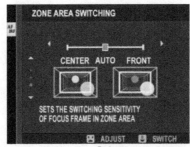

- **FRONT:** Focuses on subjects nearest the camera, within the designated zone. It helps in tracking approaching subjects or isolating a specific subject at the forefront of a zone.
- **AUTO:** The camera prioritizes the subject nearest the central zone initially, then might switch focus areas within the zone to maintain tracking. This offers some flexibility but might not be ideal to prioritize a specific area within the zone.
- **CENTER:** Focuses on subjects placed centrally within the designated zone. This is suitable for situations where your subject is probably going to remain within the central area.

Selecting the Most Appropriate Setting: Consider your subject's movement and desired focus area:
- **Approaching subject:** Use FRONT.
- **Flexible tracking within a zone:** Choose AUTO (with caution for critical focus placement).
- **Subject in the zone's center:** Select CENTER.

Remember: Zone Area Switching collaborates with the overall zone you define and the Tracking/Speed Tracking Sensitivity settings.

PRE-CONFIGURED FOCUS TRACKING OPTIONS (SETS 1-5)

The Fujifilm X100VI provides pre-configured AF-C Custom Settings (Sets 1-5) designed for various subject types. This guide summarizes the settings for each set, allowing you make the optimal choice.

Understanding the Parameters:

These pre-configured sets define three key parameters:

- **Tracking Sensitivity:** The duration which the camera refocuses on a new subject entering the frame (higher = more focus lock on current subject, lower = more responsive to new subjects).
- **Speed Tracking Sensitivity:** The camera's sensitivity to changes in subject speed (higher = better tracks accelerating/decelerating subjects, lower = less responsive to speed changes).
- **Zone Area Switching (for ZONE focus mode only):** Priority within the designated focus zone (FRONT = closest subject, AUTO = prioritize center then adjust, CENTER = subject in the center).

Pre-Configured Set Values:

AF-C CUSTOM SETTINGS	TRACKING SENSITIVITY	SPEED TRACKING SENSITIVITY	ZONE AREA SWITCHING
SET 1	2	0	AUTO
SET 2	3	0	CENTER
SET 3	2	2	AUTO
SET 4	0	1	FRONT
SET 5	3	2	AUTO

- SET 1 (Multi-Purpose): Balanced approach for various subjects with predictable motion.
- SET 2 (Ignore Obstacles): Prioritizes focus lock on the initially selected subject, even if briefly obscured.
- SET 3 (Accelerating/Decelerating Subject): Tracks subjects with frequent speed changes (e.g., cars racing).
- SET 4 (Suddenly Appearing Subject): Focuses quickly on subjects stepping into the frame abruptly.

- SET 5 (Erratically Moving & Accel./Decel. Subject): Designed for highly unpredictable subjects with erratic movements.

Choosing the Right Set:
Consider your subject's movement when selecting a set:
- **Predictable Motion:** Use SET 1 (Multi Purpose).
- **Temporary Obscuration:** Choose SET 2 (Ignore Obstacles).
- **Frequent Speed Changes:** Select SET 3 (Accelerating/Decelerating Subject).
- **Sudden Appearances:** Use SET 4 (Suddenly Appearing Subject).
- **Highly Erratic Movement:** Choose SET 5 (Erratically Moving & Accel./Decel. Subject).

SET 6: CUSTOMIZING YOUR FOCUS TRACKING

While Sets 1-5 provide pre-configured options, Set 6 empowers you to make your custom focus tracking experience. Here's how to access and modify the settings:

1) **Navigate to AF-C Custom Settings:** Use the menu controls to access the **AF/MF SETTING** tab and choose **AF-C CUSTOM SETTINGS**.

2) **Choose Set 6:** Highlight **SET 6 CUSTOM** and press the right button or the OK button to confirm selection.

3) **Adjusting Sub-settings:** You'll see three sub-settings within Set 6:

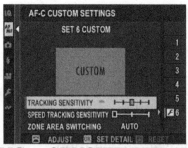

a) **TRACKING SENSITIVITY:** Use the front command dial or focus stick to adjust this value (0-4) as explained in previous guides. Higher values prioritize focus lock on the current subject, while lower values are more responsive to new subjects entering the frame.

b) **SPEED TRACKING SENSITIVITY:** Adjust this value (0-2) using the same controls. Higher values enhance tracking for subjects with frequent speed changes (acceleration/deceleration).

c) **ZONE AREA SWITCHING (for ZONE focus mode only):** Select the desired priority within the zone (FRONT, AUTO, or CENTER) via the navigation buttons or focus stick.

4) **Resetting to Defaults (Optional):** To revert the settings in Set 6 to their original values, press the **DRIVE/DELETE** button.

5) **Exiting the Menu:** Once you've adjusted the sub-settings to your preference, press **DISP/BACK** to exit the menu.

STORE AF MODE BY ORIENTATION:

It establishes how the camera remembers your focus preferences between portrait and landscape orientations:

- **OFF:** The same AF mode (single autofocus, continuous autofocus) and focus area selection apply regardless of camera orientation.

- **FOCUS AREA ONLY:** This selection can be customized independently for portrait and landscape. The AF mode itself remains the same for both orientations.
- **ON:** This offers the most flexibility. You could select separate AF modes (e.g., single autofocus for portraiture, continuous autofocus for landscapes) and focus areas for each orientation.

Select the Appropriate Setting:
Consider your shooting habits:
- **Same preferences in both orientations:** Use OFF.
- **Different focus area needs:** Choose FOCUS AREA ONLY.
- **Full customization for portrait vs. landscape:** Select ON.

AF POINT DISPLAY:

This setting controls whether individual focus points are displayed when using "ZONE" or "WIDE/TRACKING" AF modes:
- **ON:** Displays individual focus points within the selected zone or the entire frame (WIDE/TRACKING). It helps for precise focus placement.
- **OFF:** Hides the individual focus points, showing only the overall focus zone or frame coverage. This can offer a cleaner view for composition.

Selecting the Appropriate Setting: Consider your preference for visual feedback:
- **Precise focus point control:** Use ON.
- **Cleaner compositional view:** Choose OFF.

WRAP FOCUS POINT:

This setting determines focus point selection behavior when using the directional buttons:

- **ENABLE:** Allows "wrapping" focus point selection. Reaching the boundary of the focus points in one direction jumps the selection to the opposite frame. It can be faster for navigating focus points.
- **DISABLE:** Focus point selection stops at the boundary of the frame. You must use the other directional button to reach focus points on the opposite side. This might be preferable for deliberate focus point selection.

Selecting the Appropriate Setting:
- **Faster focus point switching:** Use ENABLE.
- **Deliberate focus point selection:** Choose DISABLE.

NUMBER OF FOCUS POINTS:

The quantity of focus points that can be chosen depends on this configuration in manual focus (MF) mode or when using "SINGLE POINT" autofocus (AF) mode. The X100VI offers two options:

- **117 POINTS (9 × 13):** Provides a good balance between focus point density and overall screen coverage. This is a versatile starting point for many situations.
- **425 POINTS (17 × 25):** Offers a significantly higher number of focus points for even more precise focus placement. This can be beneficial for critical focus on small details or subjects positioned off-center within the frame.

Selecting the Appropriate Setting:
- **Balanced focus control:** Use 117 POINTS.

- **Highly precise focus placement:** Choose 425 POINTS.

Remember: A higher quantity of focus points might lead to slower focus selection, especially while using the focus lever to navigate through them. Try out both options to choose the proper balance for your shooting style.

PRE-AF:

This setting manages the modality of the camera on half-pressing the shutter button:

- **ON:** The camera continuously pre-focuses, leading to faster focus acquisition on half-pressing the shutter button. However, it also consumes slightly more battery life.
- **OFF:** The camera only focuses on half-pressing the shutter button. This conserves battery life but might result in a slight delay in focus acquisition compared to having Pre-AF turned on.

Selecting the Right Setting:

- **Fast-paced action or focus-critical shots:** Use ON for potentially faster focus acquisition.
- **Slower shooting or prioritizing battery life:** Choose OFF.

Remember: The impact of Pre-AF on focus speed might be subtle in some situations.

AF Illuminator

The Fujifilm X100VI's AF illuminator is a small light that assists autofocus in low-light conditions. Below is an overview of its functionality and considerations for use:

What is the AF Illuminator?

It acts like a tiny flashlight, briefly projecting a beam of light onto your subject. This helps the camera's autofocus system

150

detect contrast and lock focus more accurately in low-light environments.

Turning the AF Illuminator On and Off:

You can activate or deactivate the AF illuminator through the camera menu. When enabled (ON), the light will automatically activate whenever the camera struggles to focus due to low light.

Limitations of the AF Illuminator:

- **Distance:** The AF illuminator's effectiveness has limitations. Should the subject be too distant, the projected light might be too weak to aid focusing. In such situations, increasing the separation from the subject might allow the camera's autofocus system to function without the illuminator.

- **Subject Comfort:** The bright light from the illuminator can be noticeable, especially at close distances. It's best to avoid situations where the light might be intrusive to your subject, such as portrait photography.

Alternatives for Low-Light Focusing:

- **Increase ISO:** While increasing ISO introduces digital noise to the image, it may occasionally be a better option than relying on the AF illuminator, especially for capturing moving subjects or avoiding startling your subject.

- **Manual Focus:** In very low-light scenarios, you might consider using manual focus with focus peaking enabled. It helps in getting accurate focus manually by highlighting sharp edges in the frame.

MASTERING PORTRAITURE: FACE/EYE DETECTION SETTINGS

The Fujifilm X100VI's Face/Eye Detection settings empower you to capture stunning portraits with precise focus and exposure. This guide explores initial segment of these settings, helping you comprehend prioritization of faces and optimize focus for beautiful portrait results.

What is Face/Eye Detection?

Imagine taking a portrait in a crowded scene. Face/Eye Detection helps the camera identify human faces within the frame. It then prioritizes these faces for focusing and exposure, making sure your subject is sharp and well-exposed even with background distractions. Additionally, Eye Detection allows you to further refine focus by targeting a specific eye within the detected face.

Understanding the Options (Part 1):

The Face/Eye Detection Setting offers several options to control how the camera prioritizes faces and eyes:

- **FACE DETECTION ON:** This enables Intelligent Face Detection. The camera detects faces, prioritizes them for focus and exposure adjustments during portrait photography. You can further customize this setting with Eye Detection options explained below.
- **EYE DETECTION SETTINGS:** Within "FACE DETECTION ON," you can choose how the camera focuses on eyes:
  - **EYE OFF:** Disables Eye Detection. When the Intelligent Face Detection is turned on, the complete face is focused on by the camera.
  - **EYE AUTO:** By default, the camera focuses on one eye within a detected face. This is a convenient option for most situations.

- ○ **RIGHT EYE PRIORITY:** It prioritizes focusing on the right eye of the subject when utilizing Intelligent Face Detection. It helps for consistent portraiture styles where you prefer focus on the right eye.
- ○ **LEFT EYE PRIORITY:** Similar to Right Eye Priority, but focuses on the left eye instead.

Selecting the Appropriate Setting:
Consider your desired level of control:

- **Basic Face Detection:** Use FACE DETECTION ON with EYE OFF for general portraiture.
- **Automatic Eye Focus:** Choose FACE DETECTION ON with EYE AUTO for convenient focus on either eye.
- **Specific Eye Focus:** Select FACE DETECTION ON with RIGHT EYE PRIORITY or LEFT EYE PRIORITY for consistent focus on your preferred eye.

Limitations:

- **Subject Movement:** If your subject moves significantly while you tap the shutter button, the focused face might not be within the green frame displayed before capture. It is very valid for fast-paced situations.
- **Exposure Modes:** In some exposure modes (e.g., aperture priority), the camera might prioritize overall scene exposure instead of optimizing exposure specifically for the face. Consider switching to a portrait-oriented mode (like portrait mode) if you want exposure tailored for your subject.
- **Subject Selection:** By default, the camera chooses one face when multiple are detected. You can tap the screen or use the focus stick to adjust the focus area on a different face.
- **Eye Switching:** Once the camera zeroes in on an eye, you can switch focus between both eyes using a custom

function button assigned to "RIGHT/LEFT EYE SWITCH."

- **Temporary Loss of Detection:** If your subject temporarily leaves the frame, the white focus frame might linger for a short while. It doesn't necessarily indicate a face is still present.
- **Burst Shooting:** Face detection might be suspended at the closing of a burst sequence depending on shooting conditions.
- **Eye Occlusion:** If a subject's eyes are obscured by hair, glasses, or other objects, the camera might prioritize focusing on the entire face instead of the eye.

Additional Notes:
- Face detection works in both portrait and landscape orientations.

SUBJECT DETECTION SETTINGS

While Face/Eye Detection excels at portraiture, your Fujifilm X100VI offers another powerful tool - Subject Detection Settings. This guide explores the rubrics of these settings, enabling you to prioritize focus on various moving subjects beyond human faces.

What is Subject Detection?
Subject Detection goes beyond traditional autofocus. It utilizes sophisticated algorithms to identify and track specific subject types within the frame. It helps to prioritize focus on these subjects, making sure they stay sharp even when moving or partially obscured.

Understanding the Options:
When you enable Subject Detection (SUBJECT DETECTION ON), you can select from various subject types the camera will prioritize:

- **ANIMAL:** Focuses on and tracks dogs and cats. Ideal for capturing playful pets or wildlife encounters.
- **BIRD:** Prioritizes focus on birds and insects. Perfect for wildlife photography enthusiasts.
- **AUTOMOBILE:** Tracks focus on car bodies or front ends, primarily those used in motorsports. Great for capturing action shots of racing vehicles.
- **MOTORCYCLE & BIKE:** Tracks focus on motorcycle and bicycle riders. Useful for capturing dynamic moments in sports photography or urban environments.
- **AIRPLANE:** Focuses on cockpits, noses, or airplane/drone bodies. Ideal for aviation enthusiasts or capturing aerial scenes.
- **TRAIN:** Tracks focus on train driver compartments or front ends. Perfect for capturing the movement of locomotives.

Selecting the Appropriate Setting:
- **Pets or Wildlife:** Use ANIMAL or BIRD for precise focus on furry or feathered friends.
- **Motorsports:** Choose AUTOMOBILE for sharp focus on racing cars.
- **Action Sports:** Select MOTORCYCLE & BIKE to track focus on riders in motion.
- **Aviation Photography:** Use AIRPLANE to capture clear images of airplanes or drones.
- **Transportation Enthusiasts:** Choose TRAIN for focused shots of locomotives.

Interaction with Face/Eye Detection:
- Activating automatic Subject Detection disables Face/Eye Detection. The camera prioritizes focusing on the chosen subject type (animals, vehicles, etc.) over human faces.

Subject Selection and Tracking:

- By default, the camera chooses one subject of the chosen type when multiple are detected within the focus area.
- Tap the screen or utilize the focus stick to move the area of focus on a different subject of the chosen type.
- Similar to Face Detection, a white frame marks the selected subject. The frame might linger for a short while after the subject leaves the frame.

Limitations:
- Subject detection might be suspended at the closing of a burst shooting sequence depending on shooting conditions.
- Subjects are in both portrait and landscape orientations.

Combining Subject Detection with Face/Eye Detection:
While Subject Detection and Face/Eye Detection don't function simultaneously, you can switch between them depending on your shooting scenario. For example:
- Use Face/Eye Detection for portraits or situations where focusing on human subjects is essential.
- Switch to Subject Detection when capturing wildlife, motorsports, or other scenarios where prioritizing focus on animals, vehicles, etc., is crucial.

FOCUS CONTROL WITH AF+MF

The Fujifilm X100VI's AF+MF (Autofocus + Manual Focus) mode empowers you to seamlessly combine autofocus and manual focus for precise control over focus placement. This guide explores the functionalities and considerations when using AF+MF.

What is AF+MF?
Imagine a situation where you've used autofocus to concentrate your subject, but you want to fine-tune the focus point. AF+MF helps to do just that! With this mode

enabled (ON), even after autofocus locks onto a subject, you can directly refine the focus point by turning the focus ring on your lens. This offers a hybrid approach, leveraging the speed of autofocus with the precision of manual focus.

Understanding the Options:

- **ON:** This activates AF+MF functionality. After autofocus locks focus, the focus ring can be utilized for further manual adjustments.
- **OFF:** Disables AF+MF. The camera behaves according to the selected focus mode (single point, continuous, etc.). Once autofocus locks, rotating the focus ring has no effect.

Additional Considerations:

- **Focus Lock and Re-engagement:** After manually adjusting focus, the camera doesn't maintain that focus point. If you don't take a picture or perform any other actions for a while, the camera reverts to the originally locked autofocus point.
- **Focus Assist Options:** While using AF+MF, digital focus assist options like DIGITAL SPLIT IMAGE and DIGITAL MICROPRISM (available through the MF ASSIST setting) are not available. These options are primarily for pure manual focus situations.
- **AF+MF Focus Zoom:** This is an additional feature available when AF+MF is enabled (ON) and SINGLE POINT is selected for AF MODE. By activating FOCUS CHECK, you can enlarge the chosen area of focus by rotating the focus ring. This allows for even more precise manual focus adjustments.

When to Use AF+MF:

Consider using AF+MF when:

- You want to fine-tune focus after autofocus locks onto a subject.

- You need precise focus control in situations where autofocus might struggle (e.g., low light, high contrast scenes).

Combining AF+MF with Other Focus Modes:
AF+MF offers a versatile approach to focusing. Experiment with using it alongside other focus modes (single point, continuous) to find the workflow that most comfortably fits your style of shooting and specific situations.

MANUAL FOCUS WITH MF ASSIST

Conquering manual focus (MF) on your Fujifilm X100VI unlocks a world of creative possibilities. This guide explores the MF Assist setting, offering visual aids to achieve precise focus when using MF mode.

What is MF Assist?
Imagine composing a beautiful shot but needing complete control over where the focus lands. MF Assist provides visual feedback to attain sharp focus manually.

Understanding the MF Assist Options:
The X100VI offers several MF Assist options to cater to different preferences:
- **DIGITAL SPLIT IMAGE:** This classic tool centrally displays a split image on the frame. When the subject is not focused, the image appears split horizontally or vertically. Rotate the focus ring till the two sections perfectly align, indicating sharp focus. Select a black and white (MONOCHROME) or color (COLOR) split image display.
- **DIGITAL MICROPRISM:** This option utilizes a grid pattern that emphasizes blurry areas. The grid appears distorted or smeared when the subject isn't focused. If the subject comes into focus on rotating the focus ring, the grid sharpens and becomes more defined.

- **FOCUS PEAK HIGHLIGHT:** This option highlights high-contrast edges within the frame. The edges won't be highlighted when the subject isn't focused. As you achieve sharp focus, the camera highlights these edges in a user-selectable color (e.g., red, blue) with an adjustable level of intensity (peaking level).

Choosing the Right MF Assist:
Consider your visual preference and focusing style:
- **Traditional Approach:** Use DIGITAL SPLIT IMAGE for a classic split-image focusing experience.
- **Emphasis on Blur:** Choose DIGITAL MICROPRISM if you prefer an illustrative depiction of blurry areas sharpening as focus is achieved.
- **High-Contrast Edges:** Select FOCUS PEAK HIGHLIGHT to focus based on sharp, highlighted edges. Experiment with different highlight colors and peaking levels for the best combination.

Additional Considerations:
- **OFF:** Disables all MF Assist options. The focus display appears normal, offering no visual aid for manual focusing.

Leveraging MF Assist Effectively:
- Combine MF Assist with focus magnification (FOCUS CHECK) for even increased accuracy at high magnifications.
- Practice using MF Assist in different lighting conditions to become familiar with how focus indicators respond.

INTERLOCK MF ASSIST & FOCUS RING

This setting controls how MF Assist interacts with the focus ring:
- **ON:** MF Assist displays only when you rotate the focus ring in manual focus mode. This assists in prolonging

battery power by not displaying the MF Assist information constantly.
- **OFF:** MF Assist remains displayed regardless of focus ring activity.

Selecting the Appropriate Setting:
Consider your preference for information display:
- **Minimize distractions:** Use ON to show MF Assist only when actively focusing manually.
- **Constant reference:** Choose OFF to have MF Assist displayed continuously for easy reference.

FOCUS CHECK

This setting controls focus magnification:
- **ON:** On rotating the focus ring in manual focus mode, the display automatically zooms in on the chosen focus area, allowing for more precise focus confirmation. Tap the focus stick to cancel focus zoom and revert to the normal view.
- **OFF:** Focus magnification is disabled. The display remains at the standard viewing magnification.

Selecting the Appropriate Setting:
Consider your need for focus confirmation detail:
- **Enhanced focus confirmation:** Use ON for enlarged viewpoint of the area of focus while adjusting focus manually.
- **Standard view:** Choose OFF if you would rather focus without magnification.

INTERLOCK SPOT AE & FOCUS AREA

This setting determines how metering interacts with the focus area:
- **ON:** While utilizing spot metering (SPOT) or multi-metering (MULTI), the camera meters the light based

on the currently selected focus area. It is perfect for ensuring proper exposure on your major subject, especially when using spot metering.

- **OFF:** Metering operates independently of the focus area selection. The camera considers the entire scene for exposure calculation.

Selecting the Appropriate Setting:
Consider your metering needs:

- **Precise subject exposure:** Use ON for spot or multi-metering linked to the focus area, prioritizing exposure for your main subject within the chosen focus frame.
- **Overall scene exposure:** Choose OFF for independent metering, where the camera considers the entire frame for exposure calculation.

INSTANT AF SETTING

This setting determines the concentration of the camera on pressing a button to focus lock or AF-ON:

- **AF-S:** The camera becomes focused on pressing this button. This is similar to how autofocus works by half-pressing the shutter button.
- **AF-C:** The camera continuously focuses while the button is held down. This is useful for capturing mobile subjects in manual focus mode.

Selecting the Appropriate Setting:
Consider your focusing needs:

- **Single focus confirmation:** Use AF-S to manually focus and then confirm focus with a single button press.
- **Continuous tracking:** Choose AF-C for maintaining manual focus on a moving subject while recomposing or holding the button down.

DEPTH-OF-FIELD SCALE

This feature on your lens indicates the range of distances that will be in sharp focus based on your aperture selection. This setting determines the reference point for the scale:

- **PIXEL BASIS:** Provides a very precise reference based on the quantity of pixels taken by the sensor. It helps in viewing your images at high resolutions on an electronic display.
- **FILM FORMAT BASIS:** Provides a more practical reference based on the traditional 35mm film format. This is a perfect starter for most photographers, especially when considering the range of the field for prints.

Selecting the Appropriate Setting:
Consider your image output and intended viewing:

- **High-resolution viewing:** Use PIXEL BASIS for the most accurate depth-of-field estimation when viewing images at high resolutions on digital displays.
- **General photography and prints:** Choose FILM FORMAT BASIS for a practical reference point similar to traditional film photography, helpful for visualizing the range of the field for printed images.

RELEASE/FOCUS PRIORITY

The RELEASE/FOCUS PRIORITY setting on your Fujifilm X100VI helps to modify how the camera prioritizes focus versus shutter response when you fully tap the shutter button. This guide explores the functionalities of this setting for both single autofocus (AF-S) and continuous autofocus (AF-C) modes.

Understanding RELEASE/FOCUS PRIORITY:
Imagine capturing a fleeting moment. This setting determines if the camera gives priority to capturing the

image immediately (RELEASE) or waiting for perfect focus before taking the picture (FOCUS). Below is an overview of the options:

1) **RELEASE:**
   a) Priority is given to shutter release speed.
   b) The camera captures the image even when focus isn't fully achieved.
   c) It is helpful for capturing fast-paced action where getting the shot is of greater significance than perfect focus.

2) **FOCUS:**
   a) Focus accuracy takes precedence.
   b) The camera only captures the image on focusing the image properly.
   c) This is ideal for situations where precise focus is critical, such as portraiture or product photography.

Independent Settings for AF-S and AF-C:
The X100VI enables you select separate RELEASE/FOCUS PRIORITY settings for both AF-C and AF-S modes:

3) **AF-S:** You can prioritize either capturing the shot immediately (RELEASE) or waiting for perfect focus (FOCUS) when using single autofocus.

4) **AF-C:** Similarly, you can choose whether to prioritize capturing continuously moving subjects even if focus isn't perfect (RELEASE) or wait for focus confirmation prior to capturing in continuous autofocus mode (FOCUS).

AF+MF OVERRIDE:

Regardless of the RELEASE/FOCUS PRIORITY setting, if you have AF+MF (Autofocus + Manual Focus) enabled (ON), you can still capture an image even if autofocus isn't locked by a complete shutter press. It is because focus can be manually achieved via the focus ring.

Selecting the Appropriate Setting:
Consider the shooting scenario and your priorities:
1) **Fast-paced action:** Use RELEASE for AF-S or AF-C to capture the moment even if focus isn't perfect.
2) **Critical focus:** Choose FOCUS for AF-S or AF-C to ensure sharp images at the expense of potential shutter delay.
3) **Manual focus flexibility:** Enable AF+MF to capture an image even with autofocus not locked, enabling you adjust focus manually.

AF RANGE LIMITER: SHARPER FOCUS, FASTER AF

The Fujifilm X100VI's AF Range Limiter is an effective instrument designed to accelerate autofocus by restricting the span of distances the camera considers when focusing. This guide explores the different options and functionalities of this setting.

What is the AF Range Limiter?
Imagine your subject is relatively close, but the autofocus keeps hunting between nearby and faraway objects. The AF Range Limiter tackles this issue by allowing you to define a specific distance range. By limiting the autofocus search to this pre-defined range, the camera achieves focus lock much faster.

Understanding the Options:
It offers several options to suit your focusing needs:
1) **OFF:** Disables the AF Range Limiter. The camera considers the entire focusing range for autofocus.
2) **CUSTOM:** This allows you to define a custom focus range:
   a) **OK:** Confirms the currently selected focus range and restricts autofocus to that range.

b) **SET:** For setting the minimum and maximum focus distances for the custom range using the focus ring or touchscreen.
   i) **Touchscreen:** Tap two objects to define the near and far ends of the desired focus range.
   ii) **Focus Ring:** Rotate the focus ring to set the maximum distance of focus to infinity, effectively limiting the smallest distance at which focus is maintained.
3) **PRESET1 & PRESET2:** These options offer pre-defined focus ranges (macro or far) without customization. The actual focus distances achieved with these presets might slightly differ from the displayed values.

When to Use the AF Range Limiter:
Consider it in situations where:
1) **Focus Hunting:** The autofocus struggles to lock onto your subject due to nearby objects or clutter in the scene.
2) **Predictable Subject Distances:** You know the general range of location for your subject (e.g., portrait photography, close-up product shots).
3) **Fast-paced Action:** The ability to lock focus quickly can be crucial for capturing fleeting moments.

Additional Considerations:
1) The AF Range Limiter settings apply to both movie mode and still photography.
2) While using the CUSTOM option, utilize the touchscreen or focus ring for setting the focus range.

TOUCH SCREEN MODE

This guide explores the functionalities of the TOUCH SCREEN MODE setting, allowing you to customize how you utilize touch controls for various shooting scenarios.

Understanding TOUCH SCREEN MODE:

This setting determines how tapping the camera's touchscreen affects focusing, shooting, and other operations. Below is an overview of the available modes:

1) **TOUCH SHOOTING:** This mode simplifies shooting. Just tap your subject to achieve focus and capture the image. In burst mode, you can hold the display to take a continuous burst of pictures.

2) **AF (Autofocus):** This mode offers further control based on the selected autofocus mode (AF-S, AF-C, or MF):

   a) **AF-S (Single Autofocus):** Tapping the screen focuses the subject and locks focus till you press the "AF OFF" icon on the screen. It's helpful for focusing on a specific point and recomposing it before capturing the image.

   b) **AF-C (Continuous Autofocus):** The camera will continually fine-tune its focus as the subject moves, provided that your finger is fixed on the screen. This is ideal for capturing mobile subjects.

   c) **MF (Manual Focus):** Even in manual focus mode, tapping the screen enables you use autofocus on the chosen point. This can be helpful for achieving initial focus before fine-tuning manually with the focus ring.

3) **AREA:** This mode allows you to select a specific point for both focus and zoom:

   a) **Focus:** Tapping the screen repositions the focus frame to the selected point.

   b) **Zoom:** While in playback mode, tapping the screen helps to zoom onto a specific portion of the picture.

4) **OFF:** Disables all touch controls. The touchscreen becomes inactive, and you'll need to rely on physical buttons and dials for camera operations.

Choosing the Right Mode:

Consider your style and preferences of shooting:

1) **Simplified shooting:** Use TOUCH SHOOTING for point-and-shoot simplicity.
2) **Precise focus control:** Choose AF (Autofocus) with the desired AF mode (AF-S, AF-C) for specific focus behavior based on your subject and shooting scenario.
3) **Selective focus and zoom:** Utilize AREA mode for precise focus point selection and image zooming during playback.
4) **Traditional controls:** Opt for OFF if you prefer relying on physical buttons and dials.

Additional Considerations:

- Disabling touch controls entirely can be achieved through the 🔧BUTTON/DIAL SETTING menu.
- Touchscreen modalities might vary slightly depending on the selected autofocus mode.

TOUCH CONTROLS FOR FOCUS ZOOM ON X100VI

This information details how touch controls function when FOCUS CHECK (focus magnification) is enabled on your Fujifilm X100VI.

Focus Check and Touch Controls:
When FOCUS CHECK is activated, tapping the touchscreen behaves differently based on the chosen TOUCH SCREEN MODE and the chosen autofocus mode (AF-S, MF).

Central Area
Below is an overview of the functionalities for the central area of the touchscreen:

Touch Screen Mode	Autofocus Mode	Operation
TOUCH SHOOTING	AF-S/MF	Capture a picture (similar to standard TOUCH SHOOTING behavior)
AF	AF-S	Initiate autofocus (AF-S only)
MF	Starts Instant AF (focuses using autofocus and then allows manual adjustments)	
AREA	AF-S	Initiate autofocus (AF-S only)
MF	Starts Instant AF (focuses using autofocus and then allows manual adjustments)	
OFF	AF-S/MF	No operation (touch controls are disabled)

Other Areas:

Tapping **outside the central area** of the screen simply scrolls the photo irrespective of the TOUCH SCREEN MODE or autofocus mode selected. This prevents accidental triggering of focus or shooting functions while using focus zoom.

Understanding Instant AF (MF Mode):

When using MF (Manual Focus) with FOCUS CHECK enabled, tapping the central area of the screen initiates

Instant AF. This means the camera briefly uses autofocus to establish focus then allows you to manually fine-tune the focus point via the focus ring.

CORRECTED AF FRAME

The Fujifilm X100VI's Corrected AF Frame is a valuable tool designed to aid focus accuracy, particularly when using the optical viewfinder (OVF) for close-up shots. This section explores its modalities.

What is the Corrected AF Frame?
Imagine you're using the OVF to frame a close-up image, but the autofocus (AF) frame doesn't seem to align perfectly with the focus. The Corrected AF Frame comes into play here. When enabled (ON), it displays an additional guide within the OVF to indicate the actual focus position for subjects approximately 50cm (1.6ft) away from the camera.

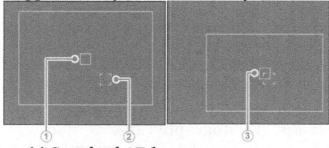

(1) Standard AF frame
(2) Focus position
(3) Green AF frame when shutter button is pressed halfway

Modalities of Operation
The standard AF frame in the OVF is a general reference point. The Corrected AF Frame provides more specific guidance:

1. **Standard AF Frame:** This frame remains present and represents the overall AF confirmation area.

2. **Corrected AF Frame (ON):** When activated, an additional frame appears within the standard AF frame. This inner frame represents the actual focus position for close-up subjects around 50cm away.

Utilizing the Corrected AF Frame:

- **Match the Subject to the Inner Frame:** For close-up shots, position your subject within the inner frame (Corrected AF Frame) to ensure acute focus on the desired point.
- **Half-Press Shutter Button:** When you half-press it to confirm focus, the standard AF frame turns green, indicating focus lock at the present distance.

Important Considerations:

- **Limited Visibility for Closer Distances:** It isn't visible for subjects closer than 50cm. In such cases, depend on manual focus or alternative focusing methods.
- **Temporary Deactivation:** You can temporarily disable the Corrected AF Frame display by pressing the central part of the focus stick. This may be beneficial if you find the additional frame visually distracting.

When to Use the Corrected AF Frame:

- **Close-up Photography:** This feature is most beneficial for close-up shots where precise focus placement is critical.
- **OVF Focusing:** If you primarily use the OVF for composing and focusing, the Corrected AF Frame offers a valuable aid for close-up work.

CHAPTER 5: SHOOTING SETTINGS

Accessing the Shooting Settings Menu:

1. Turn on your X100VI and switch to the photo shooting mode.

2. Press the **MENU/OK** button. This will display the camera's main menu.

3. Look for the 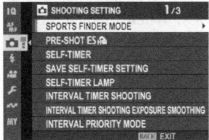 **(SHOOTING SETTING)** tab and use the navigation buttons to select it.

Exploring the Shooting Settings:

Now that you're in the Shooting Settings menu, let's break down each option and see ways it could improve your photography experience:

SPORTS FINDER MODE

Imagine you're trying to get that flawless shot of a flying bird or a sprinter crossing the finish line. These fast-moving subjects can be tricky to keep in frame. This is where **Sports Finder Mode** comes in handy.

- **What it Does:** When you activate Sports Finder Mode, the camera displays a frame within the Viewfinder or LCD screen. This frame represents the cropped area that will be captured in the resulting picture. The actual image will be zoomed in by a factor of 1.29x, similar to using a telephoto lens. The benefit? You get a wider view outside the frame, allowing you to track your subject and anticipate their movement before taking the shot.

- **When to Utilize It:** It is perfect for capturing action shots of athletes, wildlife, or anything that moves quickly. By seeing more outside the frame, your subject stays in focus and you capture the decisive moment.

PRE-SHOT PHOTOGRAPHY

Sometimes, even with Sports Finder Mode, capturing that fleeting moment can be challenging.

- **What it Does:** When enabled, Pre-Shot Photography starts capturing a burst of images on half-pressing the shutter button. This means the camera captures a few frames before you fully press the button. Consider it a safety net – you're more likely to capture the exact moment you want.
- **When to Utilize It:** It is ideal for unpredictable action shots where timing is crucial. In the event that you're trying to capture the peak of an athlete's jump or the expression on a child's face during a surprise party, Pre-Shot Photography can help you ensure you capture the exact moment.

Below are more pointers to remember:

Sports Finder Mode and **Pre-Shot Photography** work best together. Use the wider view of Sports Finder Mode to track your subject and Pre-Shot Photography to capture a burst of frames for that perfect moment.

Both these features work best on selecting the electronic shutter. The electronic type is silent and faster compared to the mechanical shutter, making it ideal for capturing action without introducing camera shake.

Remember that using Pre-Shot Photography will result in more images being saved. Ensure to have enough storage space available.

SELF-TIMER: TAKING SELFIES AND PERFECTING TIMING

The Fujifilm X100VI's self-timer offers an easy method to capture photos at a particular location in the frame, or in order to reduce shaking of the camera for sharp still lifes.

Using the Self-Timer:
1) **Accessing the Setting:** The self-timer is located in the Shooting Settings menu (**MENU/OK > A Shooting Setting**). You'll see three options: **R2 SEC (2 seconds), S10 SEC (10 seconds), and OFF**.
2) **Choosing Your Delay:**
   a) **R2 SEC (2 seconds):** It is a great option to minimize camera shake. Perfect for still life photography or capturing a group photo where everyone needs to be focused.
   b) **S10 SEC (10 seconds):** This is the classic self-timer setting, ideal for selfies or group photos where you want time to get into position. The self-timer lamp will blink just before the picture is taken, giving you a heads up.
3) **Taking the Photo:**
   a) Set your desired delay (2 seconds or 10 seconds).
   b) Compose your shot and frame yourself (if using for selfies).
   c) **Important!** Stand behind the camera on pressing the shutter button. Blocking the lens with your body can affect focus and exposure.
   d) Completely press the shutter button. The countdown will begin, and the remaining time gets displayed.

e) (Optional) To cancel the timer before taking the shot, press the **DISP/BACK** button.

Additional Tips:

- The self-timer automatically turns off when you power down the camera.
- Consider using a tripod for even greater stability, especially when using the 2-second delay for pictures of still life.
- For creative selfies, explore using the self-timer with varying aperture settings or shutter speeds to achieve unique effects.

SAVE SELF-TIMER SETTING

This setting controls whether the camera remembers your chosen self-timer delay (2 seconds or 10 seconds) after you deactivate it.

- **ON:** If you frequently use the self-timer, this is a convenient option. The camera will remember your last used delay, saving you time from having to re-select it each time.
- **OFF:** If you only use the self-timer occasionally, or prefer to choose the delay, you can keep this setting off. The camera will default to "OFF" when powered on.

SELF-TIMER LAMP

This setting controls the self-timer lamp facing the camera.

- **ON:** The lamp will blink before the picture is taken, giving you a visual cue. It helps in dim light conditions or to ensure everyone is ready for the shot.
- **OFF:** If you're shooting in dim light where you wish to be discreet, or if the blinking light might be distracting, turn it off.

Below are more pointers to consider:

- If you are not sure of the option to choose for "Save Self-Timer Setting," experiment and see what functions optimally for your workflow.
- Turning off the self-timer lamp can also be helpful when photographing wildlife or pets, as the blinking light might startle them.

INTERVAL TIMER SHOOTING: UNVEILING THE MAGIC OF TIMELAPSES

Ever seen those mesmerizing timelapse videos that showcase a sunrise or the bustling activity of a city street over time? Well, the Fujifilm X100VI provides a powerful feature – the ability to capture those stunning sequences right in the camera! This feature is called **Interval Timer Shooting**. Let's break down the first steps together:

Activating Interval Timer Shooting:

1. Navigate to the **Shooting Settings menu** by pressing **MENU/OK**. Then, select the 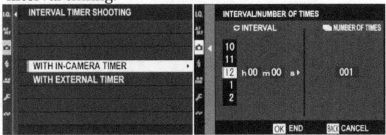 (SHOOTING SETTING) tab.
2. Find the **INTERVAL TIMER SHOOTING** option and highlight it. Press **MENU/OK** to enter the settings for interval timing.

Choosing Your Timer and Shots:

Here's where the fun begins! You'll see two main options:

- **Interval:** This determines how much time elapses between each shot. Select from a variety of settings to create fast-paced or slow-motion timelapses.

- **Number of Shots:** This determines how many photos the camera will take in total. The greater the quantity, the longer your final timelapse sequence will be.

Using the Focus Stick: The Fujifilm X100VI uses a focus stick for navigating menus. It's a small joystick which helps in navigating the selection right, left, down, or up. Use this focus stick to highlight your desired interval and number of shots.

Moving On: Once you've chosen your interval and number of shots, press **MENU/OK** again. This will take you to the next step in setting up your timelapse – choosing a starting time for your photo capture.

IMPORTANT CONSIDERATIONS FOR INTERVAL TIMER SHOOTING

While we explored the exciting world of setting up your timelapse with interval timer shooting, below are some more pointers to remember:

General Limitations:

- **Shutter Speed and Exposure:** Interval timer shooting won't work with the "bulb" shutter speed setting (used for long exposures) or with multiple exposure photography (combining multiple exposures in one image).

- **Burst Mode:** If you accidentally switch to burst mode while using the interval timer, the camera only takes one picture on pressing the shutter button.

Optimizing Your Timelapse:

- **Tripod Power:** A tripod is highly recommended for interval timer photography. This ensures your camera stays perfectly still throughout the entire capture process, resulting in a smooth and professional-looking timelapse.
- **Battery Life:** Timelapse sequences can take time to capture. Make sure you completely charge your battery to avoid any interruptions.
- **Monitoring Progress:** Want to see how your timelapse is coming along? Simply press the **PLAY** button during the capture process. This will display the captured photos. Press **PLAY** again or wait till the next interval to revert to the shooting display.

Display and Indicator:

- **Screen Saver:** In order to prolong battery life, the camera's display will turn off between shots. It will light up again a few seconds before capturing the next image. You can still activate the display at any time through the shutter button.
- **Green Blinking Light:** Don't worry if the display is off − a green blinking indicator light lets you know the camera is capturing photos during intervals.

Special Case: Infinite Captures:

If you want your timelapse to continue shooting until the storage fills up, you can configure the number of shots to "∞" (infinity). It helps to capture long-term events like sunsets or cityscapes over time.

AE BKT SETTING

Ever been unsure about the accurate exposure for a scene with high contrast or tricky lighting? The Fujifilm X100VI's **AE BKT Setting (Auto Exposure Bracketing)** is here to save the day! This powerful feature lets you capture many pictures of same scene at different exposure levels, ensuring you obtain the ideal shot. Let's dive into how it works:

Bracketing Basics:

Imagine a scene with a bright sky and a dark foreground. Using a single exposure might leave the sky blown out (pure white) or the foreground too dark. This is where bracketing comes in. By taking multiple photos with slightly different exposures, you increase your chances of capturing all the details in dark and bright areas. Later, you can select the best exposed image or even combine them for a high dynamic range (HDR) image using editing software.

Frames/Step Setting:

This controls the quantity of bracketed shots and the exposure difference between them:

- **FRAMES:** Choose how many photos you wish to take within the series of brackets (typically 3, 5, or 7).
- **STEP:** This determines how much the exposure is varied between each shot. Higher step values create a larger difference in exposure between the bracketed images.

Choosing Your Bracketing Style:

- **1 FRAME/CONTINUOUS:** This lets you decide on taking the bracketed shots one by one (1 FRAME) or in a rapid burst (CONTINUOUS). Taking them one by one allows you to recompose the frame slightly between shots, while continuous shooting is faster.

Sequence Setting:

This helps in managing the sequence which the camera captures the bracketed exposures. There are typically two options:

- **0 EV -> + STEP -> - STEP:** The camera takes a photo at the metered exposure (0 EV), then one overexposed (+ STEP), and finally one underexposed (- STEP).
- **- STEP -> 0 EV -> + STEP:** This option captures the underexposed image first, followed by the metered exposure, and finally the overexposed image.

Choosing the Right Option:
For most situations, the default settings (3 frames, 1/3 step EV, 0 EV -> + STEP -> - STEP) will work well. However, as you get more comfortable with bracketing, you could try out various settings to get the intended outcomes.

Below are some more pointers:
- Bracketing is helpful in high contrast scenes, backlit subjects, or situations where you're unsure of the perfect exposure.
- When using bracketing, make sure you have enough storage space available.

FILM SIMULATION BRACKETING (FILM SIMULATION BKT):

Love experimenting with the unique color profiles offered by Fujifilm's film simulations? This bracketing mode lets you capture the same scene with three different film simulations in one shot! This is a fantastic way to compare different looks and styles quickly and easily.

How it Works:
Navigate to the **Film Simulation BKT** option within the Shooting Settings menu. Here, the three film simulations can be chosen for the bracketed capture. For example, you might choose Provia for a natural look, Classic Chrome for

a nostalgic vibe, and Velvia for a more saturated look. On capturing the photo, the camera will capture one image with each of your chosen film simulations, giving you a variety of options to select from.

Focus Bracketing Setting:
Achieving perfect focus can be tricky, especially with macro photography or scenes with varying depths. **Focus Bracketing Setting** saves the day! This mode captures a series of photos at slightly different focus distances, ensuring at least one image will be perfectly sharp.

Two Focus Bracketing Modes:
- **AUTO:** This is the simplest option. The camera automatically determines the appropriate focus distances for the bracketing sequence.
- **MANUAL:** For more control, you can select the starting focus point and the number of focus steps (images captured at different focus distances).

Choosing the Right Option:
- **Film Simulation BKT:** It is ideal for photographers who love exploring different creative looks and want to compare film simulations quickly.
- **Focus Bracketing Setting:** Use this for macro photography, scenes with varying depths, or situations where achieving perfect focus is critical.

PHOTOMETRY: BECOMING A MASTER OF METERING

Metering is the process by which a camera measures light within a scene to determine the optimal exposure settings for your photo. The Fujifilm X100VI offers various metering options within the Shooting Settings menu, allowing you to take control and capture stunning photos in any lighting situation. Let's dive into the world of metering and explore each option:

Understanding Metering:
Metering refers to how the camera measures light within a scene to determine the optimal exposure settings for your photo. The chosen metering mode affects how much weight is given to various regions of the frame when calculating the exposure.

Important Note: The metering options you select in the Shooting Settings menu will only be active if you have **FACE/EYE DETECTION SETTING** and **SUBJECT DETECTION SETTING** turned **OFF** in the AF/MF Setting menu. These settings prioritize focusing on faces or subjects, and can sometimes override your chosen metering mode.

Metering Modes Explained:

- ⊡ **MULTI (Multi-pattern Metering):** This is the standard configuration and recommended mode for most situations. The camera intelligently analyzes the entire frame, considering color, brightness, and composition, to determine the optimal exposure. Use MULTI metering for everyday photography, landscapes, and portraits.

- ⊙ **CENTER WEIGHTED Metering:** It prioritizes the center area when measuring light. It's a good option when your main subject is positioned in the middle of the frame, and the background has similar lighting conditions.

- [•] **SPOT Metering:** It focuses on a very small, area (around 2%) to measure light. Use SPOT metering for backlit subjects, or when the background is significantly brighter or darker than your main subject. As an illustration, when photographing a flower against a bright sky, spot metering will ensure the flower is properly exposed, even if the sky is blown out (pure white).

- [ ] **AVERAGE Metering:** This mode simply takes the average light reading from the entire frame and sets the exposure accordingly. It could be helpful for achieving consistent exposure across multiple shots in similar lighting conditions. It also ideal for portraits and landscapes featuring people wearing white or black clothing.

Taking Control with Spot Metering and Focus Area:

Want even more control over metering? If you've selected **SPOT Metering** and want to ensure the camera meters the light from your specific subject, you can enable **INTERLOCK SPOT AE & FOCUS AREA** in the AF/MF Setting menu. This will link the metering to the chosen focus area, ensuring the camera prioritizes the exposure based on where you've focused.

Choosing the Right Option:

- **For most situations:** Start with **MULTI Metering**. It's the default for a reason and works well in an array of lighting conditions.
- **For backlit subjects or contrasting scenes:** Switch to **SPOT Metering** to ensure your subject is perfectly exposed.
- **For consistent exposure across multiple shots:** Try **AVERAGE Metering**.
- **For creative control:** Combine **SPOT Metering** with **INTERLOCK SPOT AE & FOCUS AREA** to ensure precise metering based on your focus point.

SHUTTER TYPES: CAPTURING QUIETLY AND ACHIEVING BLAZING SPEEDS

The Fujifilm X100VI offers a unique feature among X-series cameras: a **leaf shutter**. Unlike most cameras that use a focal plane shutter, the X100VI's shutter blades are located within the lens itself. This design offers some distinct advantages, including the ability to choose between different shutter types:

Understanding Shutter Types:
The camera's shutter manages how long the sensor is exposed to illumination, ultimately determining the brightness of your image. The Fujifilm X100VI provides three shutter options:

- **Mechanical Shutter:** This is the traditional type of shutter found in most cameras. It uses physical curtains that open and close to control exposure time. Mechanical shutters can be quite loud, especially at faster shutter speeds.
- **Electronic Shutter:** This shutter uses electronic means for controlling the exposure time by turning the sensor on and off electronically. Because electronic shutters are absolutely silent, they are perfect where noise needs to be kept to a minimum, such as photographing wildlife, concerts, or candid street photography.
- **Mechanical + Electronic:** This mode makes the camera choose between the mechanical and electronic shutter based on shooting conditions. As an illustration, the camera might utilize the mechanical shutter for flash photography, as electronic shutters typically don't work with flash.

Benefits of Electronic Shutter:

- **Silent Operation:** Electronic shutters are completely silent, allowing you to capture photos discreetly.
- **Faster Shutter Speeds:** X100VI's electronic shutter can achieve much faster shutter speeds in contrast to the mechanical shutter, allowing you to freeze ultrafast action or use wider apertures in bright conditions.

Using Quicker Shutter Speeds:
By selecting **ELECTRONIC SHUTTER** or **MECHANICAL + ELECTRONIC**, you can access shutter speeds faster than 1/4000s. To do this, simply turn the shutter speed dial to 1/4000s and then use the command dial to modify the shutter speed to even faster settings.

Potential Limitations of Electronic Shutter:
While the electronic shutter offers exciting benefits like silence and blazing-fast speeds, these are some considerations to make certain you realize the ideal picture:
- **Distortion:** Electronic shutters can sometimes cause rolling shutter distortion, which appears as wavy or skewed lines in fast-moving subjects or when panning the camera quickly. This is less noticeable using shutter speeds that are slower. Using a tripod for stationary shots or slower shutter speeds can help minimize this effect.
- **Lighting Flicker:** Electronic shutters can be sensitive to flickering light sources like fluorescent lights or LED signs. This can cause banding or a foggy appearance in the image. If you notice this happening, try changing to the mechanical shutter or using a different light source.
- **Ethical Considerations:** Since the electronic shutter is silent, be mindful of your subjects' privacy when using it in situations where silence is unexpected.

Important Note for Mechanical Shutter:
If you choose **MECHANICAL SHUTTER**, there might be slight variations in exposure accuracy at wider apertures

(f/stops). The fastest shutter speed possible also varies according to the aperture setting. For example, a shutter operating at its quickest is 1/2000s at f/2, but it increases to 1/4000s at f/4.5 and beyond.

Restrictions with Electronic Shutter:

- **ISO Range:** When using the electronic shutter, the ISO range is limited to ISO 125 – 12800. This means you might not achieve very high ISO settings for low-light situations, which can be a drawback.
- **Long Exposure Noise Reduction:** This feature is not effective using the electronic shutter; meaning you might see more noise in images captured at slower shutter speeds.
- **Flash Photography:** The electronic shutter cannot be used with flash. Should you need a flash, you'll need the mechanical shutter.

FLICKER REDUCTION

Ever notice those annoying flickering lines or banding in your photos when shooting under fluorescent lights or other artificial lighting? The Fujifilm X100VI saves the day with its **Flicker Reduction** feature! Let's explore its modalities and its usage for sharper, flicker-free photos.

Understanding Flicker:

Certain artificial lighting sources, like fluorescent lights or LED signs, flicker at a specific rate. This rapid flickering can cause inconsistencies in the way your photos are exposed, resulting in those unwanted lines or banding.

Flicker Reduction Modes:

The Fujifilm X100VI offers three Flicker Reduction modes to combat this issue:

- **ALL FRAMES:** This mode continuously analyzes the illumination and applies flicker reduction to every frame captured in a burst. While this ensures the most consistent results, it also lessens the continuous shooting frame rate (how many pictures are captured per second) of your camera.

- **FIRST FRAME:** In this mode, the camera measures the flicker rate only before the first frame is captured. It then applies an equivalent quantity of flicker reduction to all subsequent frames. This mode offers a balance between effectiveness and continuous shooting speed.
- **OFF:** Disables flicker reduction altogether. Select this choice when shooting in stable lighting conditions or if the benefits of flicker reduction don't outweigh the potential decrease in shooting speed.

Important Considerations:
- **Electronic Shutter:** Flicker reduction is automatically disabled (set to **OFF**). The reason for this is that electronic shutter itself can introduce some inconsistencies that can worsen flicker.
- **Movie Recording:** When a movie is being recorded, flicker reduction is not possible.

Choosing the Right Option:
The best Flicker Reduction mode depends on your condition of shooting:
- **For critical shots where flicker is a major concern:** Use **ALL FRAMES** for the most consistent results, even if it entails a slightly slower burst shooting speed.
- **For a balance between effectiveness and speed:** Choose **FIRST FRAME**.
- **For situations with stable lighting or employing the electronic shutter:** Turn **Flicker Reduction OFF**.

FLICKERLESS S.S. SETTING: FINE-TUNING FOR FLICKER-FREE PHOTOS

We explored how Flicker Reduction helps eliminate flickering lines caused by fluorescent lights. The Fujifilm X100VI offers another tool for combating flicker with **FLICKERLESS S.S. SETTING**.

How it Works:

When set to **ON**, this helps the camera to fine-tune the shutter speed in S (Shutter Priority) and M (Manual) modes to reduce flicker specifically caused by LED lighting and similar sources. The camera aims to match the flicker rate of the illumination by slightly modifying the shutter speed, thus minimizing inconsistencies in exposure and eliminating flicker in your photos.

Important Notes:

- **Mode Compatibility:** FLICKERLESS S.S. SETTING only works in S and M modes, where you have manual command over shutter speed.
- **Combining Features for Success:** For situations with challenging lighting, like flickering LED lights, combine **FLICKERLESS S.S. SETTING** with **CONTINUOUS** image stabilization for the best possible results.

IS MODE:

Image Stabilization (IS) is another helpful feature on your Fujifilm X100VI. It helps counteract camera shake, resulting in sharper photos, especially at slower shutter speeds or when shooting handheld. The IS MODE setting helps to control when picture stabilization is in use:

- **CONTINUOUS:** Image stabilization is always enabled, regardless of whether you half or fully press the shutter button. It is most effective for minimizing camera shake.
- **SHOOTING ONLY:** Image stabilization activates only when you half-press (in AF-C mode) or fully press to capture the image. This can save battery life compared to continuous stabilization.
- **OFF:** Disables image stabilization. Employ this if you're utilizing a tripod or if you prefer a more direct feel when shooting handheld (be aware of potential camera shakes when the shutter speeds are slow).

Things to Consider:
- Using image stabilization might introduce a slight vibration or sound as the system works to counteract camera shake.
- Depending on your shooting situation, you may strike a balance between effectiveness and battery life by choosing **SHOOTING ONLY** for image stabilization.

ISO AUTO SETTING

The Fujifilm X100VI offers a powerful **ISO Auto Setting** function which helps in controlling the camera's automatic ISO selection in various lighting conditions. Let's delve into its modalities:

Understanding ISO Auto:
ISO stands for the camera's sensitivity to illumination. An increased ISO setting helps to take photos in low-light situations, although it could introduce image noise (grain). With ISO Auto, you instruct the camera on the parameters for automatically selecting the ISO when the shooting mode dial is configured to **A** (Aperture Priority) or **S** (Shutter Priority).

Customizable Settings:

The ISO Auto Setting menu helps you configure three separate presets (**AUTO1, AUTO2, AUTO3**) with different parameters:

- **Base Sensitivity:** This is the minimum ISO for good lighting conditions. A lower base sensitivity will result in cleaner images but might not be suitable for low light.
- **Maximum Sensitivity:** This is the highest ISO for achieving a proper exposure. A higher maximum sensitivity helps to take photos in darker environments but will introduce more noise.
- **Minimum Shutter Speed:** This setting determines the minimum shutter speed in maintaining proper exposure. Greater light penetration is possible reaching the sensor, but increases the risk of camera shake.

Benefits of Customization:

By creating custom ISO Auto settings, you can tailor the camera's behavior to your specific shooting needs. For example, you might create one preset with a lower maximum ISO for cleaner images in bright daylight and another preset with a higher maximum ISO for low-light situations.

CONVERSION LENS OPTIONS

The Fujifilm X100VI allows you to attach optional wide-conversion and telephoto conversion lenses, expanding your focal length options. The camera menu offers dedicated settings for these lenses:

- **CONVERSION LENS:** Choose **WIDE** when using a wide-conversion lens, **TELE** for a telephoto conversion lens, and **OFF** if no conversion lens is attached.
- **DIGITAL TELE-CONV.:** This function helps you to take magnified pictures at different focal lengths even without a physical conversion lens. However, it comes at the cost of picture quality as it essentially crops the

sensor output. Choose from various zoom options like 2x zoom (70mm) or 1.4x zoom (50mm). **OFF** disables digital teleconverter.

NEUTRAL DENSITY FILTER (ND FILTER)

The Fujifilm X100VI boasts a built-in **Neutral Density (ND)** filter, a fantastic tool for creative photography in bright lighting conditions. Let's explore its modalities for stunning results.

Understanding ND Filters:

It is a special lens which lessens the quantity of illumination reaching the camera sensor without affecting color. It helps to achieve several creative effects:

- **Slower Shutter Speeds:** With reduced illumination to the sensor, you can utilize slower shutter speeds. This is ideal for blurring motion, creating a silky smooth effect for waterfalls, or capturing light trails from moving cars at night.
- **Wider Apertures:** The ND filter lets you use wider apertures (lower f-stops) even in bright light. It helps in achieving reduced field depth, creating beautiful background blur and isolating your subject.

Activating the ND Filter:

The ND Filter menu option allows you to turn the filter **ON** or **OFF**. The camera also uses the ND filter during movie recording, expanding your creative options for video work.

WIRELESS COMMUNICATION

The Fujifilm X100VI provides a suite of wireless communication features that can transform your photography workflow:

Connecting to Smartphones:

With your camera connected to a smartphone running the most recent version of the Fujifilm app, you can unlock a variety of remote shooting and image management capabilities:

- **Remote Control and Shooting:** Use your mobile device as a remote viewfinder and shutter release, allowing you to capture photos from a distance or from unique angles.
- **Image Transfer and Browsing:** Wirelessly transfer captured images to your phone for easy sharing or editing. You can also browse photos on your camera directly from the smartphone app.
- **Location Data Upload:** Add GPS location data to your photos directly from your smartphone, helping you document your travels and memories.

Benefits of Wireless Connectivity:

These wireless features offer an easy and effective method to control your camera, manage your photos, and improve general shooting experience.

CHAPTER 6: FLASH SETTING: STILL PHOTOGRAPHY

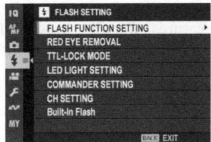

Your Fujifilm X100VI packs a built-in flash, but it offers more than just a simple point-and-light solution. By accessing the **FLASH SETTING (STILL PHOTOGRAPHY)** menu, you'll discover a range of options to control your flash and achieve creative lighting effects for your still photos. Here's a breakdown of each setting:

FLASH FUNCTION SETTING

Your Fujifilm X100VI's built-in flash offers beyond only a simple burst of light. By diving into the **FLASH FUNCTION SETTING** menu, you'll unlock a variety of modes to control how the flash fires and achieve creative lighting effects for your still photography. Here's a breakdown of all the information you require:

Understanding Flash Function Setting:
This setting helps to customize how the flash operates in various situations. Here's how to access and adjust it:

1. Tap **MENU/OK** in the photo shooting display.

2. Select the 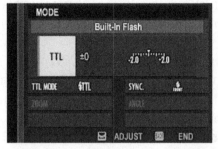 **(FLASH SETTING)** tab.
3. Choose **FLASH FUNCTION SETTING**.
The camera will display available options for the built-in flash.

Using the Focus Stick and Rear Command Dial:
- Use the focus stick for highlighting the desired setting.
- To modify the highlighted option, turn the rear command dial.
- Press **DISP/BACK** to confirm your selection.

Available Flash Modes (Options may vary):
- **TTL (Through The Lens):** The camera meters the light reflected off the subject through the lens to ascertain the ideal flash output to ensure a fair exposure. This is a good all-around mode for most situations.
- **AUTO:** The flash ignites on its own when lighting conditions are deemed insufficient for a correct exposure.
- **MANUAL:** You have total command over the flash power output, allowing for more customized lighting effects.
- **SLOW SYNC.:** The flash fires at the early stages of the exposure, followed by a slower shutter speed to capture the subject and the surrounding background light.

Important Considerations:
- **Flash Shadows:** Based on the flash angle and distance to the subject, the lens might cast shadows in your

photos. Consider adjusting the flash position or using a diffuser to soften the light.

- **Flash Limitations:** The flash won't fire in certain modes like panorama or on utilizing the electronic shutter. Additionally, some shutter speeds might not work with flash in Shutter Priority (S) or Manual (M) modes.
- **Multiple Flash Firing (TTL Mode):** In TTL mode, the flash might fire multiple times with each shot to ensure accurate exposure. Remain still until the camera finishes capturing to avoid blurry images.
- **Flash and Sound:** The flash won't fire if you have **SOUND & FLASH** set to **OFF** in the **DIAL SETTING** menu.
- **Lens Hoods:** Optional lens hoods are not recommended with the built-in flash as they might block the light and cause vignetting (darkened corners).

FLASH SETTINGS

The following are some of the flash settings you can adjust when using the camera's built in flash.

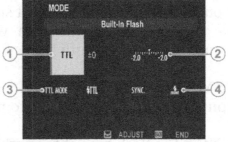

1) Flash control Mode
2) Flash Compensation
3) Flash Mode
4) Sync

1. FLASH CONTROL MODE:

This setting determines how the flash determines its power output:

1) **TTL (Through The Lens):** The camera gauges the light reflected off the subject through the lens and promptly modifies the flash power for a balanced exposure. It is the most typical and user-friendly mode for most situations.

2) **M (Manual):** You take complete command of the flash output, selecting a specific power level from 1/1 (full power) to 1/64 (lowest power) in fractions. This permits more accurate control and creative effects, but requires a deeper understanding of flash photography. Be aware that very low power settings might not achieve desired results due to limitations of the flash system. Try it out to assess the outcome before your final image.

3) **Multi:** This mode is used for advanced setups with multiple flashes. The X100VI acts as the main flash unit, controlling other wireless flash units in the system. In the absence of a multi-flash setup, you can disregard this option.

4) **⊗OFF (OFF):** Disables the flash completely.

2. FLASH COMPENSATION/OUTPUT:

This setting helps to modify the flash level based on the chosen Flash Control Mode:

- **TTL Mode:** You can adjust **flash compensation** to fine-tune the automatic flash output determined by the camera. A positive compensation value increases the flash power, while a negative value decreases it. This is helpful when the camera's automatic flash might not produce the desired result.

- **Manual Mode:** This setting directly controls the flash **output** power, allowing you choose a particular fraction of full power among the choices accessible.

3. FLASH MODE (TTL):

These modes are exclusive when the **Flash Control Mode** is configured to **TTL**. They determine how the flash fires in relation to the shutter and the overall exposure:

- **⚡TTL AUTO (FLASH AUTO):** The flash fires only when the camera deems it necessary for a proper exposure based on lighting conditions. A flash icon ⚡ pops up on half-pressing the shutter button, indicating the flash will fire.

- **⚡TTL (STANDARD):** The flash fires with each photo if possible, adjusting its power based on subject brightness for balanced exposure. The flash won't fire if it's not fully charged when you take the photo.

- **⚡TTL SLOW (SLOW SYNC.):** This mode combines the flash with a slower shutter speed. The flash fires first to lighten up the subject, followed by the slower shutter speed for capturing the ambient background light. This is ideal for situations like portraits at night, to capture both the well-lit backdrop environment and subject. Remember that the flash won't fire if it's not fully charged.

4. SYNC (H/1ST CURTAIN OR I/2ND CURTAIN):

This setting determines the timing of the flash relative to the shutter opening and closing:

- **⚡FRONT 1ST CURTAIN (recommended):** The moment the shutter opens, the flash fires, freezing the subject and the backdrop at the moment of capture. It is the

196

most typical and recommended setting for most situations.

- **REAR 2ND CURTAIN:** The flash fires shortly before the shutter closes. This creates a creative effect where moving objects appear behind the subject as streaks of light. However, this mode requires a reduced shutter speed and stable conditions to prevent shaking of the camera.

Flash Sync Speed:
The X100VI can synchronize the flash using shutter speeds of 1/2000s or slower. It indicates the flash might not fire completely if you choose a faster shutter sped, resulting in uneven illumination.

Remember:
- These settings are only applicable when the Flash Control Mode is configured to TTL.

RED EYE REMOVAL

Ever noticed those creepy red circles in your photos caused by the flash reflecting off people's eyes? The Fujifilm X100VI saves the day with its **Red Eye Removal** feature! Let's break down how it works:

What is Red-Eye?
When the camera flash fires directly at someone's eyes, the light can bounce off the red blood vessels behind their eyes, creating an unwelcome red glow in the photo (red-eye effect).

Red Eye Removal Options:
This setting within the **FLASH SETTING** menu offers two options:
- **FLASH:** This activates **flash red-eye reduction** only. The camera emits a pre-flash prior to the major

flash, which causes the pupil to constrict, reducing the red-eye effect. This works best in TTL flash control mode (explained earlier).

- **OFF:** Disables both **digital red-eye removal** and **flash red-eye reduction**. Use this if red-eye isn't a concern or if you would rather edit it out later in post-processing software.

Important Notes:
- Red-eye removal is only available when the **FLASH SETTING** is set to **FLASH**.
- Flash red-eye reduction works best with TTL flash control mode, where the camera instantly modifies the flash power based on subject brightness.

Combating Red-Eye:
While red-eye removal is a helpful feature, it's not foolproof. Below are some more pointers to minimize red-eye:
- **Bounce the Flash:** If possible, bounce the flash off a ceiling or wall instead of directing it directly at the subject's eyes. The diffused light will reduce red-eye.
- **Angle the Flash:** Slightly tilt the flash upwards to reduce the direct reflection into the eyes.
- **Use External Flash:** Some external flashes offer features like red-eye reduction or swivel heads for bouncing the light.

TTL LOCK: ACHIEVING CONSISTENT FLASH

Tired of adjusting the flash level for every photo in a series? The Fujifilm X100VI's **TTL-LOCK MODE** is available to assist! Let's explore how it works to ensure consistent flash results across multiple shots.

Understanding TTL Flash Control:

TTL stands for "Through The Lens." In TTL mode, the camera meters the light reflected off the subject through the lens to determine the optimal flash output for a balanced exposure. While convenient, adjusting the flash level manually for each shot can be time-consuming and lead to inconsistencies.

TTL Lock to the Rescue:
TTL Lock allows you to lock the flash output based on a pre-determined metering value, ensuring consistent flash results across a series of photographs. Here's how it works:

Two Lock Options:
- **LOCK WITH LAST FLASH:** The latest photo's metered value that was taken is where the flash output is locked. This is useful if you find a good flash level for a particular lighting situation and want to maintain it for subsequent shots with similar conditions.
- **LOCK WITH METERING FLASH:** The camera fires a series of pre-flashes before capturing the image. These pre-flashes help the camera meter the scene and determine the optimal flash output. The flash power is then locked based on this metering information. This option is ideal for accurate flash exposure right from the start.

Using TTL Lock:
1. Assign the **TTL-LOCK** function to a convenient camera control button (refer to your camera's handbook for customization options).
2. In the desired lighting situation, take a trial picture or use the **LOCK WITH METERING FLASH** option.
3. The flash output will be locked based on the chosen method.
4. Subsequent photos will use the locked flash level for consistent results.

Important Notes:
- **Flash Compensation:** Even with TTL Lock active, you can still adjust flash compensation to fine-tune the locked flash power for specific shots.
- **Error Message:** If you select **LOCK WITH LAST FLASH** and haven't captured any photos, the camera shows an error message as there's no previous metering value to lock.

LED LIGHT SETTING

This setting applies when a shoe-mounted flash unit with a built-in LED light. It helps to utilize the LED light for specific purposes in your still photos:
- **CATCHLIGHT:** A catchlight is a small reflection of the light source (in this case, the LED light) in the subject's eye. Adding a catchlight can make eyes appear brighter and more lively in portraits.
- **AF ASSIST:** The LED light can function as an autofocus-assist illuminator. This is helpful in low-light situations where the camera might struggle to focus via the regular autofocus system.
- **AF ASSIST + CATCHLIGHT:** This option combines both functionalities, providing focus assist and adding a catchlight to your photos.
- **OFF:** Disables the LED light entirely.

Accessing LED Light Setting:
In some X100VI models, you can access this setting within the **FLASH FUNCTION SETTING** menu. Refer to your camera's handbook for particular instructions.

COMMANDER SETTING

This advanced setting is relevant if you use clip-on flash units compatible with Fujifilm's optical wireless flash control system. The X100VI can act as a commander unit, controlling these remote flash units wirelessly:

- **Gr A, Gr B, Gr C:** These options allow you to assign different groups to your remote flashes. As an illustration, you can set one flash to Group A and another to Group B, and then control them independently from the camera via the commander mode.
- **OFF:** Disables the commander functionality.

Accessing Commander Setting:
Similar to the LED Light Setting, you might find the Commander Setting within the **FLASH FUNCTION SETTING** menu on some X100VI models. Consult your camera's manual for confirmation.

CH SETTING

This setting is crucial when using multiple wireless flash systems in close proximity to avoid interference. It determines the communication channel between the X100VI (acting as the commander) and the remote flash units:

- **CH1, CH2, CH3, CH4:** These options helps to select a specific channel for communication. Ideally, set all the commander and remote flashes within the same system to the same channel for seamless communication.

Using Separate Channels:
- If multiple photographers are using wireless flash setups nearby, each system can utilize a different channel to prevent interference with each other's flashes.

BUILT-IN FLASH

This setting helps to activate or deactivate the built-in flash:

- **ON:** Enables the built-in flash. This might be useful as a fill flash or for triggering remote flashes in commander mode.
- **OFF:** Disables the built-in flash. This is typically chosen when using external flash units fixed to the hot shoe or linked by a sync cable for full control over the lighting setup.

Using Optional Flash Units:
- The X100VI is compatible with a variety of optional Fujifilm shoe-mounted flash units that offer greater power and features compared to the built-in flash.

Third-Party Flash Units:
- The camera manual warns against using third-party flash units that exceed 300V on the hot shoe. Using incompatible flashes could damage your camera. Always ensure compatibility and voltage limitations before using third-party flash units.

CHAPTER 7: PLAYBACK MENU: MANAGING AND EDITING YOUR PHOTOS

▶️

The playback menu on your Fujifilm X100VI offers a comprehensive set of options for managing, organizing, and editing your captured photos. Experiment with these choices to improve your workflow and personalize the way you view and share your images. Here's a breakdown of each function:

RAW CONVERSION: IN-CAMERA RAW CONVERSION MADE EASY

This section provides instructions on converting RAW images to other formats directly on your Fujifilm X100VI camera, eliminating the need for a computer.

Benefits of RAW Conversion:

- RAW files capture more image data compared to JPEGs, offering greater editing flexibility and higher quality potential.
- Converting RAW in-camera enables sharing or editing of your photos without needing a computer.

The Conversion Process:

- **Display a RAW Picture:** Navigate to the image you want to convert in playback mode. Ensure it's a RAW file (usually denoted by ".RAF" extension).
- **Access RAW Conversion Menu:** Press the **MENU/OK** button while the RAW image is displayed. Go to the Playback menu, highlight **RAW CONVERSION** and press **MENU/OK** again.
- **Adjust Settings (Optional):** A list of conversion settings appears. Utilize the focus stick to navigate:
  - **Up/Down:** Highlight desired settings like image size, quality, film simulation, etc. (refer to your camera manual for specific settings available).
  - **Right:** Display available options for the highlighted setting.
  - **Up/Down:** Choose the preferred option within the setting.
  - **MENU/OK:** Confirm your selection. Repeat steps 4-7 to adjust any additional settings.
- **Preview Conversion:** Once settings are configured (or if you choose not to adjust any), tap the **Q** button. This displays a preview of the converted image based on your chosen settings.
- **Save the Converted Image:** If you're satisfied with the preview, select **MENU/OK** to save the modified picture as a new JPEG or other chosen format (refer to your camera manual for supported output formats).

Alternative Access:

You can also access the RAW conversion menu by pressing the **Q** button directly while viewing a RAW image during playback. This is a quicker way to initiate the conversion process without going through the playback menu.

RAW CONVERSION SETTINGS EXPLAINED

The following are the specific settings you can adjust when converting RAW images on your Fujifilm X100VI camera:

- **REFLECT SHOOTING COND.:** Creates a JPEG copy of the RAW image using the same settings (film simulation, white balance, etc.) that were applied when the photo was captured. This provides a quick route for getting a JPEG with your preferred in-camera settings.

- **FILE TYPE:** Choose the format for the converted image. Common options include JPEG (compressed format) for sharing or editing, and possibly TIFF (lossless format) for archiving purposes (refer to the handbook of your camera for supported output formats).

- **IMAGE SIZE:** Select the desired resolution (dimensions) for the converted image. A larger size results in higher quality but also needs additional room for storage. Choose a size suitable for your needs.

- **IMAGE QUALITY:** Adjust the compression level of the converted JPEG image (if selected as the output format). Higher quality leads to increased file sizes and vice versa.

- **PUSH/PULL PROCESSING:** Fine-tune the exposure of the converted image. This helps to adjust the brightness, if the original RAW image was slightly under or overexposed.

- **DYNAMIC RANGE:** Enhance details in highlights (bright areas) of the photo whilst maintaining shadow detail, creating a more natural contrast. Useful for high-contrast scenes.

- **D RANGE PRIORITY:** Similar to Dynamic Range, but prioritizes preserving detail in both highlights and shadows, even in high-contrast scenes. This might result in a slightly flatter overall image compared to the Dynamic Range setting.

- **FILM SIMULATION:** Trigger the appearance and feel of several films (e.g., Provia for standard color, Astia for vibrant colors, Acros for black and white). This is an effective instrument for adding a specific visual style to your converted images.
- **MONOCHROMATIC COLOR (for ACROS & MONOCHROME Film Simulations):** When using the ACROS or MONOCHROME Film Simulation options, this setting helps you select a color tint for your black and white image, like adding a slight sepia tone.
- **GRAIN EFFECT:** Simulate the grain-like film, adding a textured feel to your converted image.
- **COLOR CHROME EFFECT:** Expands the color range for highly saturated colors like red, yellow, and green, creating a more vibrant look.
- **COLOR CHROME FX BLUE:** Specifically targets the blue color channel, expanding its tonal range for richer blues.
- **SMOOTH SKIN EFFECT:** Softens skin tones, potentially beneficial for portrait photography.
- **WHITE BALANCE & WB SHIFT:** Adjust the image's color temperature for a more natural or creative white balance.
- **TONE CURVE:** Provides precise control over highlights, shadows, and midtones for detailed adjustments.
- **COLOR:** Adjust the overall color density of the image.
- **SHARPNESS:** Hone the image outlines to enhance detail or create a softer look.
- **HIGH ISO NR:** Reduces noise (mottling) that might be present in images captured at high ISO settings.
- **CLARITY:** Enhances image definition and adds a sense of depth.

- **COLOR SPACE:** Select the color space used for color reproduction (e.g., sRGB for standard web use, Adobe RGB for wider color gamut).
- **HDR MODE:** Simulates the HDR effect by merging details from highlights and shadows, reducing detail loss in high-contrast scenes. (Might not be accessible for all RAW images)
- **DIGITAL TELE-CONV.:** Uses in-camera processing to create an enlarged image with a seemingly longer focal length (may result in some loss of image quality).

Important Note:
The availability of some settings might depend on the options you chose when capturing the original RAW image.

In Conclusion:
The Fujifilm X100VI's in-camera RAW conversion functionality provides a convenient solution for converting RAW images to more usable formats without needing a computer. It helps in sharing or editing your photos on the go, enhancing your photographic workflow.

HEIF TO JPEG/TIFF CONVERSION

This option allows you to convert images captured in the HEIF (High Efficiency Image File) format to a more widely appropriate format such as TIFF or JPEG.

Benefits of Conversion:
- HEIF offers superior compression for reduced file sizes, but might not be universally supported by all devices or software.
- Converting to JPEG provides broader compatibility for sharing or editing your photos.
- Converting to TIFF offers a lossless format (preserves all image data) for archiving purposes.

Conversion Process:
1. Access the playback menu.
2. Highlight **HEIF TO JPEG/TIFF CONVERSION**.
3. Press **MENU/OK**.
4. Select the HEIF images you want to convert (via the multi selector and focus stick).
5. Choose the desired output format (JPEG or TIFF - 8-bit or 16-bit for TIFF).
6. Confirm the conversion process (refer to the handbook of your camera for detailed steps).

ERASE (DELETING IMAGES)

This option allows you to delete images. **Use caution, as deleted photos cannot be recovered.**

Deletion Modes:
o **FRAME:** Delete individual photos one by one.
o **SELECTED FRAMES:** Delete many images simultaneously.
o **ALL FRAMES:** Delete all unprotected pictures.

DELETION PROCESS (FRAME)

This mode allows you to delete individual images singly.
1. Select **ERASE** in the playback menu.
2. Choose **FRAME**.
3. Use the focus stick to navigate and highlight the image you want to delete.
4. Press **MENU/OK** to confirm deletion. (**Important:** No confirmation dialog appears before deletion, so be sure you've selected the correct image.)
5. Repeat procedures 3 and 4 to delete additional images.

Important Reminders:
• Protect important pictures before deleting to avoid unintentional loss.

- Consider copying valuable photos to storage devices for backup.

This mode helps to delete multiple photos selectively.

Selection Process:
- In the playback menu, choose **ERASE** and then select **SELECTED FRAMES**.
- Use the focus stick to navigate through your images.
- Press **MENU/OK** on each photo you wish to delete. A checkmark (√) appears on selected images.
- To deselect an image, press **MENU/OK** again on that image.

Confirmation and Deletion:
1. Once you've selected the desired photos for deletion, press the **DISP/BACK** button.
2. A dialogue for confirmation will appear.
3. Highlight **OK** and select **MENU/OK** to permanently delete the selected photos.

Important Note:
- Images included in photo books or print orders are indicated by an "S" symbol. These images might require additional confirmation steps depending on your DPOF settings.

ALL FRAMES

This mode deletes all unprotected pictures at once. **Use with extreme caution as there's no way to recover deleted photos.**
- **Confirmation and Deletion:**
  1. In the playback menu, choose **ERASE** and then select **ALL FRAMES**.
  2. A confirmation dialog will appear.

3. Highlight **OK** and select **MENU/OK** to confirm.
4. Pressing **DISP/BACK** at this stage cancels the deletion process.

Additional Reminders:

- Before deleting using **ALL FRAMES**, ensure you have no important photos remaining.
- Consider copying valuable photos to a storage device for backup.

CROP

The CROP function helps to extract a specific region of interest from your initial picture, creating a new image that focuses on that particular area. This is useful in various scenarios:

- **Reframing your shot:** If your original composition wasn't perfect, cropping can help you refine it by excluding unwanted elements at the edges of the frame. It is used to tighten the composition, focus on a specific subject within the scene, or simply straighten a slightly tilted horizon.
- **Creating a new perspective:** Cropping helps you modify the perspective of your image by zooming in or out on a particular element. As an illustration, you can crop in tightly to create a close-up portrait or zoom out to reveal more of the surrounding environment, completely altering the feel of the image.
- **Following the rule of thirds:** This is a popular composition guideline that suggests placing important elements of your image along imaginary lines intersecting at four points, dividing the frame into a 3x3 grid. Cropping can help you ensure that your subject falls within one of these intersecting

points, creating a more balanced and visually pleasing composition.

- **Cropping Process:**
    1. Navigate to the image you want to crop in playback mode.
    2. Select **CROP** from the playback menu.
    3. Zoom in and out of the image (via the rear command dial) to define your desired crop area.
    4. Move the highlighted area around the image (via the focus stick), selecting the specific portion you want to keep.
    5. Press **MENU/OK** to confirm the crop selection. A confirmation dialog will appear.
    6. Tap **MENU/OK** again to save the cropped photo.

Important Considerations:

- Higher zoom ratios during cropping result in a smaller number of pixels in the final cropped image, potentially affecting image quality.
- If the final cropped image size becomes very small (indicated by a yellow "YES"), consider if the resolution is sufficient for your needs.
- All cropped images on the X100VI maintain a 3:2 aspect ratio.

RESIZE

This function helps to make a smaller version of your original image, reducing its overall file size.

- **Resizing Process:**
    1. Display the image you want to resize in playback mode.
    2. Select **RESIZE** from the playback menu.

3. A list of available resize options will appear. The available sizes depend on the dimensions of your original image.
4. Highlight the desired resize option (e.g., Small, Medium) and press **MENU/OK**.
5. A dialog box for confirmation will appear.
6. Tap **MENU/OK** again to save the resized image as a new file.

Benefits of Resizing:
- Saves storage space on your memory card, especially useful for emailing or online sharing.
- Faster transfer times when sharing resized images.

Choosing the Right Option:
- Use **CROP** to focus on a specific detail within your image or change the composition for a different visual impact.
- Use **RESIZE** when you need a smaller version of the picture for sharing or to reduce storage space without altering the composition.

PROTECT: SAFEGUARDING YOUR PHOTOS

The PROTECT function on your Fujifilm X100VI allows you to safeguard specific images or entire folders from accidental deletion. Below is an overview of the available options:

1. FRAME:
This option selectively protect individual photos.
- **Selection Process:**
  o In the playback menu, choose **PROTECT**.
  o Highlight **FRAME** and press **MENU/OK**.
  o Use the focus stick to navigate through your images.
  o Press **MENU/OK** on each photo. A checkmark (√) appears on protected images.

o   Repeat to select multiple photos.

o   Press **DISP/BACK** to finish selecting.

2. SET ALL:

This option protects all images at once. (Use with caution as unprotected images are still vulnerable to deletion.)

- **Protection Process:**
  o   In the playback menu, choose **PROTECT**.
  o   Highlight **SET ALL** and press **MENU/OK**.

3. RESET ALL:

This option removes protection from all currently protected images.

- **Unprotection Process:**
  o   In the playback menu, choose **PROTECT**.
  o   Highlight **RESET   ALL** and press **MENU/OK**.

Important Reminders:

- Protected pictures are still deleted when your memory card is formatted. Ensure you have backups for crucial photos.
- Protecting images selected for uploading to a device removes the upload marking.
- Set or remove protection by pressing the **Fn2** button during image playback (refer to the handbook of your camera for customization of the Fn2 button functionality).

IMAGE ROTATE: KEEPING YOUR PHOTOS STRAIGHT

The IMAGE ROTATE function on your Fujifilm X100VI allows you to correct the orientation of your photos if they appear tilted or sideways during playback. Here's an in-depth description of the process:

Understanding Auto Rotate:

- Your camera might have an **AUTOROTATE PB** setting within the **DSCREEN SET-UP** menu.
- When enabled, this setting automatically corrects the image orientation during playback based on the camera's sensor position when the photo was captured.

Manual Image Rotation:

1. **Verify Image Orientation:** During playback, if a photo appears tilted, you'll need to rotate it manually.
2. **Access IMAGE ROTATE:** Select the playback menu and choose **IMAGE ROTATE**.
3. **Rotate the Image:** Use the focus stick:
   - Press **down** to rotate the photo 90° clockwise (useful for right-tilted images).
   - Press **up** to rotate the photo 90° counterclockwise (useful for left-tilted images).
4. **Confirm Rotation:** Select **MENU/OK** to save the rotation and update the image orientation for future playback on the camera.

Limitations and Considerations:

- **Protected Images:** You cannot rotate photos that are currently protected. Remove protection first if necessary.
- **External Images:** The camera might not be able to rotate images captured with other devices.
- **External Viewing:** Rotations applied in-camera won't be reflected when viewing the photo on a computer or other cameras. The photo pops us in its original orientation on those devices.

The Point?

The IMAGE ROTATE function offers an easy method to correct the orientation of your photos directly on your Fujifilm X100VI camera. Remember to check your camera's **SCREEN SET-UP** menu for the **AUTOROTATE PB** setting to enable automatic orientation correction during playback.

VOICE MEMOS: CAPTURING MEMORIES WITH YOUR VOICE

The Fujifilm X100VI lets you add another dimension to your photos – your voice! With voice memos, you can record a quick note, describe the scene, or even share a funny anecdote alongside your captured image. Here's the modalities of this nifty feature:

1. Turning on Voice Memo Recording:
First, you'll need to activate the voice memo function. Grab your camera then proceed to the playback menu. Look for the option called "Voice Memo Setting" and ensure it's switched to "ON." Now you're all set to record!

2. Choosing a Photo for a Voice Memo:
Pick the perfect photo to add a voice memo to. Snap a picture you love, or browse through your existing images in playback mode.

3. Recording Your Voice Memo:
Once you've chosen the photo, find the front command dial on your camera – it's the dial with a button in the center. To record your voice memo, simply long press the center button of this dial. Remember that voice memos are limited to 30 seconds, so plan your message accordingly! The recording will automatically stop after 30 seconds, or when you release the button.

Below are more points to remember:
- Voice memos can't be added to videos or photos that are write-protected.
- If the photo already has a voice memo, recording a new one will overwrite the old one.

- Deleting the photo will also delete the associated voice memo.

Playing Back Your Voice Memos:

Photos with voice memos are easy to identify – they'll have a small microphone icon next to them during playback. To listen to your recorded message, simply select the photo with the microphone icon and press the center button of the front command dial. A progress bar will show you how much of the memo is left to play.

Adjusting the Volume:

Want to make your voice memo a little louder? No problem! While the memo is playing, press the "MENU/OK" button to pause playback. Then, use the focus stick to adjust the volume up or down. If satisfied with the volume, press "MENU/OK" again to resume playback.

The playback volume can be adjusted for all voice memos through the camera's settings menu, under "SOUND SET-UP" and then "PLAYBACK VOLUME."

Pro-Tip: Voice memos are an excellent method of adding context or a personal touch to your photos. Consider using them to:

- Describe the scenario captured in the picture, especially if you're traveling or documenting a special event.
- Share funny anecdotes or inside jokes that wouldn't be clear from the photo alone.
- Record short audio notes for yourself, reminding you of details about the photo later.

After several trials, you'll be using voice memos to enhance your Fujifilm X100VI images.

SHINING STARS ON YOUR PHOTOS: USING THE RATING SYSTEM ON THE FUJIFILM X100VI

The Fujifilm X100VI lets you rate your photos, helping to find your favorites later on. Consider it a personal star system for your captured images! Here's the modalities of this feature:

1. Accessing the Rating Menu:

Head over to the playback menu on your camera. Find the option called "RATING" and select it. Now you're ready to start assigning star ratings.

2. Choosing a Photo and Rating It:

Use the front command dial to scroll through your photos and locate the one you wish to rate. The rear command dial then becomes your rating tool – simply turn it to select a rating between 0 (lowest) and 5 stars (highest).

For an alternative navigation method, use the focus stick to choose photos instead of the front command dial.

Pro-Tip: While you're in playback mode (viewing single photos, nine-photo thumbnails, or hundred-photo grids), you can also bring up the rating menu quickly via the "AEL/AFL" button (look for the button with a function lock symbol).

Zooming in for a Closer Look:

Want to examine a photo more closely before assigning your star rating? No problem! The Fujifilm X100VI offers touchscreen controls. Simply tap the display to enlarge or reduce your photo, allowing you to make a more precise judgment.

Here are some pointers to remember when rating photos:

- Protected photos, movies, and pictures taken with other cameras ("Gift" pictures) can't be rated.

WIRELESSLY SHARING PHOTOS WITH YOUR SMARTPHONE

The X100VI helps in transferring photos wirelessly to your paired devices using Bluetooth. Below is an overview of the process for selecting images for upload:

Accessing Transfer Function:

1. Go to the playback menu on your X100VI.
2. Choose **TRANSFER IMAGE TO SMARTPHONE**.
3. Choose **SELECT IMAGE & TRANSFER**.

Optional: Reset Upload Markings (RESET ORDER):

- If you've previously marked images for transfer, use this option to deselect all before proceeding.

Selecting Images for Upload:

- Highlight pictures you want to transfer then tap **MENU/OK** to select them for upload.
- **Filtering Images (DISP/BACK):** Before selecting, press **DISP/BACK** to display images based on specific criteria (e.g., date, rating) if desired.
- **Select All (Q button):** Quickly mark all images for upload by tapping the **Q** button.
- **Sequential Selection (AEL/AFL button):** Select any two pictures using the **AEL/AFL** button. This will automatically select all pictures between those two chosen images for upload.

Initiating Transfer:

1. Once you've selected your desired photos, press **DISP/BACK**.
2. Choose **START TRANSFER**.
3. The chosen photos will be sent via Bluetooth to your associated device.

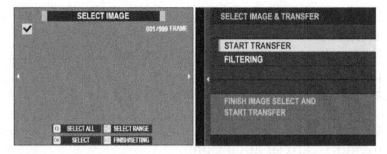

Important Notes:

* Ensure your smartphone or tablet is paired with your X100VI via Bluetooth for successful transfer.

FILTERING IMAGES FOR SMARTPHONE TRANSFER

This section dives deeper into filtering options available when selecting photos for transfer to your smartphone via Bluetooth on your Fujifilm X100VI:

Accessing Filtering:

1. During image selection for upload (as described above), press **DISP/BACK**.
2. Choose **FILTERING**.

Important Note: Selecting **FILTERING** will remove any existing upload markings on previously selected images.

Benefits of Filtering:

* This feature helps to narrow down image selection based on specific criteria, facilitating the transfer of photos that meet certain requirements.

Filtering Criteria (might differ based on firmware):

- **Date Capture:** Filter images by capture date (e.g., all photos taken yesterday).
- **Rating:** Filter based on assigned star ratings (e.g., only photos with 4 or 5 stars).
- **Folder:** Select images from specific folders in your memory card (if applicable).
- **Other Potential Filters:** Your camera model might offer additional filtering options like by image type (e.g., stills vs. panoramas) or by color (e.g., only white and black photos).

Transfer Limitations:

- Not more than 999 images can be included in a single transfer order.
- The following file types cannot be uploaded via Bluetooth:
  - Protected Images
  - Movie files (MOV)
  - RAW image files (RAF)
  - "Gift" pictures (images transferred from other cameras)

Automatic Transfer with Camera Off:

- If **IMAGE TRANSFER WHILE POWER OFF** and **Bluetooth/SMARTPHONE SETTING > Bluetooth ON/OFF** are enabled in the menu for network/USB, your camera can automatically continue uploading selected photos to your paired device even when powered off. (Refer to your camera manual for detailed instructions on enabling these settings.)

CUSTOMIZING TRANSFER BUTTON

It is possible to designate the **SELECT & SMARTPHONE TRANSFER ORDER** function to the **Fn1** button (if your X100VI model allows function customization). This provides a rapid method of accessing the image selection dialog for transfer by pressing the Fn1 button.

Wireless Communication

Your Fujifilm X100VI offers wireless communication capabilities that unlock a range of features when linked with a device running the latest Fujifilm Camera Remote app. Here's an overview of the benefits and functionalities:

Enhanced Control and Convenience:

- **Remote Control:** Control your camera then snap photos remotely using your smartphone as a viewfinder. It is vital for group photos, self-portraits, or capturing shots from difficult angles.
- **Image Transfer:**
    o Receive photos uploaded directly to your device for instant sharing or editing.
    o Browse images and download specific photos to your smartphone for further use.

Additional Features:

- **Location Data Upload:** Transfer location data (geotags) from your smartphone to your camera, embedding them into your captured photos. It is perfect for geotagging your travel pictures or documenting locations.

Customizing Fn1 Button (Optional):

If your X100VI model allows function customization, you can assign "WIRELESS COMMUNICATION" to the Fn1 button. This provides a rapid method of activating Bluetooth pairing and connect to your device via the Fn1 button.

SLIDE SHOW

The SLIDE SHOW function allows you to view your photos in an automated slideshow. It is a perfect method for sharing photos with loved ones or simply reliving your captured moments.

- **Starting the Slide Show:** Press **MENU/OK** to initiate the slideshow.
- **Navigation:**
  - o Utilize the focus stick to navigate:
    - ▪ Press right to skip to the next image.
    - ▪ Press left to revert to the previous image.
- **On-Screen Help:** Press **DISP/BACK** during the slideshow to view on-screen help if needed.
- **Ending the Slide Show:** Press **MENU/OK** at any time to stop the slideshow.

Important Note:
- The camera remains on while the slideshow is running. Manually turn off the camera when you're finished to conserve battery life.

PHOTOBOOK ASSIST: CRAFTING PHOTOBOOKS WITH EASE

The PHOTOBOOK ASSIST function on your Fujifilm X100VI allows you to transform your favorite photos into a physical photo book directly from your camera. It streamlines the procedure for creating and managing photo books directly from your camera. By going through the procedures below, you can easily select photos, design your photo book layout, and prepare it for printing to preserve your cherished memories in a tangible format.

Here's a step-by-step guide to creating a new photo book:

1. Accessing Photobook Assist:

- Navigate to the playback menu on your X100VI.
- Select **PHOTOBOOK ASSIST**.
- Choose **NEW BOOK** to begin creating a new photo book.

2. Selecting Photos:
- The camera displays your images.
- Use the focus stick to navigate through your photos.
- Tap the focus stick **up** to select an image for inclusion in your photo book. A checkmark will appear on selected images.
- Tap the focus stick **down** to deselect an image if you've chosen it by mistake.
- Tap **MENU/OK** to exit the selection process once you've chosen all your desired photos.

Important Notes:
- Images smaller than "a" size and movie files cannot be included in photo books.
- The initial photo you select will be designated as the cover image for your photo book by default.
- To choose a different image as the cover, navigate to that image and tap the focus stick **down** to specifically select it for the cover.

3. Finalizing the Photo Book:
- Once you've selected all your photos, highlight **COMPLETE PHOTOBOOK** and press **MENU/OK**.

Alternative Selection Method:
- To select all photos for your book at once, choose **SELECT ALL** instead of **COMPLETE PHOTOBOOK**.

Additional Considerations:
- A photo book can hold a maximum of 300 images.
- Any photo book that doesn't contain any pictures will be automatically deleted by the camera.

Viewing Photo Books:
1. Within the PHOTOBOOK ASSIST menu, highlight a photo book you want to view.
2. Press **MENU/OK** to open the selected book.
3. Utilize the focus stick to navigate left or right and browse through the pictures included in your book.

Editing and Deleting Photobooks:
1. Display the photo book you want to modify or delete.
2. Tap **MENU/OK** to see available options.
- **EDIT:** Choose this option to modify the photo book content. You can then follow the same steps outlined in Part 1 for selecting photos and finalizing the book.
- **ERASE:** Choose this option to permanently delete the photo book.

Important Note:
- Always be sure of your selection before deleting a photo book, as there's no way to recover it after deletion.

Transferring Photo Books for Printing:
Once you've finalized your photo book, you can transfer it to a computer or compatible printing service for physical creation. Refer to your camera manual or the instructions provided by your chosen printing service for specific transfer methods. This might involve linking your camera with your computer using USB or using an SD card reader to transfer the photo book data.

CREATING PRINT ORDERS FOR DPOF PRINTING (DPOF)

This function on your Fujifilm X100VI enables you to make a digital print order for printers compatible with the DPOF (Digital Print Order Format) standard. It helps to specify your printed photos and how many copies of each. Below is an overview of the process:

1. Accessing Print Order:
- Navigate to the playback menu on your X100VI.
- Select **PRINT ORDER (DPOF)**.

2. Setting Date Printing:
- Choose **WITH DATE** to include the capture date on your printed photos.
- Select **WITHOUT DATE** for prints without dates.
- Alternatively, use **RESET ALL** to remove any existing print orders from your camera's memory before creating a new one.

3. Selecting Photos and Copy Numbers:
- Display the image you wish to add in the print order.
- Use the focus stick **upwards or downwards** to adjust the number of copies you want printed for that specific image (up to 99 copies per image).
- To remove a photo, repeatedly tap the focus stick down until the copies reaches 0.
- Repeat procedures 3 and 4 to select all the images for printing and specify the desired number of copies for each.

4. Finalizing the Print Order:
- The maximum count of prints in your order will be displayed on the screen.
- Press **MENU/OK** to exit and confirm the print order.

Important Notes:
- Images marked with a **u** icon during playback indicate they are included in the current print order.
- A single print order can hold a maximum of 999 images from the memory card currently inserted in your camera.
- If you place a memory card with a print order created on another camera, you'll need to delete that existing order before creating a new one using your X100VI.

Transferring Print Order for Printing:

Once you've finalized your print order, you can transfer it to a DPOF-compatible printer for physical printing. Refer to your handbook for specific guidelines on how to import and utilize DPOF print orders. This might involve linking your camera to the printer via a USB cable or transferring the print order data to a PC and then to the printer.

PRINTING PHOTOS DIRECTLY TO FUJIFILM INSTAX SHARE PRINTERS

Your X100VI allows for direct wireless printing, eliminating the need for moving pictures to a computer first. Follow these steps:

Important Pre-requisite:
1) Ensure you've completed the **instax PRINTER CONNECTION SETTING** process beforehand. This involves accessing the ⚡network/USB settings menu on your X100VI, entering the SSID (name) and password of your instax SHARE printer, and establishing a connection. Refer to your camera manual for detailed instructions on this setup process.

Printing Steps:
1) **Power Up the Printer:** Turn on your Fujifilm instax SHARE printer.
2) **Access instax Printer Print:**
   a) Go to the playback menu on your X100VI.
   b) Select **instax PRINTER PRINT**. The camera will attempt to connect to the configured instax SHARE printer.
3) **Choose and Print:**
   a) Utilize the focus stick to navigate through your photos and select the image for printing.

b) Press **MENU/OK** to initiate the printing process. The selected image will be delivered to the printer, and printing begins.

Limitations:
1) Only photos captured with your X100VI can be printed directly using this method. Images from other cameras are not supported.
2) The printed area will be slightly smaller than what is displayed due to printer margins.
3) The printer's display interface might differ based on the exact instax SHARE model you're using.

DISP ASPECT (FOR HDMI OUTPUT)

The DISP ASPECT function on your Fujifilm X100VI helps to modify the aspect ratio for displaying still images on connecting to a High Definition (HD) device via an HDMI cable. Below is an overview of the available options and their effects:

Aspect Ratio Explained:
1) Aspect ratio refers to the width-to-height proportion of an image.

DISP ASPECT Options:
1) **16:9:** This conforms to the typical widescreen aspect ratio commonly used in HD televisions and monitors.
2) **3:2:** This aspect ratio is closer to the natural shape of a rectangular photograph captured on your X100VI.

Choosing the Right Option:

1) **Full Screen with Cropping (16:9):** Select this option for your photos to fill the entire screen of your HD device. However, the tops and bottoms of your photos might be cropped slightly to fit the 16:9 format.
2) **Preserving Original Ratio (3:2):** Choose this option to maintain the original aspect ratio (3:2) of your photos on the HD display. Black bars will display on the top and bottom of the screen to accommodate the difference in aspect ratio.

Important Note:
The DISP ASPECT function is exclusively accessible when your X100VI is connected to an HD device via the HDMI cable.

CHAPTER 8: NETWORK AND USB SETTINGS

The Fujifilm X100VI offers a variety of features for connecting to other devices and managing how your camera interacts with them. This section lets you control these settings.

To access these settings, simply press the **MENU/OK** button, either when you're in shooting mode or while reviewing your photos. Look for the tab labeled with a **network symbol (globe and waves)** - that's your gateway to the network and USB settings.

Let's break down each option within this menu:

CONNECTING YOUR X100VI TO YOUR SMARTPHONE VIA BLUETOOTH

The Bluetooth/SMARTPHONE SETTING menu lets you connect your Fujifilm X100VI camera to your device. You can remotely control your camera app, transfer photos easily, and even adjust camera settings - all from the convenience of your phone through the Camera Remote app.

Prior to exploring the specifics of the menu options, let us make sure the latest version is installed on your device. Keeping apps up-to-date ensures compatibility and provides you with the newest features and bug fixes.

Now, let's explore the Bluetooth/SMARTPHONE SETTING options on your camera:

1) **PAIRING REGISTRATION:** This is where the magic happens! Use this option to pair your camera with a new smartphone or tablet for the first time. The camera will search for nearby Bluetooth devices running the Remote app, making the connection process smooth and straightforward.

2) **SELECT PAIRING DESTINATION:** If you've already paired your camera with multiple devices, this option helps to choose your preferred device. An inventory of remembered devices will be displayed for your convenience. Additionally, you can choose "NO CONNECTION" if you simply want to exit the pairing menu without connecting to any device.

3) **DELETE PAIRING REG.:** It helps to easily remove an existing pairing from the camera's memory. Simply select the device you want to forget, and it will be removed from the list.

4) **Bluetooth DEVICE LIST:** This section shows a list of all devices currently paired with your camera via Bluetooth (excluding your smartphone connection). This menu is used to delete pairings with these devices if needed.

5) **Bluetooth ON/OFF:** This option controls the overall Bluetooth functionality on your camera. Selecting **ON** allows instant connection of the camera with any paired devices running the Remote app. If you're not planning to use the app or want to conserve battery life, you can switch Bluetooth to **OFF**.

6) **AUTO IMAGE TRANSFER ORDER:** Ever want to instantly share those special moments as you capture them? Turning **ON** Auto Image Transfer allows your camera to automatically upload photos to your paired device immediately you take them. It is an ideal option for social media enthusiasts or those who want a simple and rapid backup solution.

7) **SMARTPHONE LOCATION SYNC:** This setting helps to leverage the GPS capabilities of your smartphone to add location data to your photos. Enabling **ON** helps the camera to continuously download location information from your paired device while the app is running. It is beneficial for geotagging your photos, which helps you remember exactly where you captured those special memories. Just remember, location data download stops when you disconnect the app or turn off Bluetooth. The camera will also display a red location icon if the data hasn't been updated in over 30 minutes.

8) **NAME:** By default, your camera has a unique name for identification on the wireless network. This setting helps to personalize that name to something more memorable, particularly if you've got several Fujifilm cameras.

9) **IMAGE TRANSFER WHILE POWER OFF:** This powerful option lets your camera continue uploading photos to your paired device despite powering off the camera! This is a convenient feature for those who want to conserve camera battery while ensuring their photos are safely backed up. Still, remember that this option drains the camera's battery slowly while powered off. Select **ON** if this functionality is important to you, or choose **OFF** for a more conservative battery approach.

10) **RESIZE IMAGE FOR SMARTPHONE:** This setting helps you manage the photo file size you transfer to your

smartphone. Smaller file sizes upload faster and requires less room for storage on your phone. Selecting **ON** (recommended) enables image compression, which reduces the file size without significantly affecting image quality. This is a perfect option for most users who want to quickly share photos or save them on their smartphone for easy access. It's important to note that this compression only applies to photos taken at sizes L and M, and the original, uncompressed images remain safely stored on your camera's memory card.

11) **WIRELESS COM. FREQUENCY SETTING:** This option enables you choose the frequency band for your camera's Wi-Fi connection when sharing images to your smartphone. Generally, **2.4GHz** offers wider range but may be slower due to potential interfering devices using the same band. **5GHz** offers faster transfer speeds but has a shorter range and may be limited in certain regions. **If speed is your priority and you're transferring images within close proximity to your smartphone, selecting 5GHz can be beneficial.** However, confirm local regulations regarding the usage of the 5GHz band, especially the 5.2 GHz (W52) band, as it may be restricted in some areas.

12) **SELECT FILE TYPE:** This setting determines the file format used when uploading images to your smartphone. You can choose **JPEG**, which is a widely compatible format, or **HEIF**, which offers higher quality pictures with reduced file sizes in contrast to JPEG at the same quality setting. **JPEG is generally the recommended choice for most users** due to its universal compatibility. HEIF may be a good option if you value image quality and have a smartphone that supports this format.

AIRPLANE MODE

Traveling by air? Most airlines require you to disable wireless communication on electronic devices during takeoff and landing. Selecting **ON** for Airplane Mode will conveniently turn off both the camera's Wi-Fi (wireless LAN) and Bluetooth features, ensuring compliance with airline regulations. Remember to switch Airplane Mode back to **OFF** once you've reached cruising altitude and are permitted to use electronic devices again.

INSTAX PRINTER CONNECTION SETTING

Do you love capturing special moments and want to share them instantly as physical keepsakes? The Fujifilm X100VI helps you link up to compatible Fujifilm instax SHARE printers. This setting helps to configure the connection between the printer and your camera, enabling quick and easy creation of polaroid-style instant prints from your photos. Consult the instax printer documentation for detailed instructions on establishing the connection and using the printing features.

UPLOADING YOUR PHOTOS RIGHT UP TO THE CLOUD WITH FRAME.IO CAMERA TO CLOUD

This feature of your Fujifilm X100VI camera allows you to seamlessly upload your photos to the Frame.io cloud storage service. This is a fantastic option for professional photographers who need to quickly share and collaborate on images with clients or colleagues.

Below is an overview of the menu options within Frame.io Camera to Cloud:

- **CONNECT:** This initiates the connection process between your camera and Frame.io. You'll need to have a Frame.io account and be familiar with the setup process on their platform.

- **WIRELESS LAN:** This option helps to link your camera to Frame.io via a wireless LAN network (Wi-Fi). Make sure there is stable internet connection available for uploading your photos.
- **GET PAIRING CODE:** Once connected to Frame.io via Wi-Fi, you can generate a unique pairing code. This code will be used on the Frame.io platform to establish the connection with your account. **Importantly, the pairing code can only be viewed on your camera while it's actively connected to Frame.io.**
- **DISCONNECT:** When you've finished uploading your photos and are done with the session, use this option to disconnect your camera from Frame.io. This will also terminate the Wi-Fi connection.
- **SELECT FILE TYPE:** This setting helps you select which file formats you want to upload to Frame.io. You can select or deselect options like JPEG, RAW, HEIF, and more. Selecting specific file types can help you manage storage space.
- **UPLOAD SETTING:** While the details of upload settings may be specific to Frame.io, this menu likely enables you set up options like image quality or file size during upload. Consult your Frame.io account settings or documentation for additional details on these options.
- **SELECT IMAGE & TRANSFER:** This lets you manually choose individual photos or movies for upload to Frame.io.
- **AUTO IMAGE TRANSFER ORDER:** If you prefer a more automated approach, enabling this option will direct the camera to automatically mark photos and videos for upload to Frame.io as you

capture them. This is a convenient option for ensuring all your photos get uploaded quickly and efficiently.

- **TRANSFER/SUSPEND:** Once the upload process begins, use this option to pause or resume uploading photos to Frame.io as needed.
- **IMAGE TRANSFER WHILE POWER OFF:** This powerful option allows your camera to continue uploading photos to Frame.io even when it's powered off! This is a convenient feature for conserving camera battery while ensuring their photos are safely backed up to the cloud. Remember that this option drains the camera's battery slowly while powered off. Select **ON** if this functionality is important to you, or choose **OFF** for a more conservative battery approach.
- **ROOT CERTIFICATE:** Security is paramount, especially when dealing with cloud storage. This setting helps to manage root certificates, which are digital files that help your camera verify the authenticity of the Frame.io server it's connecting to. In most cases, you might not need to modify these certificates unless instructed by Frame.io support. The two options here let you:
  - **LOAD FROM STORAGE MEDIA:** If you've obtained a root certificate from Frame.io, use this option to copy it from your camera's memory card onto the camera itself.
  - **DELETE:** If a root certificate is currently loaded and you no longer need it, you can delete it using this option.
- **UPLOAD STATUS:** Curious about the progress of your photo uploads to Frame.io? This option displays the current upload status, giving you valuable information about the transfer process.

- **TRANSFER QUEUE:** This menu acts as a queue, showing an inventory of the files currently waiting to be uploaded to Frame.io. Here you can monitor the upload order and identify any potential issues that might be delaying the transfer.
- **RESET TRANSFER ORDER:** This option allows you to remove the upload marking from all files currently selected for transfer to Frame.io. It is a perfect way to start fresh with your upload selections.

CONNECTION MODE: CONNECTING YOUR X100VI TO EXTERNAL DEVICES VIA USB

The Connection Mode setting within the Network/USB menu determines how your camera interacts with external devices like computers when connected via a USB cable. Here's a breakdown of the available options:

- **USB CARD READER:** This is the most common and default setting. On linking your camera to a computer using USB with this mode selected, the camera essentially acts like a removable storage drive. This enables you to easily access and transfer photos stored on your camera's SD card to your computer for editing, sharing, or backup purposes. The camera itself remains fully functional, and you can turn it on or off without affecting the connection.
- **USB WEBCAM:** Do you love video conferencing or live streaming? This setting transforms your X100VI camera into a high-quality webcam! Linking your camera to a computer via USB with this mode enabled allows you to use your camera's superior image quality for video calls, online presentations, or even live streaming your creative endeavors. **It's important to note that using your camera as a webcam may require additional software**

on your computer, so be sure to consult your computer's documentation or software provider for specific instructions.

- **USB RAW CONV./BACKUP RESTORE:** This option offers two functionalities based on the program you use on your computer:

  o **USB RAW CONV. (needs FUJIFILM X RAW STUDIO):** If you use the FUJIFILM X RAW STUDIO software for post-processing your photos, selecting this mode allows you to leverage the X100VI's powerful image-processing machinery to quickly convert RAW image files to other formats such as TIFF or JPEG while maintaining exceptional image quality. This can significantly speed up your workflow compared to using your computer's processing power alone.

  o **BACKUP RESTORE (requires FUJIFILM X Acquire):** This mode helps you control your camera's settings using the FUJIFILM X Acquire software. You can create backups of your preferred camera settings, helping to quickly restore them to your camera if needed. It is an ideal option for photographers who have customized their camera settings to a specific workflow and want a method to quickly replicate those settings on other X100VI cameras or after a reset.

POWER UP OR TALK IT UP: MANAGING USB CONNECTIONS WITH POWER SUPPLY/COMM SETTING

The final setting within the Network/USB menu, USB Power Supply/Comm Setting, governs how your X100VI interacts with external devices in terms of power and data transfer when connected via USB. Understanding this setting ensures you maximize the benefits of your connections.

Below is an overview of the options:

- **AUTO:** This is the default and generally recommended setting. The camera intelligently switches between using the connected device for power (power delivery) or data transfer (communication) as needed. This is a convenient option that helps you concentrate on camera usage without worrying about managing power settings.
- **POWER SUPPLY ON/COMM OFF:** Choose this option to maximize your battery life. When enabled, the camera will prioritize drawing power from the connected device, minimizing the drain on your camera's battery. Remember that data transfer will be disabled in this mode. This setting is important for powering on your camera for extended periods while connected to a device that can supply power, such as a laptop.
- **POWER SUPPLY OFF/COMM ON:** This option prioritizes data transfer over power delivery. There is no power consumption by the camera on the linked device, but will exchange data with it. This is the ideal setting to transfer photos to your computer or use your camera as a webcam, even if the connected device doesn't provide external power. **Important to remember:** Some devices, like smartphones

with Lightning connectors or those that don't supply power at all, will not power on your camera via this mode. If you have doubts about a device's power capabilities, it's best to switch to this setting before connecting to avoid potential issues.

Additional Considerations:

- Regardless of the USB Power Supply/Comm Setting you choose, your camera's battery will still charge when it's powered off and linked to a device which supplies power via USB.

- The menu also offers an **INFORMATION** option that displays the camera's MAC address, Bluetooth address, and wireless network IP address. This information might be helpful for troubleshooting network connectivity issues or configuring advanced network settings.

- Finally, a **RESET NETWORK/USB SETTING** option allows you to restore all USB and network settings to their default values. This is beneficial if you come across connection problems or want to start fresh with your camera's network and USB configurations.

CHAPTER 9: CUSTOMIZING YOUR CAMERA MENUS

Imagine this: You're capturing a breathtaking scene with dramatic clouds casting magical light. You raise your camera, ready to freeze the moment, but on half-pressing the shutter, you see an annoying "Face & Eye Detection" box floating around, throwing off your focus and exposure. This setting, perfect for portraits earlier, is now hindering your composition. Frustration sets in as you navigate menus searching for the option to disable it. Precious seconds tick by, and the light might change before you find it.

Here's why customizing your menus is a game-changer:

- **Faster Access:** No more diving through endless menus! With your key settings readily available, you can adjust them on the fly, saving precious time and frustration.
- **Focus on the Moment:** Spend less time navigating menus and more time focusing on composing and capturing stunning photos.
- **Personalized Workflow:** Tailor your menus to your specific shooting style, making your camera an extension of your creative vision.

In this manner, you can quickly adjust settings like Face & Eye Detection based on the situation, instead of letting precious moments slip away.

WHICH MENUS CAN YOU CUSTOMIZE

The good news is, your Fujifilm X100VI offers two fantastic menus for you to customize: My Menu and the Quick Menu.

1) **My Menu:** This powerhouse holds up to 16 of your most-used settings across two custom pages. Think of it

as your personal cheat sheet – settings you access frequently, all in one convenient location. Imagine pressing the MENU button and seeing your customized settings right away, instead of navigating through the standard menus.

2) **Quick Menu:** This menu, activated by the Q button, allows for even faster access to 16 customizable settings. It's perfect for on-the-go adjustments you need to make frequently.

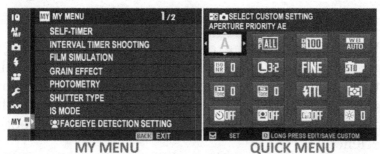

MY MENU   QUICK MENU

Before we dive in and start filling these menus with everything under the sun, let's take a strategic approach. In the next section, we'll explore some tips for thoughtfully customizing your menus to maximize your shooting efficiency.

THE Q MENU: YOUR ON-THE-GO SETTINGS HUB

The Q Menu is your secret weapon for quick adjustments, particularly with regards to crafting the unique look of your photos. This is where Fujifilm cameras truly shine with their custom image styling capabilities.

With a simple press of the Q button, you can instantly access and modify settings like Film Simulation, contrast, and more. Think of Film Simulation as different "color recipes" built into your camera. Want a classic black and white look? A vibrant and colorful one? The Q Menu puts these creative options at your fingertips.

Depending on your specific Fujifilm camera model, you can also add settings like Dynamic Range, Color adjustments, and Noise Reduction to your Q Menu.

Here's a bonus perk for newer cameras like the X100VI – the Q Menu has a transparent background. This helps you to see, in real-time, the impact of your changes on the final image. It's like having a live preview of your creative choices!

MY MENU: YOUR PERSONALIZED CONTROL CENTER

While the Q Menu excels at image styling, My Menu tackles everything else related to camera and shooting controls, essentially how you capture the image. Think of it as your personalized control center, where you can swiftly obtain and adjust settings that directly impact the shooting experience.

Since image quality settings are readily available in the Q Menu, My Menu becomes a hub for settings you change frequently but don't necessarily need for immediate adjustments. This could include:

3) **Shutter Type:** Choose between mechanical or electronic shutter for silent shooting or faster speeds.
4) **AF-C Custom Setting:** Fine-tune your autofocus behavior for different shooting scenarios.
5) **Face/Eye Detection:** Quickly turn this setting on or off depending on whether you're focusing on people or objects.
6) **Photometry:** Select how your camera meters light for optimal exposure.
7) **Sports Finder Mode:** Activate a frame overlay to help track fast-moving subjects.
8) **Interval Timer Shooting:** Capture a collection of images at specific intervals, perfect for time-lapse photography.

Recall that your particular shooting style and camera model will determine the exact settings you add to My Menu. Its customization features allow you to make it precisely what you require!

STEPS TO CUSTOMIZE THE MY MENU

Step 1: Identify Your Power Players

Before diving into customization, let's get strategic. The first step is to identify the settings you use most often – the ones you find yourself digging through menus for repeatedly. Imagine having all these frequently adjusted settings conveniently gathered on a single page, ready for instant access!

Here's the drill: Take some time to browse through your camera's menus. As you come across settings you find yourself tweaking regularly, make a mental note (or jot them down if it helps!). These are the prime candidates for your My Menu.

Things to Keep in Mind:

1) My Menu can hold up to 16 settings – plenty of room for your most-used options.
2) Some settings, particularly from the SET UP menu, won't be available for My Menu. But don't worry, there are still plenty of alternatives to select!
3) To check if you've set up My Menu, press the MENU/OK button while in shooting mode. If you see a "MY" tab, you're good to go!

Step 2: Adding Your All-Stars to My Menu

Now that you've identified your frequently used settings, it's time to add them to your My Menu! Here's a step-by-step walk-through:

1) Grab your camera and tap the MENU button. Navigate to the 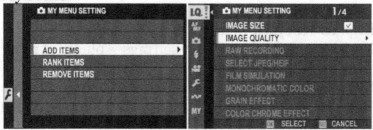 SET UP menu. Under **USER SETTING**, find **MY MENU SETTING** and select it.

2) **Housekeeping first!** You'll see options to **RANK ITEMS** (rearrange the order of items in your My Menu) and **REMOVE ITEMS** (delete settings you no longer need quick access to). Freely utilize these functions as you customize your My Menu.

3) **Time to add some magic!** Use the focus lever to highlight **ADD ITEMS** and press the MENU/OK button.

4) **Here comes the fun part!** You'll see an inventory of settings, with those compatible with My Menu highlighted in blue. Items already in your My Menu will have checkmarks next to them.

5) **Find a setting you wish to add and highlight it.** Simply press the MENU/OK button to add it to your My Menu.

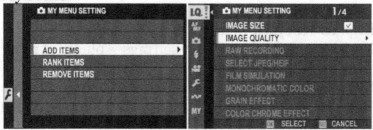

Pro Tip: As you go through the list of settings, take a moment to consider which ones you use most often and prioritize those for your My Menu. Remember, you can revert and adjust your My Menu later as your shooting preferences evolve!

Step 3: Fine-Tuning Your My Menu

Almost there! Now that you've added your favorite settings to My Menu, let's personalize the order for optimal workflow.

1) **Adding an item with a twist!** When you press MENU/OK to add a setting to your My Menu, the camera will show you your updated menu. This is your opportunity to **arrange the order** of your My Menu items. Utilize the selector buttons or joystick to move the newly added item in the list until it's where you want it. Once you're happy, press MENU/OK again to return to the menu selection screen and continue adding items.

2) **Remember, order matters!** As you continue adding items, consider the order in which you typically use them. Grouping similar settings together can create a smooth workflow. Exposure factors, like Shutter Speed and ISO, can be arranged next to each other.

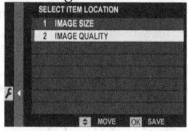

Step 4: Wrapping Up!

1) Once you've added up to 16 items to your "My Menu," click the DISP/BACK button to finish customizing it.

2) **Now, test it out!** The next time you're shooting, press the MENU button. You should see your personalized My Menu displayed, ready for swift access to your most-used settings.

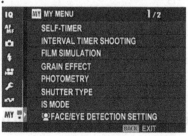

As you become more familiar with the features of your Fujifilm X100VI, your shooting tastes may change. My Menu's greatest feature is that it can change to fit you! Follow these prompts to keep your My Menu current:

Adding New Settings:

- Craving even faster access to a particular setting? Simply revisit the **USER SETTING** menu, navigate to **MY MENU SETTING**, and choose **ADD ITEMS**. Follow the familiar steps outlined earlier to add that setting to your My Menu.

Removing Underused Settings:

- Did a setting you initially thought would be essential turn out to be less-used than expected? No problem! Head back to the **MY MENU SETTING** menu and choose **REMOVE ITEMS**. Highlight the setting you wish to remove and press OK. Once you're done decluttering, press DISP/BACK.

Reordering for Optimal Workflow:

- Over time, you might discover a more efficient order for your My Menu settings. The **RANK ITEMS** option within **MY MENU SETTING** comes to the rescue! Select it, highlight the setting you wish to move, press OK, and use the controls to adjust its position. When you are content with the new order, press DISP/BACK to save your changes.

CUSTOMIZING THE Q MENU

Ready to fine-tune your Q Menu for even faster adjustments? Here's how:

On-the-Fly Editing (for cameras with a dedicated Q button):

1. **Hold down the Q button!** This is the quickest way to access Q Menu customization.
2. **Navigate and select!** Use the directional controls to highlight the setting slot you wish to adjust, then press OK.
3. **Pick your new power tool!** A list of available options will pop up. Simply highlight the new setting you wish to assign to that slot and press OK.
4. **Repeat and refine!** Continue this process until your Q Menu is customized to your liking.

Alternative Editing Method (cameras having a "soft" Q button):
For Fujifilm cameras that lack a dedicated Q button, it is still easily customizable via the camera menus.

1. Dive into the 🔧 **SET UP** menu. Navigate to **BUTTON/DIAL SETTING** and then select **EDIT/SAVE QUICK MENU**.
2. **Choose your slot!** Highlight the setting slot and press OK.
3. **Selection time!** You'll see a list of potential settings. Highlight the setting you wish to assign and press OK.
4. **Repeat for a personalized Q Menu!** Continue this process for each slot.

Remember, your Q Menu is a living document! As you become more familiar with your camera and shooting preferences, feel free to revisit the customization options to tailor your Q Menu for optimal performance.

Advanced Q Menu Customization (for newer Fujifilm models):
While older Fujifilm cameras like the X-T200 and X-S10 limit Q Menu customization to 15 slots (with the first slot reserved for shooting mode), newer models like the X-T5 and X100VI offer even more flexibility!

Tailoring the Number of Slots:

1. **Head over to the SET UP menu.** Navigate to 🔧 **BUTTON/DIAL SETTING** and then select **EDIT/ SAVE QUICK MENU**.
2. **Size matters!** Here, you'll see the option to customize the number of visible Q Menu slots. Choose between settings for four, eight, twelve, or sixteen slots. Select the option that most comfortably fits your shooting style and the number of settings you access frequently.

Seeing Through Your Adjustments:
Newer Fujifilm cameras take Q Menu customization a step further with a transparent background feature. This helps you to see, in real-time, the effects of your modifications on the final image composition right through the Q Menu. Imagine tweaking settings and seeing the visual impact instantly!

1. **Explore the menu options.** The **Q MENU BACKGROUND** option is located either in the 🔧 **SCREEN SETTING** menu or the **BUTTON/DIAL SETTING** menu, based on your specific camera model.
2. **Enable the magic!** Locate the Q Menu Background option and activate it to enjoy the benefit of a see-through Q Menu.

CHAPTER 10: THE SECRET SAUCE OF PHOTOGRAPHY: UNDERSTANDING THE EXPOSURE TRIANGLE

Ever wondered how photographers achieve those stunning images with perfect brightness and creative effects? The secret lies in the **Exposure Triangle**, the three fundamental settings on your camera that work together to control how light is captured:

SHUTTER SPEED: THE TIMEKEEPER OF LIGHT

Imagine your camera's shutter speed as a curtain that controls how long light is allowed to hit the sensor. The longer you keep the curtain open (slow shutter speed), the more light gets in, resulting in a brighter image. This is helpful in low-light situations. However, a slow shutter speed can also blur moving subjects.

Conversely, a fast shutter speed acts like a quick flash of the curtain, letting in less light but freezing action in its tracks. This is ideal for capturing sharp photos of moving objects like athletes or wildlife.

APERTURE: THE SIZE OF THE LIGHT GATE

Think of aperture as the opening of your lens, similar to the pupil of your eye. A wider aperture creates a larger opening for light to enter, making your photos brighter (good for low light or creative effects). However, a wider aperture also reduces sharpness in areas outside the focused zone, creating a pleasing background blur.

A narrower aperture acts like a smaller opening, admitting lesser illumination (which can make photos darker) but ensuring everything from foreground to background appears sharp in focus.

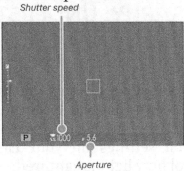

Shutter speed

Aperture

ISO: THE SENSOR'S SENSITIVITY TO LIGHT

ISO controls the sensitivity of your camera sensor to light. It's like adjusting the gain on a microphone. The sensor is more sensitive to light when the ISO is set higher, allowing you to take pictures in dim light conditions without needing a slow shutter speed (which could cause blur). However, increasing ISO can introduce unwanted grain or noise into your photos. The sensor becomes less sensitive (better for clean, high-quality images) at lower ISO settings but requires greater illumination for an appropriate exposure.

Balance is Key:
You can increase one setting to compensate for decreasing another, all while maintaining a properly exposed (bright enough) photo. For example, if it's dark outside, the shutter speed can be lowered to let in more light, but also increase ISO to avoid blurry photos due to camera shake.

Beyond Brightness: Creative Potential
While achieving a correctly exposed picture is important, the Exposure Triangle also unlocks creative possibilities. By adjusting these settings, you can:

- **Control motion blur:** A slow shutter speed can create a dreamy blur effect for waterfalls or moving vehicles. A fast shutter speed can freeze action, perfect for capturing athletes or wildlife.
- **Play with depth of field:** A wide aperture creates a limited field depth, blurring the background and making your subject stand out. A narrow aperture creates a deep depth of field, keeping everything in focus from foreground to background.

UNDERSTANDING EXPOSURE MODES

What are Exposure Modes?

Imagine exposure as a recipe for a perfect photo. It involves two key ingredients: shutter speed and aperture. Shutter speed establishes the time in which illumination reaches the sensor, while aperture decides how much illumination is permitted in at a time. These configurations combine to capture a well exposed photo, where neither the highlights are blown out (too bright) nor the shadows are completely dark. The X100VI's exposure modes help to choose how much control you have over these "ingredients."

There are four major exposure modes, each giving you a different level of control over how your photos are captured. We'll begin by explaining the first mode: Program AE (P).

PROGRAM AE (P MODE): LETTING THE CAMERA TAKE THE WHEEL

The first mode we'll explore is **Program AE (P Mode).** This is an entirely automated mode where the camera takes charge of setting the shutter speed and aperture for a picture with proper exposure.

How P Mode Works:

- In P Mode, the camera analyzes the scene and automatically selects the best blend of shutter speed and aperture to achieve a balanced exposure.
- This is a great option for beginners or whenever you want the camera to handle the technical aspects, helping you focus on composing your shot.

Making Minor Adjustments (Optional):

Even though P Mode is automatic, you can still make slight modifications to the exposure if needed. A technique called **program shift** helps to nudge the camera's chosen settings in a particular direction. Consult your camera's manual for details on program shift functionality.

P Mode Display:

- When using P Mode, you'll see a **P** displayed on your camera screen to confirm the mode is active.

- The values for the aperture and shutter speed will also be displayed, both set to **A (Auto)** since the camera is choosing them automatically.

Points to Remember:

- If the lighting conditions are extremely challenging and fall outside the camera's metering range (the range of light it can measure for proper exposure), the shutter speed and aperture displays might show dashes (---).

While Program AE (P Mode) is a convenient automatic mode, perhaps you should have more influence over the final photo. Here's where **program shift** comes in.

What is Program Shift?

This is a handy feature that helps to adjust the shutter speed and aperture combination chosen by the camera in P Mode, all while maintaining a correct exposure.

Making Adjustments:

Simply rotate the rear command dial on your camera. As you do this, you'll see the values for the aperture and shutter speed change in the viewfinder or display. By default, the camera modifies the other setting (either aperture or shutter speed) to compensate and maintain a balanced exposure.

When is Program Shift Unavailable?

Below are some situations where program shift won't be available:

- **Flash with TTL Auto:** When using a flash unit that supports Through-The-Lens (TTL) auto exposure, program shift won't work.
- **Dynamic Range Auto:** If you have the **DYNAMIC RANGE** setting in the **IMAGE QUALITY SETTING** menu set to an auto option, program shift won't be available.
- **Movie Mode:** Program shift is not functional while recording videos.

Resetting Program Shift:

If you've made adjustments using program shift and want to return to the camera's original settings, simply turn your camera off. When you turn it back on, program shift resets.

Remember: Program shift is a subtle way to influence your photos in P Mode without completely switching to a manual exposure mode. It's an excellent choice for starters who wish to experiment with a little more control.

SHUTTER-PRIORITY AE (S MODE): TAKING CONTROL OF MOTION

Program AE (P Mode) offered automatic exposure with some room for adjustment. Now, let's explore **Shutter-Priority AE (S Mode)**, which increases your control over how your subject in the image.

What is S Mode?
In Shutter-Priority AE (S Mode), you get to choose the shutter speed that you prioritize. This is especially helpful if you wish to control how motion is captured in your photos.

- **Freezing Action:** For subjects that move quickly such as athletes or wildlife, you'd choose a faster shutter speed in S Mode. This helps freeze the action and prevent blur.
- **Creating Motion Blur:** For creative effects like silky smooth waterfalls or artistic motion trails, you'd choose a slower shutter speed in S Mode. This allows more motion blur to be captured in the image.

How Does S Mode Work?
1. Set the aperture ring on your lens to **A (Auto)**. This tells the camera you want it to handle the aperture automatically.
2. Turn the shutter speed dial to select your desired shutter speed. The available shutter speeds changes based on settings and lighting conditions on your camera.

3. The camera automatically adjusts the aperture setting to achieve a balanced exposure based on your chosen shutter speed.

S Mode Confirmation:
- When using S Mode, you'll see an **S** displayed on your camera screen to confirm the mode is active.
- The shutter speed shows your chosen value.
- The aperture value will display **A (Auto)** since the camera is setting it automatically.

Shutter Speed Selection in S Mode:
In Shutter-Priority AE (S Mode), you get to choose the aperture and shutter speed which are instantly modified to obtain a perfect exposure. Here's a breakdown of how shutter speed selection works:
- **Shutter Speed Display:** Your selected shutter speed is shown on your camera screen.
  - **Faster than 1 second:** These shutter speeds are shown as whole numbers (e.g., 250 represents a split second of 1/250th). This is handy for capturing fast action and freezing motion.
  - **Slower than 1 second:** These shutter speeds are displayed with a quotation mark symbol after the number (e.g., 4" represents four seconds). These slower speeds are beneficial for creative effects like blurring motion (think silky water or light trails).
- **Impact on Light:** Remember that each time you reduce the shutter speed by half, you're letting in half the illumination. This difference in light is referred to as

a stop. On rotating the shutter speed dial, you'll see adjustments happening in full stops (like going from 1/250 to 1/125).

- **Fine-Tuning Shutter Speed (Optional):** Your X100VI might also allow for finer adjustments in increments of a third of a stop (e.g., going from 1/250 to 1/320). This provides even more precise command over shutter speed for creative effects. Consult your camera's manual for finer adjustments and how to access them (it might involve using the command dial on the rear side).

IMPORTANT TIPS FOR USING S MODE:

- **Warning Signs:** If the camera can't achieve a perfect exposure with your selected shutter speed, the aperture value on your screen will turn red. This is a warning that the image might overly brilliant or overly dark.
- **Finer Shutter Speed Control (Optional):** As mentioned earlier, some X100VI models allow for even finer shutter speed adjustments in fractions of 1/3 of a stop by turning the rear command dial. This provides even more precise control for specific effects.
- **Adjusting on the Fly:** Fortunately, the shutter speed can be modified even while holding the shutter button halfway down. This allows for quick adjustments as you compose your shot.
- **Slow Shutter Speeds and Timers:** When shutter speeds are slow, the camera will display a countdown timer on the screen while capturing the image. This helps you keep track of the exposure time.
- **Reducing Noise in Long Exposures (Optional):** If you're planning on taking long exposure photos (with slow shutter speeds), you can enable the **LONG EXPOSURE NR** option in the **IMAGE QUALITY SETTING** menu. This helps reduce unwanted noise (grain) that can appear in low-light photos captured

with long exposures. Be aware that enabling this noise reduction might slightly increase the processing time.

Key Takeaway:
By understanding how shutter speed selection works in S Mode, you can achieve different effects in your photos. Choose faster speeds to freeze action and slower speeds for artistic motion blur. The camera instantly modifies the aperture to maintain a balanced exposure based on your selected shutter speed.

LONG EXPOSURES: YOUR CREATIVITY, YOUR STYLE

Long exposure photography, also known as time exposure or slow-shutter photography, is a technique that captures a scene over an extended period of time. This helps to obtain unique effects that would be impossible with normal shutter speeds.

What is Long Exposure Photography?
1) **Capturing Time:** The shutter of the camera stays patent for a lengthy period compared to regular photos. This allows more illumination to penetrate the sensor, revealing details and effects invisible to the naked eye.
2) **Freezing Stillness, Blurring Motion:** Stationary elements in the scene (like buildings or landscapes) remain sharp, while moving elements (like cars or people) become blurred or streaked using a slow shutter speed. This creates a dreamy, ethereal effect.
3) **Examples of Long Exposure Effects:**
   a) **Light Trails:** Moving lights, such as automobile headlights or stars in the night sky, leave visible trails as they move during the long exposure.

b) **Smooth Water:** Flowing water, like waterfalls or waves, seems slick and velvety due to the blurring effect.

c) **Cloud Movement:** The movement of clouds across the sky is captured as streaks or bands, incorporating a feeling of time and motion to the image.

Things to Remember:

1) **Long exposures typically require low-light conditions.** During the day, a strong neutral density (ND) filter is recommended to reduce the quantity of illumination reaching the sensor and allow for a slower shutter speed.

2) **Only bright objects leave visible trails in long exposures.** Dark objects, like boats during the day, might disappear completely from the image. At night, however, their lights might create trails.

TIME (T) MODE: LONG EXPOSURES MADE EASY

Having gained understanding of the basics, let's dive into the specific long exposure modes your Fujifilm X100VI offers. The first is **Time (T) mode**, which is an excellent choice for capturing long exposures with precise shutter speed control.

How to Use Time (T) Mode:

1) **Configure the Shutter Speed to T:** Locate the shutter speed dial and rotate it until the **T** setting is selected.

2) **Choose Your Shutter Speed (Optional):** To pick specific shutter speed in Time (T) mode, locate your camera's rear command dial and rotate it.

3) **Capture the Image:** Once you've framed your shot and chosen your desired duration, fully press the shutter button to start the exposure. If you've set a speed of 1 s

or less, the camera will display a timer that counts down for exposures longer than one second (1s).

4) **Reduce Noise (Optional):** For long exposures, consider enabling **LONG EXPOSURE NR** in the **IMAGE QUALITY SETTING** menu. This helps reduce unwanted noise (grain) that might appear in low-light photos. Remember that enabling this might slightly increase processing time after capturing the image.

Important Tips:
1) **Tripod for Stability:** Long exposures require the camera to stay perfectly still throughout the exposure. A tripod is highly recommended to avoid blurry photos due to camera shake.
2) **Experiment and Practice:** There's no one-size-fits-all duration for long exposures in Time (T) mode. Experiment with different hold times on the shutter button to see what works best for your desired effect.

BULB (B) MODE: ULTIMATE CONTROL

Time (T) mode offered precise control over long exposure duration by how long you held the shutter button. Bulb (B) mode takes things an additional step and provides flexibility for long exposures.

How to Use Bulb (B) Mode:
1) **Configure the Shutter Speed to B:** Locate the shutter speed dial and rotate it until the **B** setting is selected. This indicates you're using Bulb (B) mode for long exposures.
2) **Manual Shutter Control:** With Bulb (B) mode, you have complete control over the exposure duration. Press the shutter button downwards to **open** the shutter and begin the exposure. The camera will keep the shutter open provided you hold the button down. The screen

will display a timer counting the entire duration of exposure.

3) **Close the Shutter (Important):** When you've achieved your desired exposure length, simply **release** the shutter button to **close** the shutter and stop capturing the image.

4) **Aperture and Bulb Mode (Optional):** While in Bulb (B) mode, setting the aperture to **A** will lock the speed of the shutter at 30 seconds. This is a useful starting point for some long exposures.

5) **Reduce Noise (Optional):** For long exposures, consider enabling **LONG EXPOSURE NR** in the **IMAGE QUALITY SETTING** menu. This helps reduce unwanted noise (grain) that might appear in low-light photos. Remember that enabling this might slightly increase processing time after capturing the image.

Important Tips:

1) **Tripod for Stability:** Even more so than in Time (T) mode, Bulb (B) mode requires the camera to be perfectly still throughout the exposure, as you're manually controlling the shutter duration. A tripod is vital to prevent hazy pictures due to camera shake.

2) **Practice Makes Perfect:** Mastering Bulb (B) mode takes practice. Try different shutter button hold times and experiment get the intended long exposure effect.

REMOTE RELEASE: HANDS-FREE LONG EXPOSURES

For even greater control and stability during long exposures, utilize a remote release with your Fujifilm X100VI.

What is a Remote Release?

A remote release is a button you can press remotely to trigger the camera shutter instead of using the shutter button on the camera itself. This may be beneficial for long exposures because it minimizes the possibility of shaking the camera.

How to Make use of a Remote Release with X100VI:
1) Your X100VI is compatible with two types of remote releases:
   a) **Fujifilm RR-100 Remote Release:** This is a remote release specifically designed by Fujifilm for your camera.
   b) **Third-Party Electronic Releases:** There are also various electronic remote releases available from other manufacturers that may be compatible with your X100VI.
2) **Connecting the Remote Release:** Locate the remote release connector on your camera. Connect the cable from your remote release (either the RR-100 or your third-party option) to this connector.

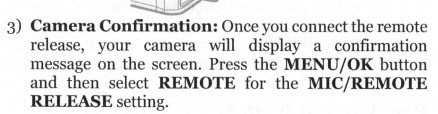

3) **Camera Confirmation:** Once you connect the remote release, your camera will display a confirmation message on the screen. Press the **MENU/OK** button and then select **REMOTE** for the **MIC/REMOTE RELEASE** setting.

Benefits of Remote Release:
1) **Minimizes Camera Shake:** You could prevent your hands from contacting the camera to activate the shutter by utilizing a remote release, which can cause slight vibrations and blurry photos during long exposures.

2) **More Control:** A remote release could be especially helpful for long exposures in the dark when it might be difficult to see the camera controls clearly.

APERTURE-PRIORITY AE (A MODE): TAKING CONTROL OF FIELD DEPTH

We've explored Shutter-Priority (S Mode) for controlling motion blur. Now, let's dive into Aperture-Priority AE (A Mode), which gives you more control over what proportion of your picture appears sharp, also known as depth of field.

What is A Mode?
In Aperture-Priority AE (A Mode), you get to choose the aperture value you want. The aperture setting you choose will affect the proportion of your image in focus (depth of field).

1) **Shallow Depth of Field:** A wider aperture (indicated by a lower f-number, like f/2.8) produces a shallow field depth. This means your subject is highly focused and clear, but the backdrop is going to be pleasantly blurred. This is ideal for creative portraits or making your subject distinct from the background.

2) **Deep Field Depth:** A narrower aperture (indicated by a higher f-number, like f/16) creates a deep field depth. This means a chunk of your image, from the forefront to the background, will appear sharp in focus. It helps with landscape photos or situations where you want everything in focus.

How Does A Mode Work?
1) Configure the value for aperture you want using the aperture ring on your lens.
2) Move the shutter speed dial to **A (Auto)**. This tells the camera to handle the shutter speed automatically.

3) The camera will then instantly modify the shutter speed to get a balanced exposure based on your chosen aperture.

A Mode Confirmation:
1) When using A Mode, you'll see an **A** displayed on your camera screen to confirm the mode is active.
2) The aperture value will show your chosen setting.
3) The shutter speed displays **A (Auto)** since the camera is setting it automatically.

UNDERSTANDING APERTURE IN A MODE:

Aperture is a setting that manages the intensity of illumination and what proportion of the image appears sharp (depth of field). While it might initially appear illogical, here's how aperture values work:
1) **Larger Aperture (Smaller f-number):** A wider aperture is indicated by a lower f-number (like f/2.8). This admits more illumination and makes a shallow field depth. It translates to a cutting-edge subject, but the backdrop becomes hazy. Great for portraits or making your subject stand out.
2) **Smaller Aperture (Larger f-number):** A narrower aperture is indicated by a higher f-number (like f/16). This admits less illumination and creates a deep field depth. This means a larger section of your picture, from foreground to background, will be sharp in focus. Great for scenes where sharpness is desired, such as landscapes.

A Mode and Aperture Selection:
In Aperture-Priority AE (A Mode), you get to choose the value of the aperture you want using the aperture ring on your lens. The camera will then instantly adjust the shutter speed to achieve a balanced exposure.

Important Points to Remember:

1) **Exposure Warning:** If the camera can't attain a decent exposure using the aperture you've selected, the shutter speed value on your screen will turn red. This might indicate a too bright or too dark picture. You might modify the aperture or switch to a different exposure mode.
2) **Metering Range:** If your subject is very dark or bright and falls outside the camera's metering range, the shutter speed will display dashes (---).
3) **Live Depth of Field Preview (Optional):** X100VI allows you to preview the field depth for your chosen aperture. If the **PREVIEW DEPTH OF FIELD** function is assigned to a button, pressing that button will show you a lens icon and the percentage of the picture which will be focused based on your selected aperture.
4) **Adjusting Aperture on the Fly:** Fortunately, the value for the aperture can be modified even while holding the shutter button halfway down. This allows for quick adjustments as you compose your shot.

Remember: A Mode is a great way to regulate the blurring effect in your picture background. As you practice with different aperture settings, you'll get more comfortable with how they affect your photos.

MANUAL EXPOSURE (M MODE): TAKING FULL CONTROL

Now, let's dive into Manual Exposure (M Mode), which gives you complete creative control over shutter speed and aperture.
What is M Mode?
In Manual Exposure (M Mode), you get to choose **both** the aperture and shutter speed for each photo. This allows for a high degree of creative freedom and customization.

1) **Intentional Effects:** M Mode lets you deliberately overexpose (brighter) or underexpose (darker) your pictures for aesthetic effects. This is helpful for setting particular moods or highlighting certain elements in your image.
2) **Exposure Meter:** This meter indicates whether your current settings will yield a correctly exposed, overexposed, or underexposed image. You can use this meter as a guide to adjust your aperture and shutter speed until you achieve the desired exposure.

Configuring Shutter Speed and Aperture in M Mode:

1) **Shutter Speed:** To choose a shutter speed, turn the shutter speed dial.
2) **Aperture:** Using your lens's aperture ring, set your preferred aperture value.
3) **M Mode Confirmation:** When using M Mode, you'll see an **M** displayed on your camera screen to confirm the mode is active.

Fine-Tuning Exposure (Optional):

X100VI allows you to adjust shutter speed in even smaller rates of 1/3 EV by turning the rear command dial. This provides even more precise control over exposure in M Mode.

MANUAL MODE: MASTERING OR MYSTERY?

Manual Exposure (M Mode) might seem like the holy grail of creative control for photographers. However, this is not always the best choice. Let's explore when M Mode shines and when automatic modes might be better suited for the situation.

Myth Busted: Auto vs. Manual

There's a misconception that skilled photographers utilize only manual mode. The truth is, even experienced photographers rely on automatic modes often to capture the desired shots. M Mode has its advantages, but it's important to know when to apply it effectively.

The Power of Manual:

1) **Creative Control:** M Mode provides total command over ISO, shutter speed, and aperture. This helps to achieve specific effects or looks in your photos that automatic modes might be incapable of managing. As an illustration, you might want to utilize a slow shutter speed to blur motion or a large aperture to provide a shallow field depth.

2) **Fine-Tuning Exposure:** While automatic modes can achieve good exposure in most cases, M Mode allows for precise adjustments for situations where light is tricky. The camera's exposure meter is a handy guide in the perfect settings.

3) **Consistent Look:** If you're taking a number of photos and want to keep up a steady look and feel, M Mode helps to lock in your desired aperture, ISO settings, and shutter speed throughout the shoot.

When to Consider Auto Modes:

1) **Fast-Paced Situations:** When shooting in quickly altering ambient lighting or capturing fast-moving subjects, automatic modes might be a better choice. They can react and adjust exposure settings quicker than you can manually.

2) **Learning the Ropes:** While M Mode is an important tool, it can be overwhelming for beginners. Automatic modes are an excellent method of learning about exposure basics and composition before diving into full manual control.

3) **Preserving the Moment:** Sometimes, capturing the moment holds significant perfect exposure. Auto modes

can be helpful in situations where you'd prefer not to miss a fleeting shot while fiddling with manual settings.

We've talked about the creative control M Mode offers, but there's another benefit: it can encourage you to slow down and take more deliberate photos.

The Downside of Speed:
Digital photography allows us to take tons of pictures quickly. This can lead to a lot of similar photos which may not be your best work.

M Mode to the Rescue:
Switching to Manual Exposure (M Mode) forces you to slow down and think more carefully about your shot. Here's why:

1) **Thinking About Settings:** In M Mode, you need to choose both shutter speed and aperture for each photo. This requires considering the scene as well as the outcome you aim to get. Are you trying to halt motion or blur it? Do you want a shallow or deep field depth?

2) **Fewer Snapshots, More Thoughtful Photos:** M Mode is more time-consuming, but it can lead to fewer, higher-quality photos that you've put more thought and intention into.

The Result: Quality over Quantity
By using M Mode, you'll likely take fewer photos, but each photo will be a more deliberate choice with the specific shutter speed and aperture you selected to get the best outcome. This can aid in the development of your photography skills and capture more creative and impactful images.

M Mode: Consistency is Key

Automatic exposure modes are great for most situations, but they can sometimes make slight adjustments to your configurations depending on what makes up your shot. If you require your photographs to all have the same precise appearance, this could be an issue.

When Consistency Matters:
1) **Sequential Shots:** If you're capturing a sequence of photos, like someone walking or an object moving, you want all the frames to share similar brightness and overall look. M Mode ensures your ISO, aperture, and shutter speed settings stay constant throughout the sequence.
2) **Image Stacking:** Some photography techniques involve combining multiple photos into a single image, like panoramas or focus stacking. In these cases, consistent exposure across all the individual photos is crucial. M Mode guarantees identical configurations for every picture.

The Manual Solution:
By setting your Shutter speed, ISO, and aperture manually, you lock in those settings regardless of how you recompose your shot within the frame. This ensures all your photos in the sequence or stack will have a uniform look and exposure.

When Making use of a Flash
Manual Exposure (M Mode) is perfect when working with studio flash. Here's why:
1) **Flash, Not Ambient Light:** Studio flash creates the main light source for your photo, not the surrounding ambient light. The camera's automatic exposure system focuses on ambient light, which is irrelevant in this case. By adjusting the aperture, shutter speed, and ISO in M

mode according to the flash power, you can guarantee that your subject is exposed consistently and accurately.

When to Skip M Mode:
While M Mode offers creative control, there are situations where automatic or semi-automatic modes might be a better choice:
1) **Capturing Moving Subjects:** If you're photographing something that's moving, like a person or animal, the lighting conditions might change as you track your subject. Automatic modes can react and modify aperture or shutter speed faster than you can manually to ensure proper exposure throughout the shot.
2) **Focus on the Moment, Not Settings:** If you're capturing a fast-paced situation or need to connect with your subject (like in portraiture), automatic or semi-automatic modes might be better. Manually adjusting settings in M Mode might distract you from capturing the moment or interacting with your subject. Consider Shutter Priority or Aperture Priority modes for more control in settings.

M Mode for Learning:
Even though there are situations where automatic modes shine, M Mode is still a valuable tool for learning:
- **Sharpen Your Skills:** Practicing with M Mode helps you understand the connection between ISO, shutter speed, and aperture. By manually choosing these settings, you acquire a better comprehension of how they affect your photos.

The Takeaway:
1) M Mode offers creative control, but it's not the optimal option at all times. Choose automatic or semi-automatic modes to focus on the moment or your subject. Use M

Mode to learn and experiment, and you'll become a more well-rounded photographer.

2) Use M Mode with studio flash for precise exposure control based on your flash settings.

3) Opt for automatic or semi-automatic modes when capturing images of mobile subjects to keep up with changing light conditions.

ISO: ADJUSTING LIGHT SENSITIVITY

ISO is another important setting that affects how light sensitive it is. The greater the ISO setting, the higher the sensitivity of the camera. This can be helpful in low-light situations, but there's a trade-off.

How ISO Works:

1) **Low ISO (e.g., ISO 200):** This is the lowest ISO configuration on most cameras and is ideal for bright lighting conditions. It captures a clean image with minimal grain (noise).

2) **High ISO (e.g., ISO 6400):** This is helpful in dimly lit areas where you might not possess adequate light for adequate exposure at a lower ISO. However, grain or noise might appear noticeable in your photos on increasing the ISO.

ISO Options on the X100VI:

Your X100VI offers three ways to adjust ISO:

1) **Auto (A):** The camera instantly adjusts ISO according to the shooting circumstances you've chosen (AUTO1, AUTO2, or AUTO3). This is a good option for starters or if you want the decision made by the camera.

2) **Command Dial (C):** Rotate the front command dial to choose specific ISO values ranging from 64 to 51200. This includes "extended" values which provides even greater light sensitivity but may introduce more noise.

3) **Manual Selection (125-12800):** You can manually choose your desired ISO value using the ISO button or menu. The selected ISO will be displayed on the camera screen.

Remember:
There is a trade-off when setting ISO. Using a higher ISO setting helps to take pictures in dim light conditions where a lower ISO setting might not provide adequate illumination for a clear exposure. However, on increasing the ISO, there is a greater likelihood of introducing visible noise or grain in your pictures. This noise can detract from the picture quality, particularly in regions with consistent color or shadow. Finding the right ISO balance depends on the specific shooting situation and your desired image quality.

EXPOSURE TRIANGLE & STOP SYSTEM

Exposure Triangle: A Move for Balance
Imagine a triangle with ISO, aperture, and shutter speed at each corner. This trio of configurations cooperate to affect the luminance of the picture. Increasing one setting needs to be balanced by decreasing another (within limits) to maintain a good exposure. The stop system helps us understand these adjustments.

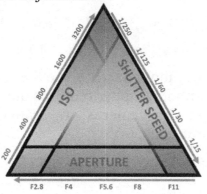

The Stop System: Keeping Things Equal
A stop is a unit used to measure changes in ISO, aperture, and shutter speed. Each full stop represents a twofold or one-half increase in the quantity of light admitted by the camera. To reduce the amount of illumination by half, for instance, raises the shutter speed by one stop. Increasing by twofold the quantity of illumination admitted is also possible by increasing the aperture by one stop.

What is the Significance of Varying Shutter Speeds and Apertures?
Even though same brightness can be gotten with different combinations of aperture, shutter speed, and ISO, every setting has a unique effect on your photo besides exposure:
1) **Shutter Speed:** This regulates the duration which the camera's sensor is exposed to illumination. Greater illumination can enter with a slower shutter speed, although moving objects may get blurry. In dim light, a faster shutter speed may necessitate a broader aperture or a higher ISO in order to freeze motion.
2) **Aperture:** It controls the amount of illumination can be admitted into your lens through the aperture. A shallow field depth produced by a larger aperture blurs the backdrop. A narrower aperture (higher f-number) creates a deeper field depth, making the image clear.

CAPTURING THE IDEAL MOMENT: MASTERING EXPOSURE FOR ACTION PHOTOS

Catching fleeting moments with moving subjects, like in sports or action photography, requires quick thinking and adjustments. Fujifilm cameras are crafted to assist you excel in these situations.

Fujifilm's Advantage: Easy-Access Controls

Unlike some cameras, Fujifilm models provide instant access to all three key exposure settings ("exposure triangle") – aperture, shutter speed, and ISO. This allows for quick changes made on the spot without having to navigate menus. Additionally, most Fujifilm cameras feature a prominent exposure compensation dial for overall brightness adjustments.

Benefits of External Controls:

1) **Quick Adjustments:** External dials helps to make changes to exposure settings rapidly, crucial for capturing fleeting moments with moving subjects.

2) **Settings at a Glance:** Even on powering off the camera, you can glance at the external dials to see your current exposure settings. This is a big advantage for photographers who need to be prepared and know their camera settings at all times.

Beyond the Dials:

While external dials are great, Fujifilm cameras offer even more control through buttons and menus. This lesson will explore three additional features that aid in achieving impressive results:

1) **Right Metering Mode:** Choosing the appropriate metering mode ensures your camera focuses on the right portion to achieve accurate exposure, especially important for moving subjects.

2) **Automatic ISO:** Letting the camera instantly modify ISO can be helpful in fast-paced situations, ensuring proper exposure even with changing light conditions.

3) **Boost Mode (if applicable):** Some Fujifilm models like the X100VI offer a Boost Mode that can enhance camera performance for capturing fast-moving subjects.

METERING MODES FOR ACTION: LOCATING THE IDEAL FOCUS

When capturing moving subjects, especially under different lighting circumstances, choosing the appropriate metering mode on your Fujifilm X Series camera is essential to getting accurate exposure. Different metering modes prioritize different areas of the frame to determine exposure.

Fujifilm Metering Modes:
1) **Multi metering (often the default):** This mode analyzes the entire scene and tries to achieve a balanced exposure. It could be a perfect starting point for many situations.
2) **Spot metering:** This mode focuses the exposure reading on a very small, specific part of the frame. It's beneficial for action shots where your subject might be backlit or in a different lighting situation than the background. You can focus and lock your subject in the exposure reading before recomposing and taking the shot.
3) **Center-weighted metering:** This mode prioritizes the frame's center for exposure but also considers the surrounding areas.
4) **(Optional) Average metering:** When calculating exposure, this option uses the full frame as a basis. Though it's less typical compared to other modes, this could be appropriate in some instances.

Accessing Metering Modes:
This is done in two ways:
1) **SHOOTING SETTING Menu:** Proceed to the SHOOTING SETTING menu and find the PHOTOMETRY option. This will display the available metering modes for you to choose from.
2) **Metering Mode Switch (on some models):** Look for a dedicated switch which helps to cycle through various metering modes.

Important Note:
The metering mode you select will only affect exposure if you have Face/Eye Detection Setting and Subject Detection Setting turned OFF in the AF/MF SETTING menu. These settings prioritize focusing on faces or subjects and might override your chosen metering mode if enabled. Ensure they are disabled for full control over exposure in action shots.

MULTI METERING: YOUR SPEEDY ALL-ROUNDER

How it Works: Multi metering analyzes the entire frame, considering brightness, color, and composition, to achieve a balanced exposure.

Ideal for: This mode is excellent for fast-paced situations where lighting might be changing rapidly, like tracking a race car through sun and shade. It's an excellent default choice unless you have specific reasons for using another mode.

When to Consider Another Mode: If Multi metering isn't giving you the desired exposure results, consider other options.

CENTER-WEIGHTED METERING: PRIORITIZING THE CENTER

How it Works: Just as the name implies, center-weighted metering considers the entire frame but prioritizes the central exposure reading.

Ideal for: This mode is useful on centrally positioning your subject, which is common in action shots. Additionally, it may be helpful if Multi metering is giving you consistently overexposed or underexposed photos.

Remember: Center-weighted metering focuses on the center, so ensure your subject is actually centrally placed for this mode to work effectively.

SPOT METERING: FOCUSING ON YOUR SUBJECT

How it Works: This is the opposite of Multi metering. It takes a light reading from a tiny area (1-2% of the frame), usually the center by default, and ignores everything else.

Ideal for: Ensuring your subject has the correct exposure, regardless of the background lighting. It is beneficial for action shots where your subject might be backlit or in a different lighting situation than the background.

Customization: Some Fujifilm cameras help to change the spot metering point from the center to another location in the frame.

AVERAGE METERING: A SIMPLE OPTION

How it Works: This mode treats the entire frame equally when determining exposure. It basically takes an average light reading from all parts and sets the exposure.

Ideal for: Average metering is a simple option that may be beneficial in situations with very bright or very dark action subjects. However, it might not be the ideal option for most action shots where balanced exposure across the frame is desired.

Note: Compared to Multi metering, Average metering lacks the advanced scene analysis for an equitable exposure.

SELECTING THE PERFECT METERING MODE:

The finest metering mode for action photography depending upon the specific lighting situation and your subject. Here's a quick recap:

1) **Multi metering:** A good all-rounder for fast-paced situations with changing light.
2) **Center-weighted metering:** Useful for centrally placing your subject.
3) **Spot metering:** Ensures proper exposure even in dimly lit areas.
4) **Average metering:** A simple option for very bright or dark subjects, but less versatile than Multi metering.

LINK SPOT METERING WITH AF POINTS

We learned that Spot metering is useful for action shots where your subject might be in off-center lighting. But by default, Spot metering measures illumination from the central frame. Here's a trick to utilize this feature more flexibly on some Fujifilm cameras:

Linking Spot Metering to AF Points:
Using this feature, the Spot metering point can be moved around the frame with your chosen autofocus point. This way, wherever you focus your camera (and presumably your subject is), the Spot metering will ensure the appropriate exposure for that specific area.

How to Link (if applicable):

1) Go to the AF/MF SETTING menu.
2) Look for an option to **Link Spot metering and AF points** (might be called something like "Spot Metering Linked").

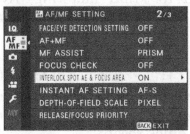

Camera Compatibility: This feature is only available on some Fujifilm X Series cameras, with X100VI, X-T3 and X-T4 having it enabled by default. Check your camera's manual to determine whether it offers this function.

Benefits: By linking Spot metering to your AF points, you can ensure precise exposure even if they're not centrally positioned. This is very helpful for action photography with off-center subjects.

AUTOMATIC ISO: HELPING TO FOCUS ON THE ACTION

Capturing action photos requires quick thinking and adjustments. Automatic ISO on your Fujifilm X Series camera can help you focus on your subject by instantly making adjustments to the ISO setting to keep up appropriate exposure.

Positives of Auto ISO:
1) **Less Work, More Focus:** By letting the camera manage ISO, you have one less setting to worry about.
2) **Balanced Exposure:** Auto ISO raises or lowers ISO as needed to achieve good exposure, ensuring your photos aren't overly brilliant or overly dark.

278

3) **Combating Blur:** With dim or uneven lighting conditions, Auto ISO can help prevent blurry photos by automatically adjusting ISO to maintain a quicker shutter speed, which freezes motion more effectively.

Finding Auto ISO:

There are three Auto ISO options (AUTO1, AUTO2, and AUTO3) that helps to customize how the camera adjusts ISO in different situations.

1) Proceed to the SHOOTING SETTING menu and find the ISO AUTO SETTING option. This will display the available AUTO modes for you to choose from.

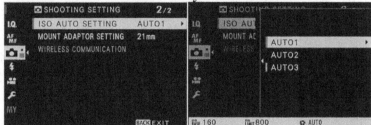

2) After choosing one of the AUTO modes, you have the option to adjust any of the following settings:
   a) Default Sensitivity
   b) Max Sensitivity
   c) Min Shutter Speed

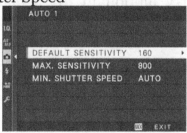

DEFAULT SENSITIVITY:

This is your chosen ISO setting for most situations. The camera will make effort to maintain this ISO to the greatest feasible extent.

It only increases the ISO if the required shutter speed for a feasible exposure falls below the speed you set in "Min. Shutter Speed" (discussed next).

MAX. SENSITIVITY:

This is the highest ISO value to automatically use by the camera. Auto ISO will choose an ISO setting between your Default Sensitivity and this maximum limit.

In essence, these two settings work together:

You set your preferred starting point (Default Sensitivity) for clean pictures with little noise.

You define an acceptable maximum ISO limit (Max. Sensitivity) to ensure faster shutter speeds in dim light or fast-moving situations, even if it introduces some image noise.

MIN. SHUTTER SPEED: CONTROLLING MOTION BLUR IN AUTO ISO

The third option is Min. Shutter Speed. This setting helps you control blurry motion in live-action pictures while utilizing Auto ISO.

How it Works:

1) You configure the slowest shutter speed you're comfortable with. Auto ISO will then adjust ISO between your Default Sensitivity and Max. Sensitivity limits to ensure the shutter speed stays above your chosen minimum.

2) This prevents the camera from dropping the shutter speed too low in dim light or fast-moving situations, which can cause motion blur.

Auto Option:

1) If you choose "Auto" for Min. Shutter Speed, the camera instantly selects a minimum shutter speed according to your lens's focal length. As an illustration, with a 200mm lens, the camera might choose a minimum of 1/200th of a second.
2) Important Note: Even with Auto Min. Shutter Speed, if the lighting is too dim and ISO is already maxed out, the camera might still utilize a slower shutter speed to obtain the appropriate exposure. This could result in some motion blur.

Finding the Balance:
A faster Min. Shutter Speed will help freeze motion but might force the camera to increase ISO more often, potentially introducing noise. A slower Min. Shutter Speed allows the camera utilize lower ISO for cleaner images but raises the possibility of motion blur.

BOOST MODE: SUPERCHARGE YOUR ACTION PHOTOGRAPHY (IF APPLICABLE)

Some Fujifilm camera models like the X100VI come with a special Boost Mode that can significantly enhance your action photography capabilities. Here's what it offers:

- **Smoother Viewfinder:** Boost Mode increases the viewfinder refresh rate from 60 frames per second (fps) to 100 fps. This reduces viewfinder blackout time, making it far simpler to track and frame fast-moving subjects as they happen.
- **Faster Autofocus:** Boost Mode also improves autofocus speed, allowing the camera to react quicker and lock focus more effectively.

Trade-off: Battery Life

The only downside to Boost Mode is that it consumes more battery power. However, the benefits for capturing sharp, focused action shots often outweigh the shorter battery life.

Turn it On!

If your Fujifilm camera has a Boost Mode, consider enabling it whenever you're shooting action subjects. The smoother viewfinder and faster autofocus can create a significant impact in capturing those fleeting moments.

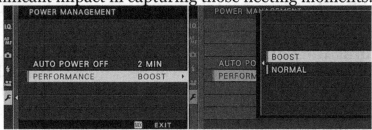

CHAPTER 11: DRIVE MODES

This mode provides access to a variety of shooting modes beyond the standard single image capture. This allows you to tailor your camera to different photographic situations.

Accessing Drive Settings:
- Press the DRIVE/DELETE button on the back of your camera.

Available Drive Settings:
1) **STILL IMAGE (S):** This is the standard single frame capture mode, perfect for everyday photos.
2) **CH HIGH SPEED BURST:** This mode captures images in rapid succession at high frame rates, ideal for freezing action or capturing fleeting moments.
3) **CL LOW SPEED BURST:** Similar to CH, but at a slower frame rate. This can be useful for situations where you want to capture a burst of images but don't need the extreme speed of CH mode.
4) **ISO BKT (ISO Bracketing):** This mode takes three pictures at varied ISO settings (one at your chosen ISO, one slightly underexposed, and one slightly overexposed) allowing you to select the best exposure later.
5) **WHITE BALANCE BKT (White Balance Bracketing):** Similar to ISO bracketing, but captures three photos with slightly varying white balance configurations to ensure accurate color reproduction under various lighting conditions.

6) **BKT (Bracketing):** This is a general bracketing mode that helps to choose which settings you want to bracket (exposure, white balance, flash).

7) **HDR (High Dynamic Range):** This mode combines multiple exposures into a single image with more detail in both highlights and shadows, useful for scenes with high contrast lighting.

8) **Multiple Exposure:** This mode helps to take multiple exposures within a single frame, creating artistic effects.

9) **Adv. MODE (Advanced Filter):** This mode provides access to various creative filters that can be applied to your photos in-camera.

10) **MOVIE:** This mode helps to record videos with your X100VI.

Remember: Not all Drive settings are available in every shooting mode.

BURST MODE / CONTINUOUS SHOOTING MODE

Capturing fleeting moments, like kids running or athletes in action, requires quick reflexes and the right camera settings. Burst mode, also known as continuous shooting mode, is your best friend in these situations.

What is Burst Mode?

It is a feature that lets you take a rapid sequence of photos by long pressing the shutter button. Instead of capturing one image at a time, your camera fires off multiple photos in quick succession. Depending on your camera's capabilities, it can capture anywhere from 3-5 to 20-60 images per second. With each photo, you raise the likelihood that you will capture that perfect moment of action.

Buffer Limit:
There's a catch! Burst mode isn't unlimited. As you capture photos, your camera's buffer (temporary storage) fills up with images waiting to be saved to the memory card. When the buffer is filled, burst mode stops working until there's free space again.

In essence:
1) Burst mode helps to capture a quick series of pictures.
2) Faster burst mode (more frames per second) raise the likelihood of catching the peak of action.
3) Burst mode is constrained by your camera's buffer, so extended bursts might stop until the buffer clears.

Choosing the Right Burst Mode Speed
Many cameras offer different burst mode speeds, allowing you to capture action at varying rates. The best option depends on a few factors:
1) **Camera Capabilities:** Some cameras simply have faster burst modes than others. Check your camera's manual for its burst mode specifications.
2) **File Format:** Shooting JPEG files allows for the fastest burst speeds and most photos per burst because JPEG files are smaller than RAW or RAW+JPEG formats. RAW files capture more image data but take longer to relay to the memory card, slowing down burst mode.
3) **Memory Card Speed:** For the best burst mode performance, use a fast UHS-I or UHS-II memory card. Slower memory cards can stifle the speed at which your camera can write images, limiting the number of photos captured in a burst.

Understanding Burst Mode Limits:

1) Your camera's manual will specify the maximum number of shots achievable in a burst depending on the factors mentioned above.
2) Once the camera's buffer fills up with captured images waiting to be saved to the memory card, burst mode becomes inactive momentarily until there's free space again.

Choosing Your Speed:
Fujifilm X Series cameras are known for their impressive burst mode capabilities, perfect for capturing action photos. These cameras offer two main burst mode speeds: High and Low.
1) **High-speed continuous:** This mode captures photos at a faster rate (typically a few extra frames every second in contrast to low speed). It's ideal for capturing extremely fast action, like race cars or birds in flight.
2) **Low-speed continuous:** This mode captures photos at a slower rate. It's a good option for slower moving subjects or for conserving battery life or memory card space. You'll be able to capture more images per burst at this slower speed.

Choosing the Right Speed:
The best burst mode speed depends on the action you're trying to capture:
1) **Ultra-fast action:** Choose high speed for subjects like race cars or flying birds where you need to capture the peak moment very quickly.
2) **Slower action:** Low speed is suitable for subjects with slower movements or when you want more images per burst.

USE BURST MODE WISELY

While in a technical sense, you can utilize burst mode continuously, it's generally recommended for specific situations. Here's why:

1) **Overkill for Static Subjects:** Burst mode isn't necessary for still subjects or slow movement. It's better to focus on composing a well-timed single shot.
2) **The Downside of Excess:** Constant burst mode can lead to:
   a) **Laziness:** You might rely on bursts to capture the moment instead of perfecting single shots.
   b) **Storage Overload:** Bursts generate a large number of images, quickly filling up memory cards and hard drives.

The Best Times for Burst Mode:
1) **Action Photography:**
   a) Sports: Activate burst mode during a game to be ready for exciting moments like slam dunks or buzzer-beaters.
   b) Wildlife and Birds: Capture those fleeting moments of animals in motion.
   c) Children's Activities: Ideal for capturing the energy of a football match.
2) **Unpredictable Events:**
   a) Graduations: Ensure you capture the exact moment your child receives their diploma.
   b) Portraits: Boost your likelihood of getting that perfect expression or pose.
   c) Street Photography: Freeze fleeting interactions like couples making eye contact.
3) **Macro Focus Stacking:** When manually concentrating on a close-up subject (like a window) at increased magnification, using burst mode can help

ensure you capture at least one image with perfect focus as you fine-tune the focus ring.

Photography Genres That Love Burst Mode:
Beyond action photography, several other genres benefit from burst mode:
1) **Sports Photography:** A natural fit for capturing the peak moments of athletic competition.
2) **Pet Photography:** Perfect for freezing those adorable yet unpredictable pet antics.
3) **Bird Photography:** Capturing birds in flight or other rapid movements.
4) **Wildlife Photography:** Similar to bird photography, burst mode helps capture unpredictable movements of wild animals.
5) **Street Photography:** Can be useful to record ephemeral moments of interaction on the street.
6) **Event Photography:** Sometimes helpful for capturing decisive moments during an event, but not always necessary.

ACTIVATING BURST MODE ON YOUR FUJIFILM X100VI

Now that you understand the benefits of burst mode, let's get you capturing those action shots on your Fujifilm X100VI!

STEP 1: TURN ON BURST MODE
1) Press the DRIVE/DELETE button on the back of your camera. This will open the Drive menu.
2) In the Drive menu, navigate and select either:
   a) **CH HIGH SPEED BURST:** Ideal for capturing very fast action at high frame rates.

b) **CL LOW SPEED BURST:** Suitable for slower action or to conserve battery life or memory card space.

Choosing Your Speed (Optional):
Some Fujifilm cameras allow you to adjust the burst mode frame rate within the Drive menu. However, the text doesn't specify if the X100VI offers this option. Consult your camera's manual to see if you are able to modify the frame rate within the Drive menu. If not, the camera will make use of the standard burst speed for the chosen mode (high or low).

Confirmation:
Once you've selected your burst mode (high or low speed), press the MENU/OK button to confirm your selection and close the Drive menu. Your camera is now ready to capture burst photos!

STEP 2: CHOOSING THE PERFECT FOCUS MODE
On activating burst mode, selecting the appropriate focus mode is crucial for capturing sharp images.

A. **AF-C (Continuous Autofocus) Focus Mode for Fast Action:** This mode is ideal for fast-moving subjects. The camera will continuously adjust focus as you partially tap the shutter button, ensuring your subject stays sharp throughout the burst.

Selecting AF-C on X100VI:
There are two ways to activate Continuous Autofocus (AF-C) on your Fujifilm X100VI:
1) **Focus Selector Switch:** Look for the focus selector switch in front of your camera. Slide the dial to the "C"

setting. This is the quick access option for Continuous AF.

2) **AF/MF Setting Menu:** Alternatively, you can access the AF/MF Settings menu for more granular control. Here's how:

a) Press the Menu button (MENU) on the rear camera.

b) Navigate through the menu tabs until you find the AF/MF SETTING option. Select it by pressing the MENU/OK button.

c) Within the AF/MF SETTING menu, find the AF MODE option and select it.

d) Choose CONTINUOUS AF from the available AF modes.

e) Press the MENU/OK button again to verify your choice and exit the menu.

B. AF-S for Static Subjects:

If you're photographing a stationary subject, you can use Single Shot Autofocus (AF-S). This mode focuses on half-way pressing the shutter button. Access Single Shot Autofocus (AF-S) using the "S" configuration on the switch for focus selection.

Remember: Continuous Autofocus (AF-C) is often advised for burst mode photography, especially with fast-moving subjects.

C. Custom AF-C Presets

While Continuous Autofocus (AF-C) is perfect for action in burst mode, a few cameras from the Fujifilm X Series (like your X100VI) offer even more advanced options: **Custom AF-C Presets.** These presets allow you to fine-tune how the camera focuses on moving subjects in burst mode. There are five pre-programmed settings for various situations, and some models even offer a sixth customized preset for ultimate customization.

Accessing Custom AF-C Presets:

1. Tap the Menu button (MENU) on your rear camera.
2. Proceed to peruse the menu tabs till you locate the AF/MF SETTING option. Select it by pressing the MENU/OK button.
3. Within the AF/MF SETTING menu, find the AF-C CUSTOM SETTINGS option and select it.

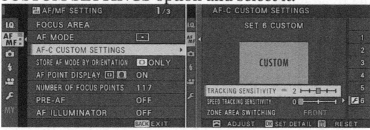

Using Presets:

Your camera will display information about the five available Custom AF-C presets. Each preset is designed for a specific type of action, such as tracking a fast-moving subject or prioritizing focus accuracy. Choose the preset that best suits your shooting situation.

User-Defined Preset (on some models):

Some X Series models offer a sixth, user-specified preset. It helps to make your custom focusing behavior for burst mode by adjusting three specific parameters within the AF system. Refer to your camera's manual for details on customizing this preset.

Remember: Custom AF-C presets are an advanced feature, and the default Continuous AF (AF-C) mode will work well for most burst mode photography. Explore these presets at your own pace as you get more comfortable with burst mode and autofocus settings.

STEP 3: CHOOSING THE APPROPRIATE CAMERA SETTINGS

Now that you've activated burst mode and selected the appropriate focus mode, it's time to optimize your camera settings for capturing sharp action shots. These settings will differ based on the specific situation, but here are some key things to consider:

1) **Shutter Speed:** This is crucial for capturing clear, non-blurry images during burst mode. A quicker shutter speed freezes action more effectively.

   a) **Recommendation:**

      i) Slower moving objects: 1/250s or faster shutter speed.

      ii) Faster moving objects: 1/1000s or faster shutter speed.

2) **Adjusting for Faster Shutter Speeds:** If you're having trouble achieving the recommended shutter speeds, here are some options:

   a) **Increase Aperture:** A wider aperture allows more camera illumination, which can assist you in achieving a quicker shutter speed. However, this will affect the field depth (the area in focus).

   b) **Raise ISO:** Boosting the ISO increases the camera's sensitivity to light, allowing for an increased shutter speed. Be aware that higher ISO can also introduce image noise (grain).

3) **Exposure Variation (Optional):** This setting controls whether the exposure (brightness) remains consistent throughout the burst sequence. By default, your camera might adjust exposure for each image in burst mode. If you want all the images in your burst to have the same exposure, set the 🔧 BUTTON/DIAL SETTING > SHUTTER AE to OFF.

STEP 4: TAKING THE BURST

Here comes the exciting part! Once you've configured your camera settings, you're ready to capture those action shots.

1) **Spot the Moment:** Keep an eye out for the perfect action.

2) **Press and Hold:** When you see the moment unfold, long press the shutter button to start the burst sequence. Your camera will quickly take a series of pictures.

3) **Burst Mode Etiquette:** Remember, use burst mode strategically to avoid filling your memory card with unnecessary photos. Ideally, wait for the key moment before initiating the burst. If you're using single-shot autofocus, it's recommended to lock focus beforehand for better results.

Burst Mode in Moderation:

As mentioned earlier, burst mode can fill up your camera's buffer (temporary storage) quickly. Burst mode will be inactive after the buffer is filled until there's free space again. So, utilize this mode in short bursts to capture the peak moment of the action, rather than long pressing the shutter button for extended periods.

SHUTTER TYPES VS BURST MODE

Modern cameras, like your Fujifilm X100VI Series camera, come equipped with two shutter options: mechanical and electronic.

Mechanical Shutter:

1) **Traditional Design:** This is the technology used in most DSLR cameras. A physical curtain shuts and opens to show the sensor on pressing the shutter button.

2) **Reliable and Familiar:** Mechanical shutters have been around for a long time and are known for their dependability.

Electronic Shutter:
1) **Modern Technology:** This newer technology eliminates the physical shutter. Instead, the camera sensor electronically controls exposure on tapping the shutter button.
2) **Speed Advantage:** Electronic shutters can achieve faster burst mode speeds compared to mechanical shutters. This can be beneficial for capturing very fast action.

Choosing a Shutter Type:
To maximize burst mode speed, use the electronic shutter.

How to Access Shutter Type Settings:
1) Tap the Menu button (MENU) on your rear camera.
2) Proceed to peruse the menu tabs till you locate the SHOOTING SETTING option. Select it by pressing the MENU/OK button.
3) Within the SHOOTING SETTING menu, find the SHUTTER TYPE option and select it.
4) Choose ELECTRONIC SHUTTER from the available shutter type options.
5) Press the MENU/OK button again to confirm your selection and exit the menu.

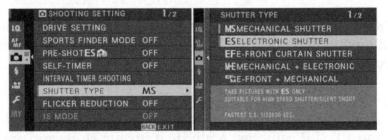

Benefits of Electronic Shutters for Burst Mode
While mechanical shutters are reliable, electronic shutters offer some significant advantages for burst mode photography:

1) **Blazing Fast Speeds:** Electronic shutters help to take pictures at incredibly high shutter speeds, exceeding the potential of mechanical shutters. It helps to halt the quickest action with incredible detail.
2) **Rapid-Fire Burst Mode:** Electronic shutters can achieve faster burst mode speeds compared to mechanical shutters. This implies you can take more images in a shorter burst, increasing the odds of filming the peak moment of the action.
3) **Silent Shooting:** They operate silently, unlike mechanical shutters with their clicking sound. It's ideal for situations where noise might be disruptive, such as weddings, concerts, or wildlife photography.
4) **Durability:** Without the wear and tear of a physical shutter mechanism, electronic shutters are stronger and less prone to breakdowns over time.

Electronic Shutters: A Speed Advantage with a Twist
While electronic shutters offer impressive burst mode speeds and other benefits, there's a potential downside to consider:
1) **Rolling Shutter Effect:** This distortion occurs when the sensor exposes the picture line by line electronically. If the subject moves quickly during this process, it can appear warped or skewed in the resulting shot. Imagine a race car with a bent body!

Minimizing Rolling Shutter:
Fortunately, it appears that camera technology is constantly improving, and some modern cameras are very effective at minimizing or eliminating rolling shutter with electronic shutters.

Choosing the Right Shutter:

1) **For Maximum Speed:** A great option for the quickest possible burst mode speeds.
2) **For Action Photography (with Caution):** If you're photographing fast-moving subjects that travel across the frame (like a race car), be cautious. Consider using either:
   a) An electronic shutter specifically designed to minimize rolling shutter.
   b) The mechanical shutter, which doesn't suffer from this distortion.

BURST MODE TIPS

Burst Mode Tip #1: Be Gentle with the Shutter Button

Burst mode helps to take a quick series of images, but proper shutter button technique is crucial for sharp photos. Here's why:

1) **Avoiding Camera Shake:** You can introduce camera shake (if you tap the shutter button too forcefully), which blurs the image. This is especially noticeable when using telephoto lenses or with reduced shutter speeds.
2) **Light Touch, Big Results:** Use a light touch, almost rolling your finger off the surface. This minimizes camera shake and helps you capture crisp, clear images.

Imagine this analogy: Think of your camera like a glass full of water. A gentle touch keeps the water steady, while a forceful press creates ripples and spills (blurry photos). By being gentle, you treat your photos with care and ensure sharp results.

Burst Mode Tip #2: Don't Forget Composition

The fast-paced world of burst mode photography might make you focus solely on capturing the action, but don't forget about composition! Here's why composition matters:

1) **Beyond the Moment:** While capturing the peak moment is important, framing the moment significantly impacts the visual impact of your photo.

2) **Compositional Questions:** As you shoot in burst mode, take a moment to consider:
   a) How can you arrange the elements for maximum visual impact?
   b) How do the different objects in your shot relate to each other?

3) **Compositional Guidelines:** Even during the peak moment, there are helpful techniques for composing strong shots. Here are two examples:
   a) **Rule of Thirds:** It suggests placing your subject off-center, creating a more visually interesting composition.
   b) **Rule of Space:** This concept entails allowing room in the frame for the movement and gaze of your subject. This adds a sense of dynamism to your photos.

4) **Storytelling Through Images:** Every photograph, even those captured in a little moment of time, has the potential to tell a story. By considering composition, you can ensure your photos are visually captivating and effectively communicate your story.

Burst Mode Tip #3: Pack Lots of Memory Cards
Burst mode gobbles up memory card space fast! Here's why:

1) **Rapid Fire, Filling Files:** Imagine capturing images at 10 frames per second (FPS) only for sixty seconds. That's a staggering 600 photos!

2) **Be Prepared for Action:** Should you intend to capture fast-paced action, make sure you have enough memory cards to handle the volume of photos.
3) **Stock Up on Storage:** I recommend getting a casing and inserting high-capacity cards (ideally 64GB or larger) in it.
4) **Think Like a Long Trip:** It's similar to taking more batteries in case of a lengthy trip. You might not need them all, but having them readily available can save you from missing out on capturing those perfect moments.

Burst Mode Tip #4: Embrace the Light
Light is crucial for sharp photos, and even more so when capturing action with burst mode. Here's why:
1) **Light and Shutter Speed:** In low light situations, the shutter speed of your camera has to be reduced to capture enough light. Unfortunately, slower shutter speeds can lead to blurry photos, especially with fast-moving subjects.
2) **Shooting for Sharpness:** For crisp, clear burst mode photos, aim for an increased shutter speed. This requires good lighting conditions.
3) **Golden Hour Glory:** The golden hours, either before dusk or soon after morning, bathe the scene in soft, warm light, ideal for taking bright action shots.
4) **Midday Might:** Midday sun delivers powerful light, but could be harsh and create unflattering shadows. Use this light with caution.
5) **Low Light ISO Boost:** If you must take pictures in dim light, consider boosting your ISO to maintain an increased shutter speed. While this might introduce some image noise (grain), it's a better alternative than blurry photos.

Remember: Good lighting is essential for sharp burst mode photography. Seek out bright, diffused light whenever possible for optimal results.

Burst Mode Tip #5: Your Low-Light Ally

While good lighting is ideal for sharp burst mode photos, there are situations where you might find yourself taking pictures in dim light. Here's a surprising benefit of burst mode in these conditions:

1) **Minimizing Camera Shake:** Tapping the shutter button can cause camera shake, which blurs photos. The more force you apply, the worse the shake.
2) **Burst Mode to the Rescue:** In low light areas, this mode helps to take sharper images. Here's why:
   a) You only have to tap the shutter button **once** to initiate a flurry of pictures.
   b) Subsequent images in the burst are less likely to be blurred by camera shake compared to the initial shot you might take while carefully stabilizing the camera.
3) **Beyond Action:** Burst mode isn't just for capturing fast action! Understanding this low-light advantage can potentially save lives when you need sharp photos in less-than-ideal lighting conditions.

HDR PHOTOGRAPHY: CAPTURING SCENES WITH RICH DETAIL

HDR (High Dynamic Range) is a powerful feature on your Fujifilm X Series camera that helps to take scenes with more detail in both bright highlights and dark shadows. Here's how it works:

1) **Multiple Exposures:** When you activate HDR mode, your camera actually takes three separate photos with varying degrees of exposure. One image is exposed

normally, one is slightly underexposed (darker), and one is slightly overexposed (brighter).

2) **Combining the Best Parts:** The camera then intelligently combines the best parts of these three exposures into a single final image. This final image retains specifics in bright and dark conditions that might be lost in a regular photo.

Activating HDR:

1) **Access the Drive Mode Menu:** Press the DRIVE/DELETE button located on your rear camera. This button typically has an image of a car with multiple frames around it.

2) **Select HDR:** Within the drive mode menu, navigate through the options until you find HDR. Select HDR to activate this mode.

Choosing an HDR Setting:

Your camera offers different HDR settings that determine the degree of exposure variation between the three captured images. Here's an analysis of the options:

1) **HDR AUTO:** This setting lets your camera automatically choose the best exposure variation for the scene.

2) **HDR200, HDR400, HDR800:** These options allow you to manually select the level of exposure variation. Higher numbers indicate a greater difference between the captured exposures.

3) **HDR800+:** This setting pushes the camera to its limits, capturing the maximum possible variation in dynamic range.

Capturing Your HDR Photo:

Once you've chosen your HDR setting, simply frame your shot and press the shutter button. The camera will capture the three images and automatically combine them into a final HDR photo.

Important Notes for Using HDR
Here are some additional things to keep in mind when using HDR mode:

1) **Hold Steady:** For optimal results, it's important to keep your camera stable while the camera captures the three HDR images. Any camera shake during this process can affect the final image quality.

2) **Moving Subjects and Changing Conditions:** HDR might not produce the desired outcome with unsteady an subject or if the lighting or composition changes significantly between the three exposures captured for the HDR image.

3) **Slight Image Crop and Resolution Reduction:** Be aware that HDR processing might slightly crop the resulting picture and reduce the overall resolution compared to a non-HDR photo.

4) **Mottling at Higher Settings:** Using stronger HDR settings (HDR400, HDR800, etc.) can sometimes introduce a mottled pattern in areas of your photo. Choose the HDR setting that best suits your scene to avoid this effect.

5) **ISO Limitations:** HDR is not compatible with extended ISO values (very high ISO settings) on your camera.

6) **Shutter Speed Variation:** The camera might modify the shutter speed slightly depending on the chosen HDR setting and ISO.

7) **Flash Not Supported:** The flash does not fire when using HDR mode.

8) **Identifying HDR Photos:** During playback, HDR photos will be identified by a special icon ( ) on your camera's screen.

Dynamic range means the distinction between the most brilliant and dimmest areas in a scene where you can still see details. Imagine a photo with a bright sky and dark shadows. A good dynamic range would capture details in places that are brilliant and dark, without them appearing blown out (too white) or crushed (completely black).

Here's an analysis of the challenge:

1) **Human vs. Camera Vision:** The human eye is incredibly powerful, able to see details in highlights that are **millions of times brighter** than the details in shadows.

2) **Camera Limitations:** Unfortunately, digital cameras aren't as capable. They can typically capture details in a range of around **4,000 to 16,000 times** the brightness difference.

3) **The Exposure Dilemma:** This limited camera range creates a challenge. If you set the exposure to capture details in the bright highlights, the shadows might appear dark and lack detail. Conversely, if you expose for the shadows, the highlights might become overexposed and lose detail (appearing completely white).

The Good News: Don't despair! There are techniques to overcome this limitation and capture more detail in your photos. We'll explore these methods in the next section.

METHOD 1: ADJUSTING THE SCENE FOR BETTER CAPTURE

This method involves manipulating the scene itself to bring the range of brightness closer to what your camera can handle. Here are two common techniques:

1) **Reflectors and Fill-Flash:** These tools help brighten dark shadow areas, making them closer in brightness to

the highlights. This reduces the overall difference in brightness within the scene, allowing your camera to capture details in both areas.

a) Reflectors: These are large, white surfaces that bounce light back into the shadows, brightening them. They're commonly used in portrait photography.

b) Fill-Flash: A flash directed at the shadows can also brighten them and reduce the dynamic range of the scene.

2) **Diffusers:** These are translucent materials placed in front of harsh light sources. They soften the illumination, lowering the intensity level of highlights and bringing them closer to the brilliance of the shadows. This technique is also useful in portrait photography with bright sunlight.

Important Note: While these methods are effective, they have limitations. Reflectors and fill-flash are more practical for smaller scenes like portraits, not for vast landscapes.

METHOD 2: EXPANDING YOUR CAMERA'S DYNAMIC RANGE

This method involves using built-in camera features to obtain a greater variety of brilliance in your photos.

1) **In-Camera HDR Setting:** Your camera has a built-in **Dynamic Range** (DR) setting located in the **IQ** **Image Quality Setting** menu (also accessible through the Q Menu). By default, this is set to 100%.

2) **Boosting Dynamic Range:** You can increase this setting to 200% to gain an extra "stop" of dynamic range. This allows your camera to obtain a larger spectrum of brightness between highlights and shadows in a single photo (compared to the 100% setting). Going

even further to 400% provides another halt of dynamic range.

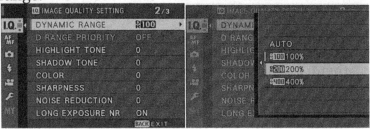

Important Considerations:

1) **Higher ISO Requirement:** To use the 200% and 400% DR settings, you'll need to set your camera's ISO to a higher level than the base ISO. For example, if your camera's base ISO is 160, you must employ ISO 640 (one stop higher) to activate the 400% DR setting.

2) **Automatic DR Option:** Your camera also offers an AUTO DR setting that automatically chooses either 100% or 200% based on the shooting conditions.

UNDERSTANDING HOW DYNAMIC RANGE WORKS ON YOUR FUJIFILM CAMERA

We learned that your camera provides a built-in Dynamic Range (DR) setting to capture more detail in both highlights and shadows. Here's a deeper dive into how it works:

1) **Underexposure for Highlights:** The camera slightly underexposes the image during capture. This prioritizes protecting the specifics in brilliant highlights, which are more prone to being blown out (appearing completely white) in a normal exposure.

2) **Shadow Boost in JPEG Processing:** On capturing the image, the camera's image processor boosts the brightness in the shadows when converting the raw sensor data into a JPEG file. This helps to recover detail that might have been lost due to the underexposure.

Dynamic Range Bracketing: Covering Your Bases
Your camera also offers Dynamic Range Bracketing as a shooting mode. This means it captures several pictures of the similar scenes at various intensities of exposure (one properly exposed, one underexposed, and one overexposed). This bracketing ensures you'll get one or more image with good detail in illuminated and dark conditions, regardless of the scene's lighting complexity. Use this option if you're unsure about the best DR setting for a particular scene.

D Range Priority for Extra Detail Recovery (X100VI and other select models)
The FujifilmX100VI Series offer an additional feature called D Range Priority. This mode builds upon the regular Dynamic Range settings by also incorporating the camera's Highlights and Shadows settings. D Range Priority works to recover even more detail in areas with blown highlights or crushed shadows (areas that appear completely black).

Accessing D Range Priority:
1) Go to the IMAGE QUALITY SETTING menu on your camera.
2) Navigate to the D RANGE PRIORITY submenu.
3) Select one of the options below:
   a) AUTO: The camera automatically selects STRONG, WEAK, or OFF based on the illumination circumstances.
   b) STRONG: This setting aggressively recovers detail in highlights and shadows. It also introduces more image noise.
   c) WEAK: This setting offers a more subtle approach to detail recovery, with less risk of increased noise.
   d) OFF: Disables D Range Priority.

IMAGE QUALITY SETTING 2/3
I.Q. DYNAMIC RANGE R400
AF MF D RANGE PRIORITY OFF
HIGHLIGHT TONE 0
SHADOW TONE 0
COLOR 0
SHARPNESS 0
NOISE REDUCTION 0
LONG EXPOSURE NR ON
BACK EXIT

I.Q. D RANG
AUTO
STRONG
WEAK
OFF
COLOR
SHARPN
NOISE F
LONG E

UNLOCKING EXTRA DETAIL: RAW FILES

For the ultimate dynamic range, consider taking pictures in RAW format instead of JPEG. Here's why:

1) **RAW Captures Everything:** RAW files include every piece of information obtained by your camera's sensor, unlike JPEGs which discard some information. This extra data gives you more flexibility to recover details in illuminated and dark conditions during post-processing using editing software.

2) **Editing Highlights and Shadows:** RAW processing software helps to modify the whites/highlights and blacks/shadows sliders. This helps you recover details that might be lost due to overexposure (blown out highlights) or underexposure (crushed shadows) in the original capture.

Bracketing for HDR: Capturing the Full Range

If you need even more dynamic range than a RAW file can offer, then bracketing combined with HDR processing is the ultimate solution:

1) **Bracketing Multiple Exposures:** This technique involves capturing an array of three photos of similar scenes at varying degrees of exposure. One image might be properly exposed, another slightly underexposed, and another slightly overexposed.

2) **HDR Magic:** Software like Adobe Photoshop can then combine these bracketed exposures into one HDR (High Dynamic Range) image. This HDR image packs in a

much greater variety of brightness information than a single RAW file, leading to a much detailed and realistic illustration of the scene, closer to what your eye sees.

3) **Displaying and Editing HDR Images:** Ideally, you'd view an HDR image on an HDR-compatible TV to see its full potential. However, you can also edit the HDR image into a standard JPEG format for viewing on regular displays. This edited JPEG will still offer a greater dynamic range and richer detail compared to a single RAW or JPEG image.

In short, RAW format and bracketing for HDR processing are powerful tools for capturing scenes with the most detail possible in illuminated and dark conditions.

CLASSIC OPTION: FILTERS FOR LANDSCAPE PHOTOGRAPHY

Don't forget about tried-and-true glass or resin filters! Landscape photographers have long relied on these filters to attain a greater dynamic range in their shots.

1) **Graduated Neutral Density (ND) Filters:** These filters are darker at the top and gradually fade to clear at the bottom. They're perfect for landscape scenes where the sky is much brighter than the foreground (think mountains or beaches). The filter helps darken the bright sky, bringing it closer in brightness to the land, so the entire scene falls within the camera's dynamic range. This helps to shoot in sky and landscape without blowing out the highlights.

2) **Choosing the Right ND Grad Filter:** These filters come in different strengths (how dark the top portion is) and with varying degrees of softness in the transition zone between the dark and clear areas. Choose the filter that best suits the brightness difference in your scene.

3) **Fujifilm X100VI's Built-in ND Filter:** This model actually has a built-in neutral density filter, giving you

this dynamic range advantage without needing an additional attachment.

What have we said?
While modern cameras and software offer powerful tools for expanding dynamic range, traditional filters remain a valuable option, especially for landscape photographers.

UNDERSTANDING DYNAMIC RANGE VS. HDR IN PHOTOGRAPHY

1) **Dynamic Range Explained:** Dynamic range means the distinction between the locations with the most and least light in a scene where you can still see details. Imagine a photo with a brilliant sky with deep shadows. A scene with good dynamic range would allow you to see specifics in the sky and shadows, without them appearing blown out (white) or crushed (black).

2) **Fujifilm's Dynamic Range Optimization:** When you use this setting, it modifies a JPEG image internally to reduce the overall contrast. This means the bright areas won't appear completely white, and you'll possess the ability to view some specifics and color in those highlights.

Similarities: Controlling High-Contrast Scenes
Both Dynamic Range optimization and HDR aim to improve photos taken in scenes with high contrast. These are scenes where:
1) The sky is very bright.
2) The foreground (landscape, buildings, etc.) is much darker.

The goal is to capture specifics in the bright and dark scenery in a single photo.

1) **Increasing Dynamic Range:** By using Dynamic Range or HDR, you're essentially expanding the

camera's dynamic range. This helps to capture specifics in dark and illuminated areas without losing information due to overexposure or underexposure.

2) **Preserving Details:** Both techniques help retain texture, color, as well as specifics in the extreme brightness and darkness of the scene.

Key Differences: How They Work

It's important to understand that even though HDR and Dynamic Range achieve similar results, they work in very different ways:

1) **Dynamic Range (In-Camera JPEG Processing):** This is a simpler approach. The camera processes a single JPEG image captured at a single exposure level and reduces the contrast to recover some detail in the highlights.

2) **HDR (Multiple Exposures and Processing):** This is a more advanced technique. The camera captures multiple images of similar scenes at various intensities of exposure (one for highlights, shadows, and midtones respectively). Special software then combines these exposures into an HDR image with a greater dynamic range, revealing details in dark and bright areas.

3) **Dynamic Range (DR):**

   a) **Underexposed Capture:** The camera intentionally takes a slightly underexposed image to protect the highlights from being blown out (appearing completely white).

   b) **Selective Brightness Boost:** The camera's processor then selectively increases the brightness in most parts of the picture (excluding the brightest highlights). This recovers specifics in the shadows and midtones without affecting the highlights.

   c) **Higher ISO Requirement:** Because the initial image is underexposed, Dynamic Range settings often require a higher ISO setting. Higher ISO can introduce image noise, so it's a trade-off to consider.

4) **High Dynamic Range (HDR):**
   a) **Multiple Exposures:** Unlike Dynamic Range which uses a single image, HDR captures three images of similar scenes with various exposures. One image is exposed normally, one is marginally too exposed to capture specifics in shadows, and one is slightly underexposed to protect the highlights.
   b) **In-Camera Processing:** The camera's processor then merges these three exposures in one HDR image. This final image has a significantly larger dynamic range in comparison to the individual exposures, resulting in a photo with details in both highlights and shadows.

The final image (Photo 1) has a larger DR compared to photos 2 (underexposed) & Photo 3 (overexposed)

Limitations:

1) **Not a Magic Solution:** HDR as well as dynamic range have limitations. If the scene has an extreme distinction between sections that are dark and those that are bright, neither technique could potentially recover all the details perfectly.

2) **Similar Outcome, Different Methods:** While the final images from HDR and Dynamic range might look similar, the way they achieve those results is fundamentally different.

DYNAMIC RANGE SETTINGS EXPLAINED

Understanding camera settings can sometimes feel overwhelming, but I'll break down the Dynamic Range (DR) options in a way that's easy to understand.

Finding the DR Settings:
Look for the IMAGE QUALITY SETTING menu on your camera. The **Dynamic Range** Setting options will be located there.

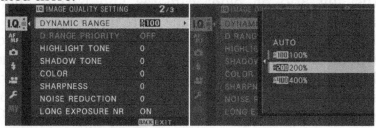

DR Settings Explained:

1) **DR 100 (Off):** This setting is like turning off Dynamic Range altogether. The camera captures the image at the chosen exposure level without any additional processing to raise the dynamic range.

2) **DR 200 (One Stop Extra):** This setting attempts to recover an additional "stop" of dynamic range. Imagine a photo with dark shadows and a brilliant sky. One stop of extra dynamic range means the camera can potentially capture more specifics in the highlights (sky) and shadows without one overpowering the other. This setting is ideal for scenes with moderate contrast to recover some detail in the shadows without affecting the highlights too much.

Important Note: Using DR 200 needs a minimal ISO setting. This ISO requirement is usually 400 on older Fujifilm X cameras and 320 on newer models. Higher ISO can introduce image noise, so it's a trade-off to consider.

3) **DR 400 (Two Stops Extra):** This setting is even more aggressive than DR 200. It attempts to recover two stops of additional dynamic range, helping to take specifics in dark and bright conditions in high-contrast scenes. Imagine a photo with a brilliant sky and dark foreground elements. DR 400 is possibly useful in recovering details in both areas. However, remember that this setting requires a higher minimum ISO (usually 800 on older cameras and 640 on newer models), which can introduce more image noise.

4) **DR AUTO:** This is a convenient option for situations where the contrast in your scenes varies. The camera instantly selects DR 100 (no processing) or DR 200 (one stop extra) depending on the conditions. DR 400 is unavailable in Auto mode. The minimum ISO requirement for DR AUTO is 400 (older cameras) or 320 (newer models).

Choosing the Right DR Setting:
1) Start with DR 100 (Off) for scenes with normal contrast.
2) In case you have moderate contrast and want to recover some shadow detail, try DR 200.
3) For high-contrast scenes with very bright highlights, DR 400 might be necessary; however, be mindful of the higher ISO requirement and potential for noise.
4) Use DR AUTO for scenes with varying contrast where you want the camera to make the decision for you (between DR 100 and DR 200).

HIGH DYNAMIC RANGE (HDR) SETTINGS
We've covered Dynamic Range (DR) settings, and now let's explore the options for High Dynamic Range on your Fujifilm X Series camera.
Finding the HDR Settings:

The location of the HDR settings depends on your specific camera model:

1) **Cameras having a DRIVE button (e.g., X100VI):**
   a) Press the DRIVE/DELETE button on your camera.
   b) In the drive mode menu that appears, select HDR.
2) **Cameras having a Drive Mode Dial:**
   a) Go to the SHOOTING SETTING menu on your camera.
   b) Within the SHOOTING SETTING menu, navigate to the DRIVE SETTING submenu. Here, you'll find the HDR options.

HDR Settings Explained:
The camera manual may be light on details regarding HDR settings, but let's compare them to the Dynamic Range (DR) options we learned about earlier:

1) **HDR 200% (One Stop Extra):** This setting incorporates one stop of additional dynamic range, just like DR 200. It's a good choice for scenes with moderate contrast or whenever you desire a subtle HDR effect that won't drastically alter the natural look of the image.
2) **HDR 400% (Two Stops Extra):** This setting is more aggressive than 200%, adding two stops of dynamic range. It's suitable for scenes with higher contrast where you want to recover more detail in both highlights and shadows.
3) **HDR 800% (Three Stops Extra):** This is the strongest standard HDR option, adding three stops of dynamic range. It's ideal for very high-contrast scenes where you need significant detail recovery in places that are both brilliant and dark. The resulting HDR effect will be more noticeable than with the lower settings, but it should still look natural and avoid an artificial appearance.

4) **HDR 800%+: (Extreme HDR with D Range Priority):** This is a powerful setting that combines the strengths of HDR 800% and the D Range Priority feature (available on some models) set to STRONG. D Range Priority helps recover even more specifics in bright and dark conditions. According to Fujifilm, this setting is designed to capture the maximum possible dynamic range in your scene. But remember that the resulting image might have a more processed or artificial look due to the extreme adjustments.

5) **HDR AUTO:** This is a convenient option that lets the camera choose HDR 200% or 800% depending on the degree of contrast it detects in the scene. The most extreme option, HDR 800%+, is unavailable in Auto mode.

Choosing the Right HDR Setting:

1) Start with lower settings (HDR 200% or 400%) for scenes with moderate contrast or if you prefer a subtle HDR effect.

2) Use HDR 800% for high-contrast scenes where you need significant detail recovery.

3) Choose HDR 800%+ cautiously, as it might create a more artificial-looking image due to the extreme adjustments.

4) Use HDR AUTO for scenes with varying contrast to make the decision for you (between HDR 200% and 800%).

Beware of the "Muddy" Look with HDR 800%

While other HDR setting produce more natural-looking results, the strongest option, HDR 800%+, can introduce a noticeable effect, especially in the shadows. This effect can sometimes make the shadows appear muddy or lacking detail.

Combating the Mud

Here's a trick to improve the look of photos taken with HDR 800%+:

1) **Adjust Clarity and Sharpness:** Increase the Clarity setting to +3 and the Sharpness setting to +2. These adjustments can help add some "punch" back into the image and counteract the muddy look caused by the extreme HDR processing.

Remember:

1) Use HDR 800%+ sparingly, as it can create unnatural-looking images due to the strong processing.

2) Apply Clarity and Sharpness adjustments only with HDR 800%+ to avoid overdoing the effect.

CHOOSING BETWEEN DYNAMIC RANGE AND HDR

Both Dynamic Range (DR) and HDR help you capture details in highlights and shadows of high-contrast scenes, especially useful when shooting JPEGs (not RAW). But in what situation is one better than the other to use?

Dynamic Range (DR):

1) **Ideal for:** Use DR when you're shooting handheld or if there's motion in the scenery. This is because DR works with a single image, making it faster and less prone to alignment issues that can happen with HDR.

2) **Faster Processing:** DR requires processing only one image, so it's quicker than HDR.

3) **Less Prone to Alignment Issues:** With handheld shooting or movement in the scene, slight camera shake can cause misalignment in the multiple images captured for HDR. DR avoids this issue.

High Dynamic Range (HDR):

1) **Ideal for:** Use HDR on a tripod and there's minimal movement in the scene. This ensures the multiple images captured for HDR align perfectly.

2) **More Detail Recovery:** HDR generally offers an array of dynamic range compared to DR, potentially recovering more specifics in dark and bright conditions.

In Summary:
1) **For handheld shooting or scenes with movement:** Choose Dynamic Range (DR) for its speed and single-image processing.
2) **For tripod use and static scenes:** Choose this range for its potential to recover even more detail in high-contrast situations.

RAW FILES AND HDR: IMPORTANT INFORMATION YOU SHOULD KNOW

1) **RAW with HDR: Double the File Size:** Shooting in HDR mode while also capturing RAW files creates two files:
   a) A processed HDR JPEG image.
   b) A RAW file that's three times greater than the usual RAW file.
2) **Why the Big RAW File?** This extra-large RAW file combines three separate photos within the single .RAF file:
   a) The original photo you captured based on your chosen exposure settings.
   b) An underexposed version by the configured stops for HDR (to recover shadow details).
   c) An overexposed version (to recover highlight details).
3) Essentially, the camera takes a variety of exposures and embeds them all into a single RAW file for you to process later. This gives you more flexibility to recover details in highlights and shadows during editing, even when shooting in HDR mode.

316

4) **Software Doesn't See All the Data:** Even though the large RAW file captured in HDR mode contains three exposures, most editing software like Lightroom, Photoshop, and Capture One can only access the data from the original photo you captured (the first exposure). The additional underexposed and overexposed data embedded within the RAW file isn't utilized by these programs. This makes it difficult to extract and edit them individually for more control in these programs.

5) **Fujifilm HDR RAF vs. DNG Conversion:** Fujifilm has a specific format for these HDR RAW files called "Fujifilm HDR RAF." Some sources suggest converting this format to the more widely-used Adobe DNG format in Lightroom. Supposedly, there's a checkbox option during conversion ("Embed original Raw file") that allows Lightroom to use all three exposures within the HDR RAF file.

6) **Limited Benefit in DNG Conversion:** However, tests show that checking or unchecking the "Embed original Raw file" box during DNG conversion in Lightroom makes no discernable change in the resulting picture. In other words, Lightroom doesn't seem to effectively utilize the extra exposure data in the Fujifilm HDR RAF file, regardless of the conversion setting.

7) **Alternative: Exposure Bracketing:** Fujifilm cameras offer an "Exposure Bracketing" feature that takes several pictures at various exposures (similar to what the camera does internally for HDR). This provides you with separate RAW files for each exposure, enabling more control during editing in post-processing software.

8) **HDR's Convenience vs. Bracketing's Flexibility:** While the HDR function on Fujifilm cameras is readily available and simple to operate, it sacrifices some

control over the individual exposures. Exposure Bracketing offers more flexibility for fine-tuning in editing software, but requires you to manually capture the bracketed images.

PANORAMIC PHOTOGRAPHY

Ever wanted to capture a breathtaking vista or a sprawling scene in its entirety? Panoramic photography lets you achieve that!

WHAT IS PANORAMIC PHOTOGRAPHY?

Panoramic photos create an image with a much wider field of view than a standard image, closer to what you see with your own eyes (estimated to be around 160° horizontally by 75° vertically). This results in an aspect ratio of 2:1. Panoramic images can also be even wider, like 3:1, 4:1, or even capturing a full 360° view.

TAKING PANORAMAS:

1) Look for the DRIVE/DELETE button on your camera.
2) Press the DRIVE/DELETE button and proceed to the drive mode menu.
3) Within the drive mode menu, select "Adv." (Advanced) and then "PANORAMA".

Choosing the Panoramic Angle:

4) Once you've selected Panorama mode, use the focus stick (or focus lever) on your camera to move left. This will display the available panoramic angle options.
5) Choose the desired angle by highlighting it and pressing the MENU/OK button.

Capturing Your Panoramic Image:

6) After selecting the panoramic angle, use the focus stick (or focus lever) on your camera to move right. This will display the available panning direction options.
7) Choose the path you wish to pan the camera (left or right) by highlighting it and pressing the MENU/OK button.
8) Taking the Panoramic Shot:
   a) Firmly tap the shutter button to begin recording the panorama. You don't need to hold the button down during the entire process.
   b) Slowly pan the camera in the direction indicated by the arrow on your camera screen. The camera instantly stops recording when it captures the entire panoramic image based on the guides displayed.

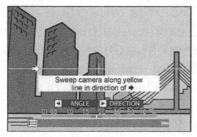

TIPS FOR FLAWLESS PANORAMAS:

1) Maintain a steady, slow panning motion in a small circle.
2) Keep your camera level (parallel) or upright (at a right angle) to the horizon.
3) If you're not pleased with the outcome, alter the panning speed.
4) For better stability, brace your elbows against your sides while panning.
5) A tripod is strongly advised for capturing sharp, clear panoramic images.
share

AREAS OF CONSIDERATION WHEN SHOOTING

1) **Don't Release the Shutter Early:** Make sure to long press the shutter button until the camera finishes capturing the entire panorama. Releasing it prematurely will stop the recording and you might miss sections of the scene.

2) **Incomplete Panoramas:** Even if you long press the shutter button, there's a slight chance the camera might not capture the entire scene planned for the panorama.

3) **Stitching Imperfections:** Panoramic images are created by stitching multiple photos together. In some rare cases, the camera may be unable to flawlessly blend these images, resulting in stitching errors.

4) **Low-Light Blurry Photos:** Panoramic shots can be more prone to blur in low-light conditions because the camera has to capture multiple images while panning.

5) **Panning Speed Matters:** Panning too quickly or too slowly can disrupt the capture process and lead to a failed panorama. The camera will also stop recording if you pan in the wrong direction.

6) **Slight Angle Variations:** The actual panoramic angle captured might be slightly wider or narrower than the angle you selected.

7) **Subjects to Avoid for Panoramas:**
   a) Moving objects: People walking, cars driving, etc. will appear blurry or distorted in the resulting picture.
   b) Close-up subjects: Panoramas are not ideal for close-up shots.
   c) Featureless scenes: Skies, fields of grass, or walls with little variation won't create an interesting panoramic image.
   d) Fast-moving subjects: Waterfalls, waves, or anything in constant motion could be hard to capture effectively in a panorama.

e) Scenes with changing brightness: Avoid panoramas of scenes with a mix of very bright and very dark areas, as the exposure might be off in different sections of the picture.

8) **Exposure and Shutter Speed:** If you have "🔧 BUTTON/DIAL SETTING > SHUTTER AE" set to "ON," the exposure for the entire panorama will depend on the first frame captured. This might be a perfect choice for scenes with varying lighting conditions.

ADDING ARTISTIC EFFECTS WITH ADVANCED FILTERS

Want to add some creative charm in your pictures? Your Fujifilm camera has a built-in set of Advanced Filters that let you achieve various artistic effects directly in-camera.

USING ADVANCED FILTERS

1) Locate the DRIVE/DELETE button on your camera.
2) Press the DRIVE/DELETE button and proceed to the drive mode menu.
3) Within the drive mode menu, select "Adv." (Advanced) and then "ADVANCED FILTER".
4) An inventory of available filters displays on your camera screen. Browse through the options and choose your desired outcome.
5) Once you've selected a filter, simply frame your shot and take the picture! The camera will apply the chosen filter effect to your image.

Note: Remember that Advanced Filters are applied during image capture and affect the JPEG image only. The RAW file (if enabled) will not have an impact on the filter.

EXPLORING THE BUILT-IN FILTERS

Let's delve into the different Advanced Filters and the creative effects they produce:

1) **TOY CAMERA:** Take your photos back in time with this filter, creating a nostalgic look reminiscent of old-school toy cameras.

2) **MINIATURE:** Want to transform your scene into a miniature model? This filter creates a diorama effect by blurring the upper and lower sections of the picture, making it appear like a tiny world.

3) **POP COLOR:** Boost the vibrancy and saturation of colors for a high-contrast, eye-catching look.

4) **HIGH-KEY:** This filter produces bright and airy images with low contrast, ideal for light and cheerful scenes.

5) **LOW-KEY:** For a more dramatic and moody effect, choose the LOW-KEY filter. It creates a dark and shadowy image with minimal highlights.

6) **DYNAMIC TONE:** This filter offers a more artistic approach. It manipulates the spectrum of tones of your image for a dreamlike or fantasy-inspired look.

7) **SOFT FOCUS:** Soften the entire image for a gentle and diffused effect, creating a more ethereal or romantic mood.

PARTIAL COLOR FILTERS FOR CREATIVE BLACK AND WHITE WITH A POP

Your Fujifilm camera also offers a series of "Partial Color" filters within the Advanced Filters menu. These filters add a unique twist to pictures in black and white:

1) **Partial Color Filters:**
   a) **Red**
   b) **Orange**
   c) **Yellow**

d) **Green**
e) **Blue**
f) **Purple**

2) These filters capture your image in black and white, but with one specific color remaining intact throughout the entire photo. For example, the "Partial Color (Red)" filter will turn everything black and white except for red objects, which will retain their original color. This creates a striking visual effect that draws attention to the colored elements within the scene.

Keep in mind:

1) The standard of the resulting picture with Partial Color filters can be influenced by the subject matter and the settings of your camera. In some cases, there might be visible grain or slight variations in brightness or color hue.

CHAPTER 12: UNVEILING THE ESSENTIALS: YOUR FUJIFILM X100VI ACCESSORY KIT

The Fujifilm X100VI features a thoughtful selection of accessories to get you started on your photographic journey. Let's delve into each item and explore how it contributes to your creative process:

- **Li-ion Battery NP-W126S:** This is the heart of your camera's power. Consider investing in a spare battery for extended shooting sessions, especially if you anticipate being away from a charger for long periods.
- **USB Cable:** This trusty cable connects your X100VI to your computer for image transfer and charging. While the included cable is perfectly functional, some photographers prefer third-party options with braided exteriors for enhanced durability.
- **Shoulder Strap:** This provides a comfortable and secure way to carry your camera. For a more stylish touch, some photographers opt for aftermarket straps made from premium leather or canvas.
- **Metal Strap Clip and Clip Attaching Tool:** These handy tools enable you to attach the shoulder strap to your camera body.
- **Protective Cover:** This safeguards your camera from minor bumps and scratches while it's stored in your bag.
- **Lens Cap:** This essential accessory protects your precious lens from dust, fingerprints, and scratches. Consider a magnetic lens cap for quicker, one-handed operation.
- **Hot Shoe Cover:** When not employing a supplementary flash unit, the hot shoe cover keeps your camera's hot shoe clean and protected.

- **Owner's Manual:** This comprehensive guide unlocks the capabilities of your X100VI. Take some time to familiarize yourself with its capabilities and functions – you might be surprised by hidden gems!

These core accessories provide a solid foundation for your photographic adventures. As you explore your creative vision, you can expand your X100VI's capabilities with additional accessories – we'll delve into those in the next part!

LENS ADD-ONS

BROADENING YOUR HORIZONS: THE FUJIFILM TCL-X100II TELE CONVERSION LENS

The fixed lens of the Fujifilm X100VI provides an exceptional focal range suitable for a multitude of situations. Yet, consider the possibility that you crave a bit more telephoto punch for capturing portraits or distant details? Enter the **Fujifilm TCL-X100II Tele Conversion Lens (A)**.

This compact and lightweight teleconverter seamlessly attaches to your X100VI, multiplying your lens's focal distance by an estimated factor of 1.4. In photographer's terms, this translates to a new effective focal length of around 50mm, equivalent to the traditional 35mm film format. This slight increase allows you to:

- **Craft flattering portraits:** The lens with a 50mm field of view offers a classic choice for portraiture, offering a natural perspective that's pleasing to the eye.
- **Zoom in on details:** Get closer to faraway subjects, perfect for capturing wildlife, architectural features, or distant action shots.

Maintaining Image Quality:

Fujifilm designed the TCL-X100II to maintain the exceptional image quality you expect from your X100VI. The lens construction utilizes high-quality elements to minimize any potential image degradation. Additionally, your camera automatically recognizes the attached teleconverter and adjusts accordingly, ensuring sharp and accurate results.

Aesthetics and Convenience:

The TCL-X100II complements your X100VI beautifully, available in both black and silver to match your camera's finish. It's also incredibly compact and lightweight, maintaining the camera's excellent portability. While it adds a bit to the overall size, it remains highly manageable and won't weigh down your bag.

Performance and Usability

Fujifilm has outdone itself with the TCL-X100II's optics. It maintains the X100VI's exceptional image quality, delivering sharp results even with maximum aperture settings. There's virtually no perceivable optical difference, aside from the delightful shift to a 50mm perspective. The camera's automatic recognition of the attached teleconverter is another thoughtful touch that streamlines the shooting experience.

As a photographer, using the TCL-X100II has been refreshing. It's a joy to see 50mm portraits and vertical compositions come alive on the X100VI. For individuals who, like me, primarily use 35mm lenses horizontally, The lens with a 50mm field of view opens doors for captivating vertical images without distortion. Having both focal lengths readily accessible with the X100VI truly expands creative possibilities, making it an even more versatile travel companion.

Considering the Downsides: Optical Viewfinder and Alternatives

The Fujifilm TCL-X100II isn't without its drawbacks. It's crucial to be cognizant of a potential trade-off:

- **Optical Viewfinder Obstruction:** The teleconverter does block a portion of the optical viewfinder. This might serve as a minor annoyance or even a dealbreaker for photographers who rely heavily on the optical viewfinder for composing their shots.

Alternative Solutions:

- **Electronic Viewfinder:** The X100VI's excellent electronic viewfinder remains fully functional with the TCL-X100II attached. If you're comfortable using the EVF, this might serve as a workaround for the optical viewfinder obstruction.

Overall Take:

Despite this potential drawback, the Fujifilm TCL-X100II remains a compelling accessory for many X100VI users:

- **Versatility Boost:** It offers a valuable focal length extension, providing a more telephoto perspective for portraits and distant subjects.
- **Exceptional Performance:** The image quality remains outstanding, and the camera seamlessly integrates with the teleconverter for a smooth shooting experience.
- **Compact Portability:** It maintains the X100VI's attractive compact size, rendering it an excellent travel companion.

The Final Verdict:

If you're looking to add some telephoto reach to your X100VI without sacrificing portability, and you're comfortable utilizing the electronic viewfinder occasionally, then the TCL-X100II is a fantastic choice. However, if the optical viewfinder is essential to your shooting style, you might like to consider alternative options.

Here's a quick tip: If you're unsure about the teleconverter, try renting one first. This permits you to experiment utilizing the focal length and see if it suits your shooting style before committing to a purchase.

Recap: TCL-X100II's Strengths and Weaknesses

Let's break down the benefits and drawbacks of the Fujifilm TCL-X100II Tele Conversion Lens in a way that's easy to understand:

Pros:

- **Telephoto Power:** This is the star of the show! You get a delightful 50mm focal length (35mm equivalent), perfect for portraits, capturing details at a distance, and adding a slight compression effect.
- **Sharp Shooter:** Fujifilm's optics shine through. The TCL-X100II maintains impressive sharpness across the entire image, from the center to the corners.
- **Built to Last:** The all-metal construction exudes quality and durability. This converter is engineered to endure the demands of everyday photography.
- **Clean Performance:** No chromatic aberrations or distortion to mar your images. This means you'll get true-to-life colors and straight lines where they should be.

Cons:

- **Bulkier Build:** Compared to the X100VI's sleek body, the TCL-X100II adds some size and weight. While still compact, it might feel a bit less pocketable.
- **Price Point:** The cost can be a consideration, especially considering it's a converter without aperture

or focus control. It's essentially high-quality glass and metal for the added focal length.

EXPANDING YOUR HORIZONS: THE FUJIFILM WCL-X100II WIDE CONVERSION LENS

The Fujifilm X100VI's 35mm lens is fantastic for a broad array of subjects. Yet, consider the possibility that you crave even more expansive vistas or want to capture the entirety of a cramped scene? Introducing the **Fujifilm WCL-X100II Wide Conversion Lens, model A**.

This ingenious accessory seamlessly attaches to your X100VI, widening your field of view:

- **Broader Perspective:** The WCL-X100II effectively converts your 35mm lens to a wider 28mm focal length (35mm equivalent). This enables a broader scene composition in a single frame, ideal for landscapes, architecture, and tight indoor spaces.
- **Landscape Prowess:** You've rightly mentioned the advantage for landscape photography. The 28mm focal length is a favorite among landscape photographers due to its capacity to render wide-ranging vistas captured through a natural look, often emphasizing foreground elements.
- **Effortless Integration:** Fujifilm has ensured a smooth user experience. The camera spontaneously recognizes the attached WCL-X100II and corrects any potential aberrations, ensuring sharp and accurate results.

Maintaining Image Quality:

A common concern with conversion lenses is a potential decrease in image quality. Here's the good news:

- **Fujifilm's Engineering Feat:** Fujifilm has impressed with the WCL-X100II's design. It maintains the

X100VI's exceptional image quality. Sharpness and image fidelity remain on par with the native 35mm lens. This constitutes an important achievement, as some converters can introduce softness or other image artifacts. The WCL-X100II stands out due to its capacity to deliver exceptional wide-angle images without compromise.

Practical Considerations:

Attaching the WCL-X100II does add a bit of bulk to the X100VI. While it remains compact, it might not slip as easily into some smaller bags or jacket pockets. This is a factor to consider For photographers who give precedence to extreme pocketability. On the positive side, the converter's metal construction beautifully complements the X100VI's design, creating a visually cohesive unit.

The WCL-X100II utilizes a threaded connection instead of a bayonet mount. While a bayonet mount might be faster for swapping lenses, the threads are very well-machined and smooth, making attachment a swift and reliable process.

My Overall Take:

The WCL-X100II is a fantastic accessory that I highly recommend. The wider 28mm perspective unveils a universe of creative possibilities, particularly for landscape and architectural photography. While there's a slight trade-off in portability, the image quality remains outstanding, and the converter's sleek design maintains the X100VI's premium aesthetic. Should you be in the market to expand your X100VI's capabilities and embrace wider vistas, the WCL-X100II is definitely worth considering."

PROTECTORS FILTERS (PRF-49 / PRF-49S)

- **Safeguarding Your Lens:** These filters act as a shield for your precious X100VI lens, repelling dust, scratches, and fingerprints. This is especially valuable when shooting outdoors or in environments with potential hazards.

- **Super EBC for Reduced Flare:** The Super EBC (Electron Beam Coating) is a noteworthy feature. It minimizes harmful reflections and stray light, helping to maintain sharp and contrasty photographs, particularly during capture towards strong light sources.
- **Mounting:** It's significant to highlight that these filters require the dedicated adapter ring AR-X100 / LH-X100 for attachment to your X100VI.

LENS HOOD (LH-X100):

- **Combating Lens Flare:** The lens hood is another essential protective accessory. It extends forward from the lens, blocking incidental light from penetrating the lens at extreme angles. This helps to prevent lens flare, a common issue that can cause unwanted ghosting and reduced contrast in your images.
- **Improved Contrast:** By minimizing lens flare, the lens hood promotes sharper and more contrasty photographs, particularly during capture in bright or backlit conditions.
- **A Detachable Accessory:** The LH-X100 lens hood is detachable, allowing you to remove it when not needed for a more compact profile.

These filters and lens hood provide a layer of defense for your X100VI's lens, helping to maintain its optimal efficiency and visual clarity. They're a worthwhile investment for any photographer who wants to safeguard their camera.

THE UNSUNG HERO: AR-X100 ADAPTER RING

While not the most glamorous accessory, the AR-X100 adaptor ring Is significant in expanding your X100VI's filtration and lens hood capabilities. Here's why it's important:

- **Filter Compatibility:** The X100VI's lens has a specific thread diameter. The AR-X100 adaptor ring acts as a bridge, allowing for the fitting of 49mm circular filters, such as UV protectors or polarizers (sold separately). These filters provide essential protection or creative effects for your photography.
- **Lens Hood Connection:** The AR-X100 adaptor ring also serves another critical function: it replaces the stock lens ring and creates a bayonet mount for the LH-X100 lens hood (discussed previously). This lens hood assists to combat light diffraction and maintain sharp, contrasty images.

ILLUMINATING POSSIBILITIES: EXTERNAL FLASHES FOR FUJIFILM X100VI

The Fujifilm X100VI's built-in flash offers a convenient lighting solution. But for photographers seeking more control and power, external flashes open up creative possibilities. Let's examine certain aspects of the popular shoe-mount flash options from Fujifilm:

FUJIFILM EF-X500:

- **Powerhouse Performance:** The EF-X500 boasts a powerful guide number of 50 (ISO 100/m), ensuring ample illumination for various lighting situations.
- **High-Speed Sync (FP Mode):** This is a game-changer. The EF-X500 allows flash firing at any shutter speed, even faster speeds typically used for freezing motion or achieving shallow depth-of-field with a broad aperture setting. This offers creative flexibility, especially under the glaring sun.

- **Multi-Flash Mastery:** Get creative with lighting setups! The EF-X500 supports multi-flash configurations, granting you the ability to adjust the illumination on your focal point and surroundings independently for dramatic effects.
- **Effortless TTL Control:** Fujifilm's TTL (Through-The-Lens) metering ensures accurate flash exposure, both in single-flash and multi-flash scenarios. This eliminates the need for complex manual adjustments, letting you focus on capturing the moment.

CHOOSING THE RIGHT FLASH:

The EF-X500 is an adaptable alternative for photographers who demand power, high-speed sync, and multi-flash flexibility. However, Fujifilm offers other flash options to consider, every one boasting unique advantages:

- We'll explore details about the EF-X20, EF-60, EF-42, and EF-20 in the next section, providing a more comprehensive comparison to help you find the perfect flash for your needs.
- Consider factors like portability, guide number, features like bounce flash, and budget when making your choice.

THE FUJIFILM EF-X20 FLASH: COMPACT POWERHOUSE

- **Pocket-Sized Powerhouse:** Don't let its size fool you! Despite its compact and lightweight design, the EF-X20 packs a punch with a guide number of 20 (ISO 100/m). This provides ample illumination for various indoor and close-up shooting situations.
- **Intelligent i-TTL Flash Control:** Fujifilm's intelligent i-TTL metering shines here. The EF-X20 automatically adjusts the flash output to perfectly match the scene's lighting, ensuring accurate exposures and minimizing the necessity of complex manual

adjustments. This permits you to concentrate on capturing the moment with confidence.

- **Premium Design and Ergonomics:** Matching the X100VI's aesthetics, the EF-X20 is crafted from high-quality metal materials, creating a cohesive look. The ergonomic design features a responsive dial for intuitive control over flash settings.
- **Built-in Diffusion Panel:** For softer, more flattering lighting, the EF-X20 features a built-in wide diffuser. This diffuser scatters the light output, creating an effortlessly authentic and even illumination on your subject.
- **Advanced Wireless Capabilities:** The EF-X20 boasts a built-in "Slave Mode" for advanced off-camera flash setups. This permits you to trigger the EF-X20 wirelessly from another compatible flash unit, opening doors for more creative lighting arrangements.

In the Next Part:

We'll explore the EF-X20's control elements in detail, including the exposure setting dial, wide panel lever, and wireless slave flash selector. This will provide a more profound comprehension of the way to utilize the EF-X20's features to achieve your desired lighting effects.

Exposure Setting Dial:

This versatile dial offers two control modes:

- **TTL Auto Mode:** Under these settings, the EF-X20 utilizes Fujifilm's intelligent i-TTL metering. You can adjust flash compensation within a range of -1EV to +1EV in precise 1/3 stop increments. This permits you to tweak the flash output relative to the ambient light to achieve a specific degree of brightness in your image.
- **Manual Mode:** For amplified control over the flash power, the manual mode provides a selection of output levels: 1/1, 1/2, 1/4, 1/8, 1/16, 1/32, and 1/64. This granular control empowers you to create specific

lighting effects, from dramatic highlights to subtle fill light.

A noteworthy feature is the dial's ability to display settings even when the flash is powered off. This allows for quick confirmation of your chosen settings before you start shooting.

Switch for wide panel adjustment:

The EF-X20 comes equipped with a built-in wide diffuser panel. This diffuser helps to soften and spread the flash output, creating an effortlessly authentic and flattering light on your subject. Here's how the lever functions:

- **Lowered Position:** For standard flash operation, the lever remains in its lowered position. The flash fires directly without affecting the beam width.
- **Raised Position:** Elevate the lever to activate the wide diffuser panel. This is uniquely advantageous for wider-angle shots (down to a 20mm focal length equivalent in 35mm format) as it ensures even light distribution across the entire frame.

Mounting Lock Releasing Button:

It's the end of an era for fiddling with levers and screws! The EF-X20 features a new and improved mounting mechanism:

- **Simplified Attachment:** Simply place the flash unit on the X100VI's hot shoe. The mounting lock releasing button automatically engages, securely fixing the flash in place. There's no longer a requirement to manipulate a locking bar or tighten a screw, making attachment effortless and convenient.

Wireless Slave Flash Selector:

The EF-X20 transcends its on-camera capabilities. It can also function as a wireless slave flash unit in multi-flash setups, opening doors for more creative lighting possibilities. This selector switch allows you to configure the EF-X20 for various wireless scenarios:

- **Master Flash Mode (X):** Under these settings, the EF-X20 acts as the main flash unit, triggering other compatible slave flashes wirelessly.
- **Slave Flash Mode (N-MODE or P-MODE):** When set to N-MODE, the EF-X20 fires in response to light pulses from a "non-preflash" master flash. Should the primary light source flash utilizes a preflash for exposure metering, set the EF-X20 to P-MODE for proper synchronization.

With this wireless capability, you can position the EF-X20 off-camera to achieve indirect lighting effects, adding depth and dimension to your images.

FUJIFILM EF-X60 FLASH: POWER AND FLEXIBILITY IN A COMPACT PACKAGE

While the EF-X20 Is a superior pick for portability, photographers seeking even more power and versatility might consider the **Fujifilm EF-X60 flash**. Here's how it stacks up:

- **Powerhouse Performance:** Small but mighty, the EF-X60 packs a serious punch with a maximum guide number of 60 (ISO 100/m at 200mm flash setting). This translates to ample illumination for various lighting situations, from bouncing flash off-camera to overpowering bright sunlight.
- **Bounce Flash Mastery:** The EF-X60's head offers exceptional flexibility. It may be inclined upward by 90 degrees or swivelled 180 degrees left or right. This permits you to reflect the flash light off walls or ceilings, creating softer, more natural-looking lighting and avoiding harsh shadows on your subject.

- **Adjustable Coverage:** The EF-X60 adapts to your lens choice. Its flash can illuminate areas from 24mm to 200mm. Additionally, the built-in diffuser can be used to widen the coverage to approximately 16mm, ideal for wider-angle shots.
- **Intelligent Auto Zoom:** Convenience meets versatility with the EF-X60's auto zoom function. This feature automatically adjusts the flash coverage to match the viewing angle of your mounted lens. This ensures even light distribution and prevents vignetting (corner darkening) in your images.

Exposure Control:

The EF-X60 caters to both automatic and manual flash operation:

- **TTL Mode:** For effortless flash control, the EF-X60 supports Fujifilm's TTL metering system. Under these settings, the flash output is automatically adjusted to achieve the optimal exposure for your scene. Optimal for situations where precise lighting control is desired without extensive manual adjustments.
- **Manual Mode:** For photographers who crave amplified control over the flash power, the EF-X60 offers a manual mode. This permits you to select specific power output levels, providing creative freedom to experiment with various lighting effects.

High-Speed Sync (FP Mode):

The EF-X60 pushes the boundaries of flash photography with its High-Speed Sync (FP Mode) capability. This mode allows flash synchronization at shutter speeds as fast as 1/8000th of a second. This is significantly faster than a camera's typical flash sync speed, which is often limited to around 1/250th of a second.

Benefits of FP Mode:

- **Overpower the Sun:** With FP Mode, you can overpower bright sunlight, facilitating the utilization of wider apertures for shallower depth-of-field, even in daylight conditions. This is an innovative breakthrough for portrait photographers who desire blurred backgrounds outdoors.
- **Freeze Motion with Flash:** The high-speed capability of FP Mode also allows you to freeze motion more effectively. This is useful for capturing sharp images of fast-moving subjects, even when using flash.

Wireless Flash Freedom:

The EF-X60 goes beyond on-camera flash limitations. It boasts a built-in receiver compatible with the Nissin Air System (NAS) of wireless radio communication. This opens doors for creative off-camera flash setups:

- **Remote Flash Capability:** Pair the EF-X60 with the optional Fujifilm Wireless Commander EF-W1 (to be released) or the Nissin Air10s remote flash controller. This permits you to trigger the EF-X60 wirelessly from a distance, placing it in various locations for more creative lighting effects.
- **Overcoming Obstacles:** Unlike traditional optical flash triggers that rely on line-of-sight, radio communication can bypass obstacles. This permits you to position the EF-X60 even in situations where direct visibility to the camera is limited.

Optical Wireless Mode:

The EF-X60 offers an **optical wireless mode** as a backup or alternative to radio communication. This mode enables the activation of EF-X60 wirelessly utilizing the **Fujifilm EF-X500** flash as the control unit.

Benefits of Optical Wireless Mode:

- **Reliable in Certain Environments:** This mode could be exceptionally handy in situations where radio signals might be weak or unreliable, such as environments with a lot of metal structures or radio interference.
- **Redundancy:** Having both radio and optical wireless options provides a layer of redundancy. If you experience radio signal issues, you can seamlessly switch to the optical mode to maintain remote flash control.

Things to Consider:
- **Line of Sight Required:** Unlike radio waves that can travel around obstacles, optical wireless communication relies on a direct line of sight between the commander unit (EF-X500) and the EF-X60 flash.
- **Limited Range:** The range of optical wireless triggering is generally shorter compared to radio communication.

In Conclusion:
The Fujifilm EF-X60 flash is a compelling option for all those photographers who want a powerful, versatile, and feature-rich on-camera and off-camera flash solution for their Fujifilm X100VI. With its high guide number, bounce flash flexibility, intelligent exposure modes, FP Mode, and wireless capabilities, the EF-X60 empowers you to create professional-looking images with creative lighting techniques.

Compared to the EF-X20:
- The EF-X60 offers a higher guide number (60 vs. 20) for more powerful illumination.
- The EF-X60's tiltable and swiveling head provides greater flexibility for bounce flash techniques.

- The EF-X20 is sleeker and not burdensome, making it a better choice for extreme portability.

Choosing the Right Flash:
The decision between the EF-X20 and EF-X60 depends on your priorities:
- If compactness is paramount and you primarily use on-camera flash, the EF-X20 is a great choice.
- If you need more power, bounce flash flexibility, and don't mind a slightly larger size, the EF-X60 is a compelling option.

THE FUJIFILM EF-42 FLASH: A CLASSIC OPTION FOR X100 CAMERAS

This flash, while not the latest model, remains a viable option for photographers using Fujifilm X100 series cameras like the X100VI. Here's a breakdown of its key features:

Versatility and Power:
- **TTL Compatibility:** The EF-42 offers complete TTL (Through-The-Lens) metering support, ensuring accurate flash exposures for your X100VI camera. This is particularly helpful for achieving natural-looking lighting without the requirement for complex manual adjustments.
- **Tilting Flash Head:** Providing flexibility for bounce flash techniques, the EF-42's flash head can tilt upwards by 90 degrees and rotate 180 degrees left or 120 degrees right. Using bounce flash, you can diffuse the light through reflection against walls or ceilings, resulting in a more appealing and authentic glow on your subject.

User-Friendly Controls:
- **Focal Length Display:** The EF-42 features a unique focal length display that can be switched between digital

(APS-C) and 35mm film equivalent formats. This can be helpful for photographers familiar with either system.

- **Intuitive Controls:** The EF-42 is designed with user-friendly controls, making it easy to adjust flash settings and navigate its various functions.

Automatic Convenience:

- **Auto Guide Number:** The EF-42's guide number (a measure of flash power) automatically adjusts based on the mounted lens' focal length (ranging from 24mm to 42mm). This ensures proper flash output for balanced exposures.
- **Auto Zoom:** Complementing the auto guide number, the flash head automatically zooms between 24mm and 105mm to match the lens's field of view. This prevents vignetting (corner darkening) and ensures even light distribution in your images.
- **Wide Panel Option:** For wider-angle coverage (down to 20mm equivalent), the EF-42 features a built-in wide panel diffuser. This diffuser scatters the flash light for a softer and more natural look on your subject.

Manual Flash Control:

For photographers who prefer strict supervision over the flash output, the EF-42 offers comprehensive manual adjustments:

- **EV Compensation:** Fine-tune the flash exposure in 7 steps ranging from -1.5EV to +1.5EV. This feature allows for the fine-tuning of flash intensity in harmony with the surrounding light, ensuring the ideal luminosity for your photos.
- **Power Ratio Options**: Choose among seven intensity settings for the flash: maximum, half, quarter, eighth, sixteenth, thirty-second, and sixty-fourth. This granular control provides the flexibility to create a variety of

lighting effects, from dramatic highlights to subtle fill light.

Additional Features:

- **Near Infrared Assist Beam:** In low-light situations, the EF-42 automatically activates its near-infrared assist beam. This helps your camera's autofocus system lock onto your subject, ensuring you shoot sharp images even when you're in challenging lighting conditions.

Technical Specifications:

- **TTL Flash:** Yes (ensures accurate automatic flash exposure)
- **Guide Number:** 42 (ISO 100, meters/feet) - This indicates the flash's power; higher numbers enable illumination of farther subjects.
- **Angle of Coverage:** Not specified by the manufacturer, but likely covers a moderate field of view suitable for most X100 lenses.
- **Bounce Flash Angles:** As mentioned earlier, the flash head offers excellent flexibility for bounce flash techniques:
    o Tilts upwards by 90 degrees
    o Rotates 180 degrees to the left
    o Rotates 120 degrees to the right
- **Shooting Distance (Zoom Range):** Not explicitly specified, but the auto zoom function likely adjusts the flash coverage to match the mounted lens' focal length.
- **Recycling Time:** The duration required for the flash to recharge after a full-power discharge:
    o Alkaline batteries: 3.5 seconds
    o NiMH rechargeable batteries: 3.0 seconds
- **Battery Life:** The number of flashes you can expect on a single set of batteries:
    o Alkaline batteries: Approximately 220 flashes

o NiMH rechargeable batteries: Approximately 240 flashes

In Conclusion:

The Fujifilm EF-42 flash provides a harmonious equilibrium between user-friendly features and manual control options. While it might not boast the most high-tech specifications compared to newer models, it offers sufficient power, automatic features like bounce flash and autofocus assist, and a user-friendly interface. This renders it an ideal choice for photographers in search of a dependable and versatile flash to complement their X100 camera.

Compared to Newer Flashes:

The EF-42 might not offer the same high guide number or advanced features as newer flash models like the EF-X500 or EF-X60. However, it remains a well-rounded and functional flash option For photographers who give precedence to compatibility with their X100 camera and value user-friendly controls.

Finding the Right Flash:

The decision between the EF-42 and newer flashes depends on your needs:

• If you prioritize affordability, compatibility with your X100 camera, and a favorable combination of usability, the EF-42 is a suitable choice.
• If you require higher flash power, more advanced features like high-speed sync, or wireless flash capabilities, consider newer models like the EF-X500 or EF-X60.

FUJIFILM WIRELESS COMMANDER EF-W1

The Fujifilm Wireless Commander EF-W1 is an innovative breakthrough for photographers aiming to explore the full potential of off-camera flash with their Fujifilm cameras, particularly the X100VI. Let's dive into what this commander unit offers:

Radio-controlled wireless communication system:

- **Goodbye, Line of Sight Limitations:** Unlike traditional optical flash triggers that rely on direct visibility, the EF-W1 utilizes radio-controlled wireless communication. This liberates you from the constraints of line-of-sight, allowing you to position your flash units out of the camera's view, even behind obstacles.
- **Remote Flash Control:** Effortlessly trigger and control remote flash units, like the EF-X60, wirelessly from the EF-W1 commander. This opens doors for creative multi-flash setups for more dramatic and nuanced lighting effects.

Versatile Flash Control:

- **Mode Maestro:** The EF-W1 commander provides comprehensive control over your remote flash units. You can trigger them in various modes, including:
  - TTL: For automatic flash exposure control with compatible flashes.
  - Manual: For precise manual adjustments over flash power.
  - FP High-Speed Sync: To synchronize flash with high shutter speeds, ideal for overpowering sunlight or freezing motion.
- **Group Management:** Organize your remote flashes into up to four distinct groups. This permits you to assign different settings to each group, enabling more complex and creative lighting arrangements in your scene.

Enhanced Usability:

- **Bright Ambient Light Compatibility:** The radio communication system of the EF-W1 effectively bypasses limitations of bright ambient light. This

344

permits you to use flash even in sunny outdoor conditions, achieving balanced exposures or creative fill-flash effects.

- **Broadened Photographic Horizons:** The EF-W1 transcends the restrictions of on-camera flash. By enabling off-camera flash setups, you can create more sophisticated lighting, adding depth, dimension, and dramatic flair to your images.

NAS Compatibility:

The EF-W1 boasts an additional level of versatility thanks to its support for the Nissin Air System (NAS) of radio-controlled wireless communication:

- **Broadened Flash Options:** Beyond controlling Fujifilm EF-X60 flashes, the EF-W1 commander extends compatibility to various NAS-based speedlights produced by Nissin Japan Ltd. This opens doors to a wider selection of flash units you can integrate into your wireless flash setup.
- **Unified System:** If you already own Nissin NAS-compatible flashes, the EF-W1 commander seamlessly integrates them into your Fujifilm X or GFX camera system. This obviates the requirement for separate triggering systems, streamlining your workflow.

Fine-Tuning Flash Output:

The EF-W1 goes beyond basic flash triggering. It empowers you to meticulously control the flash output for precise lighting effects:

- **Granular Power Adjustments:** Whether using TTL or Manual settings, the EF-W1 enables you to adjust flash output in precise 1/3EV increments. This level of control provides exceptional precision for reaching the required degree of brightness in your image.
- **Extensive Manual Power Range:** For photographers who crave ultimate control, the Manual

mode offers an impressive power range. You can modify the flash output down to 1/256th power, enabling the creation of subtle lighting effects or dramatic shadows.

My Take:
The Fujifilm Wireless Commander EF-W1 is a comprehensive wireless flash control solution. With its NAS compatibility, meticulous power adjustments, and multi-group management capabilities, it lets you create professional-quality lighting setups that elevate your photography.

ENHANCE YOUR VIDEO & PHOTOGRAPHY WITH THE FUJIFILM TG-BT1 TRIPOD GRIP

The Fujifilm TG-BT1 Tripod Grip with Bluetooth is a versatile accessory designed to elevate your X-series camera's capabilities for both videography and photography. Here's a breakdown of its key features:

IMPROVED VIDEO STABILITY:

- **Ergonomic Grip:** The contoured design of the TG-BT1 provides a comfortable and secure hold for your camera, ideal for extended video shooting sessions. This minimizes camera shake and contributes to smoother, more professional-looking footage.
- **Angled Head:** The grip features an adjustable head that can be tilted at various angles. This permits you to comfortably frame your shots from different perspectives, whether shooting low-angle vlogs or capturing high-angle overhead scenes.
- **Tripod Conversion:** For ultimate stability, the TG-BT1 transforms into a compact tabletop tripod. This renders it perfect for static shots, group photos, or capturing long exposure images without camera shake.

WIRELESS CONVENIENCE (WITH BLUETOOTH-COMPATIBLE X-SERIES CAMERAS):

- **Remote Shutter Release:** The integrated Bluetooth connectivity removes the necessity to physically touch your camera to start and stop video recordings. This minimizes camera shake and allows for smoother recording initiation, especially useful for self-portraits or vlogging.

- **Remote Image Capture:** Beyond video control, the TG-BT1 also functions as a remote shutter release for still photography. This proves advantageous for taking group pictures that include yourself, or for reducing camera tremors in delicate low-light conditions.

- **Zoom Control (with compatible lenses):** For cameras with electronically controlled zoom lenses, the TG-BT1 allows remote zoom adjustments. This provides greater flexibility for framing your shots or creating smooth zooming effects in your videos.

OVERALL VERSATILITY:

The TG-BT1 transcends its video-centric features. Its comfortable grip and tripod functionality make it a valuable companion for photographers as well. With its compact size and portability, it's a convenient accessory to have in your camera bag for various shooting scenarios.

COMPATIBILITY:

It's significant to highlight that the full range of wireless remote-control features (remote shutter release, video recording start/stop, zoom control) might only be available with specific Bluetooth-compatible Fujifilm X-series cameras. Ensure to verify your camera's manual or specifications for confirmation.

EFFORTLESS DIRECTIONAL CONTROL:

The TG-BT1 boasts exceptional versatility in terms of positioning your camera:

- **Quick Angle Adjustment:** The grip enables seamless and effortless tilting of the camera head, ensuring you can comfortably frame your photographs from diverse standpoints. This is essential for capturing lively video sequences or crafting imaginative photographs.
- **Portrait Perfection:** Featuring 90-degree locking positions, the TG-BT1 enables you to toggle to a vertical orientation with optimal stability. Optimal for portrait imagery or capturing content for social media stories and vlogs.
- **Flexible Tilt Function:** The quick tilt function provides rapid adjustment of the camera angle, allowing you to react swiftly to changing shooting scenarios. This is beneficial for capturing fleeting moments or maintaining stable focus on moving subjects.

BUILT FOR TOUGH CONDITIONS:

The TG-BT1 is engineered to resist environmental conditions:

- **Dust and Moisture Resistant:** The overall design of the grip incorporates features that minimize dust and moisture ingress. Additionally, the cable-free operation ensures camera connector covers remain closed, further enhancing weather resistance.
- **Peace of Mind:** Whether you're shooting outdoors or in unpredictable environments, the TG-BT1's weather resistance ensures tranquility, allowing you to concentrate on capturing your creative vision.

COMFORT AND CONVENIENCE:

The TG-BT1 prioritizes both comfort and simple operation:

- **Contoured Design:** The carefully crafted grip offers exceptional stability and comfort during extended shooting sessions. This minimizes fatigue and permits you to concentrate on capturing stunning visuals.
- **Intuitive Button Layout:** The buttons on the grip are strategically placed for easy access and intuitive operation. This minimizes fumbling and permits you to control your camera functions seamlessly.

DUAL FUNCTIONALITY:
The TG-BT1 transcends its role as a grip:
- **Tripod Transformation:** The cleverly integrated legs of the grip unfold to form a compact and stable tabletop tripod. This frees up your hands for vlogging, capturing self-portraits, or shooting group photos.

Overall, the Fujifilm TG-BT1 Tripod Grip is a well-rounded accessory that can boost your X-series camera's capabilities for both videography and photography. Its versatility, user-friendly design, and weather resistance make it a valuable companion for recording breathtaking imagery in various shooting scenarios.

FUJIFILM GRIP BELT GB-001: SIMPLE YET EFFECTIVE CAMERA HOLD

The Fujifilm Grip Belt GB-001 might seem like a basic accessory, but it offers a practical solution for photographers using Fujifilm X-series cameras. Here's a breakdown of its benefits:

ENHANCED GRIP AND SECURITY
- **Padded Comfort:** The GB-001 wraps around your hand's back comfortably. This provides a more secure

strap hold on your camera, especially when shooting with one hand. This is beneficial for various situations, such as:

- o Capturing street photography on the go.
- o Shooting from awkward angles or low positions.
- o Maintaining a steady grip while using the camera's zoom lens.
- **Reduced Camera Shake:** By providing a more secure hold, the grip belt helps minimize camera shake. This has the potential to enhance image clarity, particularly in low-light conditions or when utilizing slower shutter speeds.

COMPATIBILITY

- **X-Series Focus:** The GB-001 is designed for compatibility covering a broad spectrum of Fujifilm X-series cameras. This makes it a versatile accessory for X-series users who want to improve their camera handling.
- **Grip and Battery Grip Friendly:** An additional benefit is that the grip belt can be utilized together with select camera hand grips and battery grips for compatible models. This allows for further customization and potentially even more secure handling depending on the specific grip you use.

SIMPLE AND LIGHTWEIGHT SOLUTION

The GB-001 is a straightforward and lightweight solution for improving your camera hold. It's easy to attach and detach, making it a convenient accessory to carry in your camera bag.

My Viewpoint:

Given the Fujifilm Grip Belt GB-001 might not be a high-tech accessory, it can serve a valuable purpose for photographers who want a simple and effective way to improve their grip on their X-series camera, especially for those users who value a more secure one-handed shooting experience.

FUJIFILM NP-W126S LI-ION BATTERY: POWERING YOUR X-SERIES CAMERA

This battery is a reliable and essential power source for your Fujifilm X-series camera:

- **High-Performance:** This rechargeable lithium-ion battery delivers the power you need to capture numerous imagery and recordings with one battery cycle.
- **Extended Shooting:** Whether you're shooting for hours or just want a spare battery for peace of mind, the NP-W126S ensures you don't miss a crucial shot due to a low battery.
- **Vertical Power Booster Grip Compatibility:** The NP-W126S is compatible with vertical power booster grips for your X-series camera. These grips not only provide an additional battery compartment but also enhance ergonomics for vertical shooting.
- **Improved Heat Management (for Newer Cameras):** In newer Fujifilm X-series cameras like the X100VI, the NP-W126S is engineered to operate in unison with the camera's internal systems for better heat management. This can potentially contribute to optimal camera performance.
- **Backward Compatibility:** The NP-W126S is backward compatible with older X-series cameras that use the NP-W126 battery. However, you won't see any performance enhancements in those older models.

FUJIFILM BATTERY CHARGER BC-W126S: KEEPING YOUR X-SERIES CAMERAS POWERED UP

The Fujifilm Battery Charger BC-W126S is an essential companion for any Fujifilm X-series photographer. Here's why:

- **Dedicated Battery Charger:** This mains-powered charger is specifically designed to recharge both the NP-W126 and NP-W126S lithium-ion batteries used in X-series cameras.
- **Universal Compatibility:** Whether you have the older NP-W126 battery or the newer NP-W126S, the BC-W126S charger can handle both, ensuring you have a convenient charging solution for your X-series batteries.
- **Charging Time:** The BC-W126S charger typically takes around 150 minutes to fully charge an NP-W126S battery. Although this may not be the fastest charging solution, it provides a reliable and safe way to replenish your batteries.

My Take:
The Fujifilm Battery Charger BC-W126S is a straightforward and practical accessory for X-series users. Its compatibility with both NP-W126 and NP-W126S batteries and its reasonable charging time render it a dependable option for keeping your camera batteries charged and ready to go.

Additional Considerations:
- **Travel Compatibility:** It's essential to ensure the charger is compatible with the voltage and plug standards of your destination if you plan to travel with it.

- **Third-Party Options:** While the BC-W126S is a reliable option, there might be third-party chargers available that offer faster charging times. However, it's crucial to choose reputable brands and chargers specifically designed for your battery type to avoid potential damage.

FUJIFILM LEATHER CASE LC-X100V: PREMIUM PROTECTION AND STYLE FOR YOUR X100V

The Fujifilm Leather Case LC-X100V is a luxurious and practical accessory designed specifically for the Fujifilm X100VI camera. Here's a breakdown of its key features:

Protective Elegance

- **Premium Leather Construction:** The case is crafted from high-quality leather, offering a touch of elegance and sophistication to your X100VI. This material also provides a degree of protection against scratches, bumps, and minor impacts.
- **Tailored Fit:** The case is meticulously designed to fit the X100VI camera body perfectly. This ensures a snug and secure fit, minimizing the risk of the camera moving around inside the case.

Functional Design

- **Battery and Media Access:** A key benefit of the LC-X100VI is that you can swap the battery and SD card without detaching the case entirely. This enables for fast and convenient access to these essential components without interrupting your shooting flow.
- **Quickshot Compatibility:** The case is categorized as a "Quickshot" case, indicating that you can take pictures with the camera partially exposed. This allows for rapid response whenever it's necessary to capture a fleeting moment.

Overall Value:

The Fujifilm Leather Case LC-X100V caters to photographers who appreciate both style and practicality. It offers a layer of protection for your X100VI while complementing its classic design. The ability to swap batteries and media cards without removing the case entirely adds to its functional appeal.

Camera Case Importance:

Camera cases are essential accessories for photographers. They provide vital protection for your camera equipment, especially during transport or storage. A good camera case can shield your camera from dust, scratches, bumps, and even minor impacts. This can greatly prolong the durability of your camera and safeguard your investment.

Beyond Protection:

While protection is a primary function, camera cases can also offer additional benefits:

- **Organization:** Some cases come with compartments or pockets for storing extra batteries, memory cards, or cleaning cloths. This keeps your essential camera accessories organized and readily accessible.
- **Carrying Comfort:** Many camera cases come with straps or carrying handles, making it easier and more comfortable to carry your camera around.

Recap: The Fujifilm Leather Case LC-X100V is a premium choice for X100VI owners who want to combine style with practicality. While not all camera cases boast such luxurious materials, their core function of safeguarding your valuable camera equipment remains essential for photographers at any skill stage.

FUJIFILM MIC-ST1 STEREO MICROPHONE: ENHANCING YOUR X-SERIES VIDEO AUDIO

This Microphone is a compact and convenient accessory designed to improve the audio quality of your HD videos captured with select Fujifilm X-series cameras. Here's an in-depth examination of its features:

CLEARER AUDIO FOR YOUR VIDEOS:

- **Hot Shoe Mount:** The MIC-ST1 easily attaches to your camera's hot shoe, a universal mounting point on upper side of the camera. This enables for fast and convenient microphone placement for optimal audio recording.
- **Unidirectional Stereo Recording:** The microphone captures audio in a unidirectional pattern, focusing on the sounds coming from in front of the camera. This helps to minimize unwanted background noise and enhance the clarity of the subject's voice or the primary audio source you're recording.

COMPACT AND USER-FRIENDLY DESIGN:

- **Unobtrusive Size:** The small and lightweight design of the MIC-ST1 ensures it doesn't add significant bulk or weight to your camera setup. This renders it perfect for situations where portability is a concern.
- **Locking Screw:** A locking screw secures the microphone firmly in place on the hot shoe, preventing accidental detachment during shooting.
- **Foam Windscreen:** The included windscreen helps to diminish the impact of wind noise and surrounding environmental disturbances, ensuring cleaner audio recordings outdoors or in windy conditions.
- **Simple Connectivity:** The microphone connects to your camera using a 2.5mm audio cable. An adapter

from 2.5mm to 3.5mm is also provided for wider compatibility.

In essence, the Fujifilm MIC-ST1 Stereo Microphone is a practical and affordable solution for those users who want to capture noticeably better audio quality in their HD videos.

Additional Considerations:

- **External Recorders:** For professional-grade audio or more control over audio recording, some X-series cameras might allow connection to external audio recorders via the hot shoe or the camera's dedicated microphone input.
- **Directional Microphones:** For more advanced videographers, directional microphones with tighter pickup patterns might offer even greater control over audio capture. However, the MIC-ST1 remains a good starting point for capturing improved audio quality compared to the camera's built-in microphone.

FUJIFILM RR-100 REMOTE RELEASE: CAPTURE SHARPER IMAGES WITH STABLE SHUTTER RELEASE

The Fujifilm RR-100 Remote Release is a compact and versatile accessory designed to assist you in capturing crisper photos, especially in situations where minimizing camera shake is crucial. Let's explore its key features:

COMBATING CAMERA SHAKE:

- **Wired Connection:** Unlike wireless remote releases, the RR-100 utilizes a physical cable with a 2.5mm jack that plugs directly into your camera's remote port. This wired connection eliminates potential signal reception issues and ensures a reliable connection for triggering the shutter.

- **Reduced Camera Movement:** By using a remote release, you can trigger the camera shutter without having a physical contact with the camera itself. This minimizes camera shake caused by pressing the shutter button on the camera body, which can create blurry images, especially at slower shutter speeds or when using telephoto lenses.
- **Ideal for Specific Scenarios:** The RR-100 is perfect for various photographic situations that benefit from minimizing camera shake, such as:
  - Long exposure photography (landscapes, seascapes, star trails).
  - For close-up and macro photography, where stability is paramount to prevent any detrimental camera motion.
  - For self-portraits, where it's preferable to operate the camera remotely to eliminate any potential for camera shake.

Functional Design:

- **Two-Stage Shutter Button:** The RR-100's shutter button offers a two-stage functionality:
  - Half-press to autofocus: This facilitates concentrated attention on your subject precisely before capturing the image.
  - Full-press to capture: By tapping the button all the way down, you trigger the camera shutter without any additional camera movement from your hand.
- **Locking Feature:** For long exposure photography, the shutter release button can be locked in the depressed position. This frees you from having to press the button down for extended periods, reducing the risk of unintentional camera movement.

- **Right-Angle Adapter:** The included right-angle adapter adds a bend to the connection point, providing additional strain relief on the cable and potentially offering more comfortable handling of the remote release in certain shooting scenarios.

My Take:
The Fujifilm RR-100 Remote Release is a simple yet effective tool for photographers aiming to capture sharper images by minimizing camera shake. Its wired connection, two-stage shutter button, and locking feature make it a valuable companion for long exposure photography, close-up work, and various other situations where a stable shutter release is critical.

Additional Considerations:
- **Wireless Option:** Fujifilm also offers wireless remote releases like the EF-W1 Commander, which provides more freedom of movement compared to the wired RR-100. However, wireless options might introduce potential signal reception concerns.
- **Camera Compatibility:** Ensure the RR-100 is congruent with your specific Fujifilm camera model before purchasing. Although compatible with the X100VI, it might not be so for others.

FUJIFILM SOFTWARE ECOSYSTEM

Asides its hardware, Fujifilm has various software solutions designed to work your X-series camera photography. Here's a breakdown of some key options:

OFFICIAL FUJIFILM SOFTWARE

FUJIFILM X App

This free mobile app allows you to remotely control your Fujifilm camera through Wi-Fi. You can use it for functions like:

- Live view framing and remote shutter release.
- Image transfer to your smartphone or tablet.
- Geotagging your photos.

FUJIFILM X Acquire

This free desktop software simplifies transferring pictures and videos from your X-series camera to your computer. It additionally provides fundamental capabilities for sorting and viewing images.

FUJIFILM X RAW STUDIO

This application, which may require a purchase or be available for trial, serves as a specialized platform dedicated to the manipulation of RAW image files taken with your X-series camera. It offers tools for:

- Non-destructive modification to exposure, white balance, color, and other image parameters.
- Applying Fujifilm's signature film simulations for a unique aesthetic.
- Basic image editing features like cropping and noise reduction.

THIRD-PARTY SOFTWARE OPTIONS

Capture One

This professional-grade RAW image processing software is renowned due to its outstanding visual clarity, advanced editing tools, and tethered shooting capabilities (real-time image viewing and control while connected to your camera). While not a free option, Capture One offers a powerful solution for photographers who demand the most from their RAW files.

RAW FILE CONVERTER EX enhanced by SILKYPIX technology

Another third-party option, SILKYPIX offers RAW image processing software specifically tailored for Fujifilm cameras. It provides tools for adjustments, film simulation application, and basic editing functionalities.

CHOOSING THE RIGHT SOFTWARE

The choice of software depends on your requirements and financial plan:

- **Basic Needs:** If you primarily shoot JPEGs and prefer a simple workflow, the free X Acquire software and basic editing tools in your operating system might suffice.
- **RAW Editing Enthusiast:** For photographers who shoot RAW and want more control over image processing, the Fujifilm X RAW STUDIO or third-party options like Capture One or SILKYPIX RAW converter offer an expanded selection of editing options.
- **Professional Workflow:** Professional photographers might require the advanced features and tethered shooting capabilities offered by Capture One.

Remember, the camera is just one section of the photography equation. By taking advantage of the software options available, you can unlock the capabilities of your Fujifilm X-series camera and create stunning imagery.

CHAPTER 13: KEEPING YOUR FUJIFILM X100VI RUNNING SMOOTHLY: A TROUBLESHOOTING GUIDE

Even the most amazing cameras can encounter occasional hiccups. With the aid of this troubleshooting guide, you can quickly resume taking beautiful pictures with your Fujifilm X100VI by identifying and fixing frequent problems with it. Don't hesitate to contact your local Fujifilm distributor for further assistance if you can't find the solution.

POWER AND BATTERY

1. Problem: The camera won't turn on.
Your Fujifilm X100VI is a powerful creative tool, and similar to any electronic device, it needs a little TLC to keep it running smoothly. Let's tackle the most common reason a camera might not turn on: the battery.

Possible Solutions:
- **Fresh Start:** Just like you wouldn't take a road trip on an empty tank, it's a smart move to fully charge your battery before your first shoot. The X100VI battery doesn't come pre-charged, so plug it in using the provided charger before you head out.
- **Power Up:** Even the most enthusiastic photographers can forget to check the battery gauge. If your camera struggles to turn on, pop in a freshly charged battery or your spare (photographers often carry spares for long shoots).
- **Double-Check:** Batteries can sometimes be inserted incorrectly. Check your camera's manual (it's usually downloadable online if you are unable to locate the

physical copy) for a diagram showing the correct battery orientation.

- **Secure Fit:** Make sure the battery compartment cover is firmly latched. A loose compartment can prevent the camera from making proper contact with the battery.

Photographer's Tip: Carrying a spare battery is a great habit to get into, especially for important shoots or when you'll be out for extended periods. Many external battery packs can be utilized to charge your X100VI on the go, so consider this as an option if you're a frequent traveler.

2. Problem: The monitor stays dark after turning on the camera.

- **Solution: Halfway Press:** If you turn the camera off and then on very quickly, the monitor might not have enough time to activate. Try keeping the shutter button pressed halfway down for a second or two after turning on the camera. This should give the monitor time to boot up.

3. Problem: The battery seems to drain quickly.
Modern cameras are packed with features, but those features can drain your battery. Here are some things to remember:

- **Cold Snap:** Batteries don't like extreme temperatures. If it's a cold day and your battery is draining quickly, try warming it up in a pocket close to your body before inserting it back into the camera.
- **Clean Connections:** Just like any electrical connection, dirty battery terminals can prevent a good flow of power. Use a soft, dry cloth to gently clean the metal contacts on both the battery and the camera.

Photographer's Insight: The PRE-AF setting keeps the autofocus system constantly engaged, even while the camera is partially switched off. While this can aid in quick focus in certain situations, it can also drain the battery. If you're not actively using autofocus all the time, consider turning PRE-AF off in the camera's menu.

- **Battery Life:** Like all rechargeable batteries, the capacity of your X100VI battery will diminish over time. Investing in a new battery could be necessary if you've had your old one for a while and it seems to be losing its charge more quickly. If you're looking for a replacement, consult the instructions for your camera.

4. Problem: Camera Shuts Down unexpectedly:

Nothing is more annoying than having your camera shut down unexpectedly. Here's what to do if your X100VI decides to take a power nap:

- **Power Up:** The most common culprit for a sudden shutoff is a low battery. Make sure your battery is charged or swap it out for a fresh one.

5. Problem: The camera refuses to turn off.

Sometimes, technology has a mind of its own. If your X100VI is refusing to power down, check the indicator lamp on the camera's body. It might be busy writing data to the memory card or processing an image. Give it a moment to finish its task and then try turning it off again. If the light remains stubbornly lit, consult your camera's manual for troubleshooting steps specific to that indicator.

6. Problem: The camera isn't charging when connected via USB.

Having trouble charging your X100VI via USB? Don't worry, below are some things to check:

- **Battery Check:** Make sure the battery is actually inserted into the camera. It sounds obvious, but sometimes the simplest things can be overlooked!

- **Double-Check:** Double-check that the battery is placed in the proper direction. Refer to your camera's manual for a diagram if needed.
- **Connection Confirmed:** Verify that the USB cable is securely plugged into both the camera and your computer.
- **Wake Up Call:** When your PC is in sleep mode or is turned off, the camera might not recognize the connection. Turn on or wake your computer, then disconnect and reconnect the USB cable.

7. **Problem: The battery charger isn't showing any signs of charging.**
Even the most well-maintained camera needs a reliable charger to keep it going. If you're having trouble juicing up your X100VI battery, below are some things to check:
- **Battery Check:** Make sure the battery is inserted into the charger. Although it might seem apparent, a minor oversight can be the culprit!
- **Double-Check:** Just like with the camera, ensure the battery is inserted in the correct orientation. Refer to your camera's manual for a diagram if needed.
- **Plugged In?** This might seem basic, but double-check that the charger is securely plugged into a working electrical outlet.
- **Fully Connected:** When using a plug adapter for your charger, make sure it's securely fastened to both the charger and the outlet.

8. **Problem:** The charger seems plugged in, but nothing's happening.

Solution: If you're using a plug adapter for your charger, make sure it's securely connected to both the charger and the power outlet. A loose connection could be interrupting the flow of electricity.

9. Problem: The battery seems to be taking too long to charge.

If your battery seems to be taking too long to charge, there's no need to panic. Here's a tip:

- **Room Temperature Recharge:** Extreme temperatures can affect charging speed. Try charging your battery at room temperature (ideally between 64°F and 75°F or 18°C and 24°C).

10. Problem: The indicator light blinks, but the battery doesn't charge.

Solution: Corrosion or dirt on the battery terminals can prevent a proper connection. Carefully clean both the battery terminals and the contact points in the charger with a soft, dry cloth. Sometimes, a simple cleaning can solve the problem.

11. Problem: Cleaning didn't help, and the indicator light keeps blinking.

Solution: Like all batteries, your Fujifilm X100VI's battery has a limited lifespan. If it's been through many charging cycles and continues to exhibit charging issues, it might be time to invest in a new battery.

12. Seeking Professional Help: When the Problem Persists

Solution: If you've tried cleaning and suspect a faulty battery, but the indicator light persists in blinking without charging, it's best to contact your authorized Fujifilm dealer for further assistance. They can diagnose the issue and recommend the best course of action.

13. Problem: The camera isn't showing the power supply icon when connected to a USB cable.

Solution: This could be a setting issue. Ensure "POWER SUPPLY ON/COMM OFF" is selected in the "USB POWER SUPPLY/COMM SETTING" menu. On enabling this setting, the camera prioritizes charging via USB over establishing a computer connection.

LANGUAGE BARRIER? SWITCHING TO ENGLISH

Problem: The camera menus and displays are in a language you don't understand.

Solution: No worries, it's a simple fix! Access the user settings menu:

1. Locate the "MENU" button (usually labelled). Press it.
2. Navigate through the menus till you get to the 🔧 SET UP Menu.
3. Look for the "USER SETTING" option and select it.
4. Within the "USER SETTING" menu, find the "LANG" (Language) option and select it.
5. A list of languages will appear. Choose "ENGLISH" and confirm your selection.

Voila! Your camera's menus and displays should now be in English, making navigation and setting adjustments a breeze.

SHOOTING ISSUES

Even during a perfect photo opportunity, technical glitches can happen. Here's how to diagnose and resolve some common shooting problems with your Fujifilm X100VI:

1. **Problem:** Nothing happens on pressing the shutter button. No image is captured.

Possible Solutions:

- **Memory Card Full:** The camera can't record new photos if the memory card is full. Insert a fresh memory card or delete some existing photos to free up space.
- **Card Needs Formatting:** New memory cards or cards used in other cameras might require formatting before use with your X100VI. Formatting creates a file system the camera can recognize. Consult your camera's manual for formatting instructions (usually found in the menu).
- **Dirty Connections:** Corrosion or dirt on the memory card's metal contacts can hinder communication with the camera. To guarantee an excellent connection, carefully clean the contacts with a soft, dry cloth.
- **Damaged Memory Card:** If it happens that cleaning is ineffective, the memory card may be harmed. Check to see whether the issue still persists by trying to insert another memory card.
- **Battery Blues:** A dead battery can prevent the camera from functioning. Charge your battery or swap it for a fully charged one.
- **Auto Power Off:** Your camera might have an auto power-off feature to conserve battery life. If it turns off automatically, simply turn it back on to resume shooting.

2. **Problem:** You see a grainy pattern with speckles (noise) in the monitor or viewfinder on half-pressing the shutter button.

Solution: This is most likely normal and doesn't affect the final image! When taking pictures in dimly lit areas with a narrow aperture, the camera increases gain (sensitivity) to provide a clear preview in the display. This can cause the appearance of noise, which isn't present in the actual photos you capture. Relax, take the picture, and enjoy your noise-free image!

3. **Problem:** The camera doesn't detect a face, despite the fact that you can clearly see it in the viewfinder.

Possible Solutions:
- **Hidden Features:** Sunglasses, hats, long hair, or other obstructions can confuse the camera's face detection system. Try removing or repositioning these items to give the camera a clearer view of the face.
- **Tiny Faces, Big Frustrations:** If the subject's face takes up a little portion of the frame, the camera might have trouble detecting it. Reframe your shot to bring the face closer and make it more prominent in the composition.
- **Looking Away? No Detection!** Faces facing the lens directly or partially are the main types of faces that the camera recognizes. You may not notice faces if the subject looks off to one side or none at all. For best detection, kindly advise your subject to turn slightly more toward the camera.
- **Double-Check the Settings:** Ensure "FACE/EYE DETECTION SETTING" is turned "ON" in your camera's menu. This feature might be accidentally disabled.
- **Keeping it Level:** The camera's face detection system works best when held level. Tilting the camera significantly can affect its ability to recognize faces.
- **Lighting Matters:** Poor lighting conditions can make it difficult to detect faces. If possible, try shooting in brighter environments or using additional lighting.

4. **Problem:** The camera isn't detecting any subject at all, not just faces.
- **Peek-a-Boo Subject:** If your subject is partially hidden behind objects or out of frame, the camera might

struggle to detect it. Try repositioning yourself to get a clearer view of the entire subject.

- **Tiny Subject, Big World:** When your subject occupies a very small portion of the frame, subject detection might not work as effectively. Get closer to zoom in or use your telephoto settings (if your camera has it) to make the subject more prominent.
- **Detection Deactivated?** Confirm that "SUBJECT DETECTION SETTING" is set to "ON." You may have unintentionally disabled this function.
- **Lighting Blues:** Similar to face detection, low lighting might make it more difficult to recognize subjects. Shoot in brighter conditions or use additional lighting if possible.

5. Problem: The flash doesn't fire when you take a picture, despite the fact that you intended to use it.

Possible Solutions:
- **Double-Check the Settings:** Make sure the flash isn't set to "OFF" in the menu. Depending on the shooting mode, you might have different flash options available. Consult your camera's manual for specific flash settings and adjustments.
- **Silent Shutter Surprise:** The electronic shutter allows for silent shooting, but it's often not compatible with the flash. If you need the flash, switch to a mechanical shutter setting in the menu (consult your camera's manual for specific instructions).
- **Battery Blues:** A low battery can prevent the flash from functioning properly. Ensure your battery is charged or swap it out for a fresh one.
- **Rapid Fire Not Supported:** Some flash modes might not be compatible with bracketing or continuous shooting modes. Try switching to single frame mode and see if the flash fires correctly.

- **Finding the Sweet Spot:** The flash has a limited range. If your subject is too distant, the flash might not reach them effectively. Move closer or use a flash diffuser attachment to broaden the flash's reach.
- **Making Room for the Light:** Your fingers or the camera strap might accidentally block the flash window, preventing light from reaching the subject. Hold the camera securely, making sure the flash window is unobstructed.
- **Shutter Speed Showdown:** The quickest shutter speed that can be utilized with the flash is the sync speed. If it happens that your shutter speed exceeds the sync speed, it could happen that the camera will not be able to properly fire the flash before it closes. To give the flash ample time to fill the scene with light, consider utilizing a slow shutter speed.

6. **Problem:** Your images are not sharp or clear.

Potential Remedies:
- **Cleaning Up Your Act:** Your photos may appear soft if your lens is filthy. Gently clean the front and rear lens elements with a microfiber cloth specifically designed for cleaning lenses. Avoid touching the glass using your fingers, since skin oils can cause streaks.
- **Mind Your Fingers:** Double-check to ensure your fingers or the camera strap aren't accidentally blocking the lens, which can obviously lead to blurry photos.
- **Focus Fixation:** The camera might not have achieved proper focus before you took the picture. The focus frame will usually turn green when focus is locked. If it's red, the camera is struggling to focus. To autofocus, press the shutter button halfway before fully pressing it to capture the image.

7. **Problem:** Your photos appear grainy or mottled with colored speckles (noise).

Solution: Not all noise is bad news! Sometimes, it appears when using slow shutter speeds in low-light conditions. While using editing software for post-processing, this is a common feature of digital cameras and can usually be reduced.

- **Heat and Noise:** Noise in photos might also result from using your camera a lot in hot conditions. Before continuing to shoot, turn off the camera and let it cool if you notice a temperature alert.

Pixel Perfect (Maybe):

- **Pixel Mapping:** Your camera might have a feature called "pixel mapping." This process helps lessen the look of hot pixels, which are bright spots that can appear in images due to sensor issues. Consult your camera's manual for instructions on how to perform pixel mapping (if available).

8. **Problem:** The camera displays a temperature warning.

Solution: This is a safety measure to prevent damage from overheating. Turn off the camera and find a cool, shaded spot for it to rest and cool down. Once it reaches a normal operating temperature, you can resume shooting.

Hot Camera, Don't Shoot!

PLAYBACK TROUBLES

Even during playback, you might encounter some issues with your Fujifilm X100VI. Here's how to address common problems you might face:

1. **Problem:** When you playback photos taken on a different camera, they appear grainy or low quality on your X100VI.

Solution: This is normal. Cameras compress images to save storage space. The compression algorithm used by your X100VI might not be optimized for pictures taken on another camera, resulting in a slight loss of quality during playback on your X100VI. The original photos on the other camera should still be fine.

2. **Problem:** The playback zoom function isn't available for certain images.

Solution: This might occur for photos that were resized in another camera or created on a different device altogether. The zoom function works best with original, unedited images captured by your X100VI.

3. **Problem:** You can't hear any sound during movie playback.
    - **Volume Check:** First, ensure the playback volume isn't muted or set too low. Your camera ought to have controls for volume during playback.
    - **Microphone Mishap:** The possibility exists that something is obstructing the microphone, rendering sound recording while replaying unfeasible. Verify that neither your fingers nor the camera strap are blocking the microphone openings on your camera.
    - **Speaker Snooze:** The sound may also be muffled if the speaker is blocked. When playing back, make sure the camera is held appropriately and that the speaker is not obstructed.
    - **Sound Deactivation:** Make sure that the camera is not in silent mode, as this could prevent sound from being recorded or played back.

4. Problem: You've selected pictures for deletion, but some remain after pressing "ERASE ALL FRAMES."

Solution: Some photos might be write-protected, preventing their deletion. You'll need to unprotect them using the camera or device where they were originally protected. Consult the manual for that device for specific instructions on unprotecting files.

5. Problem: After opening the battery compartment while the camera was on, you notice the file numbering has reset unexpectedly.

Solution: It's important to always turn the camera off prior to opening the battery compartment. Doing so while the camera is powered on can interrupt internal processes and cause the file numbering to reset. Moving forward, power down the camera before opening the compartment to avoid this issue.

CONNECTION CONUNDRUMS

Connecting your Fujifilm X100VI to a TV might be a fantastic method to share your photos and videos on a larger screen. But occasionally, plans don't work out. Here's how to deal with typical connectivity problems:

1. Problem: When you attempt to play back videos or images, the camera's monitor becomes black.

Possible Solutions:
- **TV Time:** If you connect your camera to a TV, the images will likely be displayed on the TV screen instead of the camera's monitor. This is a normal behavior. Disconnect the camera from the TV to see the playback on the camera's monitor.

- **Eye Sensor Activated:** Your camera might have an eye sensor that instantly transitions between the monitor and the viewfinder depending on your eye position. If "EYE SENSOR" is chosen in the "VIEW MODE SETTING" menu for playback, the monitor might turn off when you move your eye from the viewfinder. To use the monitor, put your eye closer to the viewfinder or choose a different "VIEW MODE SETTING" option, such as "MANUAL."

2. **Problem:** You've connected your camera to the TV, but there's no picture or sound.

Possible Solutions:
- **Double-Check Connections:** Ensure the HDMI cable is securely plugged into both the camera's HDMI port and the TV's HDMI input. The transmission may be interrupted by a loose connection.
- **Input Matters:** Make sure your TV's input is set to the HDMI port where the camera is connected. Choosing the accurate input channel may require using the TV remote since many TV's have multiple HDMI inputs.
- **Volume Up!:** The volume of the TV may be set too low or muted, which would be the easiest to fix. Use the TV remote to adjust the volume to an audible level.

3. **Problem:** Despite connecting your camera to the computer using a USB, your computer is not detecting it.

Solution: Several factors could be responsible:
- **Connection Check:** Initially, confirm that the USB cable is firmly inserted into the USB ports on both your computer and the camera. If you can, try using an alternative USB cable to rule out a malfunctioning one.

- **Communication Mode Mishap:** Your camera might have a setting called "CONNECTION MODE." Ensure it's set to "USB RAW CONV./BACKUP RESTORE" before connecting the USB cable. Consult your camera's manual for specific instructions on navigating the connection mode settings.

4. **Problem:** You're using FUJIFILM X Acquire software or FUJIFILM X RAW STUDIO, but it's not detecting your camera properly.

Solution: This might be related to the camera's connection mode setting mentioned above. Double-check that "CONNECTION MODE" on the camera is set to "USB RAW CONV./BACKUP RESTORE" before connecting the USB cable.

5. **Problem:** You're trying to connect your X100VI to an iPhone, iPad, or smartphone, but it's not working.

Possible Solutions:
- **Power Supply Setting:** If you're using a Lightning cable to connect to an iPhone or iPad that doesn't provide power output, make sure the camera's "USB POWER SUPPLY/COMM SETTING" is set to "POWER SUPPLY OFF/COMM ON." This setting allows for communication without relying on the mobile device for power.
- **Smartphone Compatibility:** The connection procedure for smartphones can vary based on the kind of connector it uses. Consult your camera's manual or search online for specific instructions on connecting your X100VI to your particular smartphone model.

Connecting your Fujifilm X100VI to your smartphone wirelessly allows for convenient photo transfer and sharing. Here's how to address common issues you might encounter:

1. **Problem:** You're unable to establish a wireless connection between your camera and your smartphone.

Solution: Below are some things to check:

- **Distance Matters:** Wireless connections have a limited range. Ensure your smartphone is positioned sufficiently close to the camera throughout the connection process. After bringing the devices close together, try again.
- **Radio Interference:** Wi-Fi signals can be interfered with by radio waves emitted by microwaves, cordless phones, and other wireless appliances. When you see less Wi-Fi congestion, move your smartphone and camera from such devices and reconnect.

2. **Problem:** Despite having a wireless connection between your smartphone and camera, pictures are not getting uploaded.

Possible Solutions:

- **Smartphone Sharing a Connection?** Smartphones can only connect to one device at a time. Your phone may not connect to your X100VI to transfer images if it is already connected via Bluetooth to another device, such as a camera or headphone. End any existing Bluetooth connections on your smartphone and try connecting to the camera again.
- **Too Many Cooks (or Smartphones) in the Kitchen?** If there are multiple smartphones in the vicinity, they might interfere with the connection. Try

moving to a location with fewer wireless devices and connect again.

- **Camera Compatibility:** The camera might not be able to upload photos captured on other devices. Ensure the images you're trying to transfer were originally taken with your X100VI.
- **Movie Mishap:** Uploading movies can take longer than photos due to their larger file sizes. Be patient and allow the transfer to complete. Additionally, some smartphone models might not support playback of certain movie formats. Consult your smartphone's manual for information on compatible video formats.

3. **Problem:** You've transferred photos to your smartphone, but they aren't showing up in the gallery app.

Solution: The issue might be related to the image size. Your camera helps to resize images before transferring them to your smartphone. Enabling "Resize Image For Smartphone" in the "Bluetooth/Smartphone Setting" menu can help ensure the transferred photos are a size compatible with your smartphone's gallery app. While disabling this setting allows for transferring larger, original images, it might take longer and some phones might not be able to display very large photos.

MISCELLANEOUS ISSUES

1. **Camera Unresponsive**
- **Possible Cause:** Temporary camera malfunction or low battery.
- **Solutions:**
  - Remove the battery and reinsert it.

o Charge the battery or use a fully-charged spare battery.

2. Camera Not Functioning as Expected

- **Solution:** If the above solutions for unresponsiveness don't work, remove and reinsert the battery. If the problem persists, consult your Fujifilm dealer.

3. No Sound

- **Possible Causes:** Volume is muted or sound is disabled.
- **Solutions:**
  o Adjust the camera's volume using the controls.
  o Ensure "OFF" is not selected for "SOUND & FLASH" in the camera menu.

4. Q Button Not Working (TTL Lock Active)

- **Possible Cause:** The quick menu is locked because TTL lock is active.
- **Solution:** End TTL lock using the camera's controls.

INDEX

4

4K recording 35
4K/60fps 35

6

6.2K recording 35
6.2K/30fps 35

A

Accessory 324, 331
ACROS 105, 106, 206
Action Photos 272
Adapter Ring 331
Advanced Filters 321, 322
AE BKT Setting 178
AEL (exposure lock) 25
AEL/AFL Button 61
AF Frame 169, 170
AF Illuminator 150, 151
AF Mode 81, 137
AF POINT DISPLAY 135, 148
AF Range Limiter 164, 165
AF/MF SETTING... 58, 74, 134,
    146, 275, 278, 290, 291

AF+MF 135, 156, 157, 158,
    163, 164
AF-assist illuminator 27
AF-C Custom Settings 97, 137,
    138, 140, 144, 146
AFL (focus lock) button 25
Airplane 155, 233
AIRPLANE MODE 233
Aperture 76, 88, 188, 249,
    260, 262, 263, 264, 265,
    269, 272, 292
Aperture ring 29
Aperture-Priority AE (A
    Mode) 262, 263
ASTIA/SOFT 104
Auto Image Transfer 231
Auto Power Off 367
Automatic ISO 273, 278
Average Metering 276

B

Battery.40, 41, 42, 44, 45, 46,
    122, 177, 281, 361, 363,
    364, 367, 369
Battery chamber 32
Battery Charger 352
Battery latch 31
Battery Life 46, 177, 281, 363

Battery-chamber cover......31
Battery-chamber cover latch
......................................31
Bird 155
Black and White 105, 322
Black and White Simulations
......................................105
Boost Mode 273, 281, 282
Bracketing.......178, 179, 180,
283, 284, 305, 306, 317
Brightness 60, 250, 309
Built-in Flash 201
Bulb (B) Mode...................259
Burst Mode 177, 284, 285,
287, 288, 293, 294, 295,
296, 297, 298, 299

C

Cable channel cover for DC
coupler...........................31
Camera Parts 22
Cameras...................313, 372
Capture62, 70, 112, 220, 242,
258, 287, 302, 309, 317
Capture One 317, 359, 360
CARD.................................236
Center-Weighted Metering
......................................276
CH Setting 201
Charging.......................44, 46
Clarity.......103, 120, 131, 315
Classic Chrome 104

CLASSIC CHROME 104
CLASSIC Neg 104
CLASSIC Neg. 104
Clock............................48, 51
Cloud 233, 258
Color Chrome 107
Color Chrome Effect........107
Color Chrome FX Blue......107
Color Filters 322
Color Simulations 104
Color Space..............103, 121
Color Temperature. 109, 110,
113, 114
Command Dials 65, 68, 72, 76
COMMANDER SETTING ...200
Compression 101
Connection 52, 236, 364, 373,
374, 376
Connection Conundrums. 373
Continuous. 64, 89, 137, 138,
161, 166, 284, 289, 290,
291
Continuous AF 290, 291
Control 56, 61, 66, 70, 77, 80,
81, 82, 83, 94, 97, 110,
113, 115, 118, 182, 191,
198, 221, 242, 251, 254,
256, 259, 262, 264, 266
Control Ring......................70
Controlling.........59, 280, 308
Controls.... 79, 106, 167, 272,
273
Conversion Lens Options. 189
CROP 210, 211, 212

Custom Presets 122

CUSTOM SETTING . 81, 83, 85,
   122, 123, 124, 125, 126,
   127, 129, 130, 131, 135,
   146, 291

Custom Settings .. 85, 93, 122,
   123, 124, 125, 127, 128,
   130, 131

Custom Toolkit 124

Customizable 67, 70, 188

D

D RANGE PRIORITY .. 117, 118,
   205, 305

date .. 50, 133, 218, 220, 225,
   230

Daylight 110

Default Sensitivity 279, 280

Default Setup 95

DEPTH-OF-FIELD SCALE ... 136,
   162

Design & Build 32

Diopter adjustment control
  25

DISP (display) / BACK button
  25

DISP ASPECT............227, 228

Display Modes 74

DPOF Printing...................224

Drive Modes 63, 283

DRIVE/DELETE button 25, 63,
   147, 283, 288, 300, 313,
   318, 321

Dynamic Range 64, 81, 90,
   115, 116, 117, 126, 205,
   242, 253, 284, 299, 302,
   303, 304, 305, 306, 308,
   309, 310, 311, 312, 313,
   315, 316

E

EDIT/SAVE 85, 86, 87, 123,
   124, 125, 129, 130, 131,
   247, 248

Electronic Rangefinder (ERF)
  55

Electronic Viewfinder (EVF)
  54

ERASE 130, 208, 209, 224,
   373

ETERNA/CINEMA............. 105

EV Compensation 341

EVF 27, 33, 53, 54, 55, 73, 82,
   93, 94, 327

Exploring 50, 63, 76, 171, 322

Exposure....60, 61, 62, 64, 76,
   88, 97, 126, 153, 176, 178,
   185, 245, 249, 250, 251,
   257, 264, 265, 266, 267,
   268, 271, 272, 278, 284,
   292, 302, 317, 318, 321

Exposure Compensation ...60, 76, 97

Exposure compensation dial
....23

Exposure Compensation Dial
....60

Exposure Control 337

Exposure Modes 153, 251

Exposure Setting..............334

Exposure Triangle ...249, 250, 271

External Devices..............236

External Flashes..............332

Eye 55, 57, 152, 153, 154, 197, 198, 240, 374

Eye sensor 25

Eye Sensor 55, 57, 374

F

Face/Eye 82, 89, 152, 154, 155, 156, 242, 275

Features And Specs 22

File Formats......................35

Film Simulation77, 81, 89, 90, 91, 97, 103, 106, 126, 179, 180, 206, 241

Film Simulation Bracketing
......................................179

Film Simulations .35, 36, 103, 106, 206

Filters....... 190, 220, 307, 322

Fine-Tuning60, 63, 89, 93, 94, 110, 112, 115, 187, 244, 253, 256, 265, 266

Flash 27, 28, 69, 81, 110, 185, 192, 193, 194, 195, 196, 197, 198, 200, 201, 202, 253, 268, 301, 302, 303, 333, 335, 336, 338, 340, 341, 342, 343, 344, 345

Flash Compensation/Output
.... 195

Flash Control Mode 195, 196, 197

Flash Function Setting81, 192

Flash Mode..... 193, 194, 196, 336

Flash Mode (TTL) 196

FLASH SETTING192, 193, 197, 198

Flicker Reduction 185, 186, 187

FLICKERLESS S.S. SETTING 187

Fn1 button 23, 28, 221

Fn2 button 27, 213

Focal plane mark 22

Focus ...56, 57, 58, 61, 62, 63, 66, 67, 68, 73, 76, 88, 89, 90, 96, 97, 132, 134, 136, 137, 139, 140, 143, 144, 146, 149, 153, 156, 157, 158, 160, 163, 164, 165, 166, 167, 176, 180, 182, 193, 240, 269, 274, 278, 287, 289, 370

Focus Area . 73, 136, 137, 182

Focus Check 96, 167

FOCUS CHECK ... 67, 135, 157, 159, 160, 167, 168

Focus Control ... 137, 139, 156

Focus mode selector 29

Focus Ring 165

FOCUS RING 135, 159

Focus Stick ... 57, 58, 176, 193

Focus stick (focus lever) 25

Focus Tracking .. 89, 140, 144, 146

Focus Zoom 157, 167

Formatting 43, 49, 50, 367

Frame.io ... 233, 234, 235, 236

frames per second (fps) 35, 281

Freezing 61, 254, 257

Front Command Dial 65

Fujifilm X Acquire ... 237, 359, 375

Fujifilm X RAW Studio 237, 359, 375

Fujifilm X100VI 38, 40, 41, 42, 43, 44, 45, 46, 47, 48, 50, 53, 80, 95, 99, 113, 117, 122, 124, 127, 128, 130, 131, 132, 134, 137, 140, 144, 150, 152, 154, 156, 158, 162, 164, 167, 169, 173, 175, 176, 178, 180, 183, 185, 187, 188, 189, 190, 192, 197, 198, 203, 205, 207, 212, 213, 214, 215, 216, 217, 219, 221, 222, 224, 227, 229, 233, 240, 246, 258, 260, 288, 289, 293, 307, 361, 365, 366, 371, 373, 376

Fujifilm XApp 359

Function Button.... 90, 95, 96, 101

Function Buttons ... 90, 95, 96

G

GRAIN EFFECT 106, 206

H

H/1ST CURTAIN or I/2ND CURTAIN 196

HDMI Micro connector (Type D) 30

HDR .. 64, 178, 207, 284, 299, 300, 301, 303, 306, 307, 308, 309, 310, 312, 313, 314, 315, 316, 317

HDR Photography 299

HEIF 102, 103, 207, 208, 232, 234

HEIF file format 36

High ISO NR 81, 120

High-Speed Sync..... 332, 337, 344

Hot shoe 22

Hot Shoe Mount............. 355

Hybrid optical/electronic
    viewfinder.....................33

I

IBIS.............................34, 35
Image .. 64, 81, 88, 91, 97, 99,
    100, 102, 114, 122, 124,
    125, 128, 130, 131, 187,
    188, 191, 204, 207, 213,
    214, 221, 258, 268, 301,
    303, 318, 377
Image Format 102
Image Quality 99, 100, 114,
    122, 124, 125, 127, 128,
    130, 131, 205, 253, 256,
    259, 260, 303, 305, 311
Image Rotate 213
Image Size 81, 91, 97, 99
Image Stabilization 187
In-Body Image Stabilization
   34
Indicator lamp 25
Indicator Lamp 68
Information............ 43, 54, 89
INSTANT AF SETTING 135, 161
instax 226, 227, 233
Intelligent Auto Zoom......337
INTERLOCK MF ASSIST 135,
    159
INTERLOCK SPOT AE 135, 160,
    182
IS MODE...........................187

ISO . 23, 34, 59, 62, 65, 76, 78,
    81, 83, 84, 85, 88, 96, 97,
    116, 118, 120, 126, 151,
    185, 188, 189, 206, 245,
    250, 266, 268, 269, 270,
    271, 272, 273, 278, 279,
    280, 281, 283, 292, 298,
    301, 304, 309, 311, 312,
    332, 333, 336, 342
ISO Auto Setting 97, 188, 189
i-TTL Flash Control.......... 333

J

JPEG.....86, 87, 88, 91, 92, 95,
    101, 102, 103, 204, 205,
    207, 208, 232, 234, 237,
    285, 304, 306, 307, 308,
    309, 316, 321
JPEG/HEIF 102
JPEG/TIFF................. 207, 208

L

Landscape Photography .. 307
Language 48, 50, 366
Language Barrier 366
LCD Brightness.................. 82
LCD Monitor 55
LED Light Setting...... 200, 201
Lens .. 27, 189, 193, 194, 195,
    199, 253, 324, 330, 331,
    332

Lens Flare.........................331
Lens Hood........194, 331, 332
Light......45, 59, 61, 110, 113,
    115, 151, 177, 249, 250,
    255, 257, 268, 270, 296,
    298, 299, 320, 370
Li-ion Battery NP-W126S.324
Location 191, 221
LOCK 198, 199, 200
Lock Releasing Button 335
Long Exposure NR...........120
Long Exposures256, 257, 258,
    260

M

Manual Focus.. 151, 156, 158,
    163, 166, 168
Mastering.... 79, 95, 134, 152,
    260, 265, 272
Max. Sensitivity...............280
Memory Card.. 40, 41, 42, 43,
    49, 285, 297, 367
Memory card slot 31
MENU/OK button . 25, 48, 49,
    52, 71, 87, 99, 114, 171,
    204, 229, 243, 244, 261,
    289, 290, 291, 294, 318,
    319
Menus.................71, 87, 240
Metering. 161, 180, 181, 182,
    264, 273, 274, 275, 277
MF Assist.... 89, 158, 159, 160

MIC/REMOTE RELEASE 261
Microphone... 23, 24, 30, 372
Microphone/remote release
    connector 30
Min. Shutter Speed.. 280, 281
Miscellaneous.................377
MONOCHROMATIC COLOR
    ....106, 206
Monochrome 105
Movie ..56, 64, 76, 77, 80, 82,
    83, 84, 87, 88, 97, 125,
    127, 129, 130, 131, 186,
    220, 253, 377
Movie Mode 253
Movie Optimized Control . 76,
    77, 83, 84, 88
MOVIE SETTING 76, 125, 127,
    129, 130, 131
Multi Metering 275
Multitasking.....................65
My Menu 240, 242, 243, 244,
    245, 246

N

Navigating 52, 71, 79, 84
ND filter.....................96, 190
Network.......... 229, 236, 238
Neutral density (ND) filter 33,
    258
Neutral Density Filter 190
Noise Reduction 81, 120, 126,
    185, 242

Nostalgic Neg..................104
NP-W126S battery......33, 44, 352
NP-W235 battery..............33

O

On/Off switch 23
Optical Viewfinder 53
OVF ... 33, 53, 54, 55, 79, 169, 170

P

Pairing...........................51, 52
Panoramic Photography ..318
Photobooks..............222, 224
PHOTOMETRY 275
Photos....... 60, 187, 203, 212, 213, 216, 217, 218, 223, 225, 226, 233, 267, 301, 320
Pixel Mapping ..121, 122, 371
PLAY (playback) button 25
Playback.... 52, 56, 65, 67, 74, 79, 203, 371
Playback Menu.................203
Playback Troubles 371
Portraits..........131, 136, 287
Portraiture 152
Power Supply/Comm Setting 238, 239
PRE-AF 135, 150, 362

Preset 123, 291
Presets............. 132, 290, 291
Pre-Shot Photography 172, 173
Print Orders..................... 224
Pro.....53, 58, 66, 68, 71, 101, 110, 216, 217, 244
PRO Neg. Hi 104
PRO Neg. Std 104
Program AE...... 251, 253, 254
Program Shift 253
Protect..................... 208, 212
Protectors Filters............. 330
Provia 104
PROVIA 104
Provia/Standard 104

Q

Q (quick menu) button...... 25
Q Button....80, 82, 84, 85, 86, 87, 92, 378
QUALITY SETTING 99, 114, 122, 124, 125, 127, 128, 130, 131, 253, 256, 259, 260, 305, 311
Quick Access Tool 70
Quick Adjustments 80, 273
Quick Menu 67, 80, 82, 84, 85, 87, 96, 240, 241

R

Rating System 217
RAW Conversion 203, 204, 205
RAW File Converter EX 360
RAW Files 306, 316
RAW Recording 101
RAW Shooters...................89
Reala Ace 35, 104
REALA ACE 104
Rear command dial...........25
Rear Command Dial 66, 96, 193
Record 216
Red Eye Removal :............197
RELEASE/FOCUS PRIORITY
....................136, 162, 163
Remote ... 191, 221, 229, 230, 260, 261
Remote Flash Control 344
Remote Image Capture ...347
Remote Release 260, 261
Remote Shutter Release..347
Reprogramming 89
Resize............................377
RESIZE 211, 212, 231

S

SD 41, 43, 224, 236, 353
SDHC..................................43
SDXC 43

SELECTED FRAMES .. 208, 209
Self-Timer .. 82, 173, 174, 175
Self-timer lamp 27
Sensitivity Dial............. 23, 59
SEPIA 105
Settings50, 51, 65, 71, 76, 86, 99, 114, 122, 123, 124, 125, 126, 128, 129, 130, 131, 134, 152, 163, 171, 173, 175, 179, 180, 181, 188, 195, 204, 205, 241, 246, 267, 269, 273, 283, 290, 292, 294, 301, 311, 312, 313, 368, 369
Sharing 103, 218, 376
Sharpness106, 119, 126, 298, 315
Shooting Experience.......... 77
Shooting Issues............... 366
SHOOTING SETTING 171, 175, 275, 294, 313
Shutter button 23
Shutter Speed59, 66, 76, 176, 184, 189, 190, 245, 249, 255, 256, 258, 259, 265, 272, 281, 292, 298, 301, 321, 370
Shutter Speed Dial 23, 59
Shutter-Priority AE... 254, 255
Single 55, 136, 137, 161, 166, 290
Single Point............... 55, 136
Skin Effect...................... 108
Slide Show 222

Smartphone .. 49, 51, 52, 218, 219, 229, 375, 376, 377

Smartphone Transfer 219

Speaker 31, 32, 372

Speed Tracking 140, 142, 143, 144, 145

Sports Finder Mode 171, 172, 242

Spot Metering.182, 276, 277, 278

Standard 70, 196

Stereo Microphone .355, 356

Stereo Recording 355

Still Photography..............192

Stop System 271, 272

Storage 41, 102, 287, 298

Strap eyelet 22

Subject detection 73, 369

Subject Detection Settings
..................................154

T

Tele Conversion Lens......325, 328

Through-The-Lens ..253, 333, 340

Time.. 44, 48, 50, 51, 59, 122, 129, 244, 249, 257, 258, 259, 260, 373

Time (T) Mode 258

Time Zone 48

Timelapses 175

Tone Curve 118, 126

Tool 39, 57

Touch Function Gestures... 77

TOUCH SCREEN MODE ... 136, 165, 166, 167, 168

Touchscreen ... 73, 74, 76, 79, 85, 165, 167

Transfer ... 191, 218, 220, 221

Tripod Conversion 346

Tripod Grip 346, 349

Tripod mount 31

Troubleshooting 361

TTL Auto Mode...............334

TTL Control.....................333

TTL Lock... 198, 199, 200, 378

TTL Mode 194, 195, 337

U

UHS-I 285

UHS-II 285

USB connector (Type-C) 30

USB Settings 229

USER SETTING49, 50, 51, 244, 246, 366

V

Velvia................. 92, 104, 180

Video Capabilities............. 35

Videos......................... 80, 82

View 47, 53, 63

Viewfinder 53, 54, 57, 61, 63, 96, 97, 171, 281
Viewfinder Window....25, 27, 53
Vision 302
Voice Memos 215, 216

W

White Balance. 77, 81, 84, 89, 91, 93, 97, 108, 109, 110, 111, 114, 126, 283
Wide Conversion Lens 329
Window 53
Wireless Communication 190, 221

Wireless Transfer............. 376
Workflow...... 91, 96, 97, 131, 240, 246

X

X-Trans CMOS 5 sensor 34

Z

Zone 136, 137, 140, 143, 144, 145
Zone Area 143, 144, 145
ZONE CUSTOM SETTING. 134, 137
Zoom Control 347

BIBLIOGRAPHY

FUJIFILM Corporation. (2023). *FUJIFILM GFX100 II FF230001 Owner's Manual.* Retrieved from fujifilm-dsc.com: https://fujifilm-dsc.com/en-int/manual/gfx100ii/

FUJIFILM Corporation. (2024). *FUJIFILM X100VI FF230003 Owner's Manual.* Retrieved from fujifilm-dsc.com: https://fujifilm-dsc.com/en/manual/x100vi/index.html#gsc.tab=0

Cavazzana, L. (n.d.). *FUJIFILM FILM SIMULATION MODES COMPARED (+ RECIPES & TIPS).* Retrieved from shotkit.com: https://shotkit.com/fujifilm-film-simulation-modes/

Peltier, J. (2021, March 15). *Customizing Fujifilm's Menus for Efficient Photography*. Retrieved from jmpeltier.com: https://jmpeltier.com/customizing-fujifilm-menus/

Roesch, R. (2021, April 5). *Two Fujifilm X-Trans IV Film Simulation Recipes: Kodachrome II*. Retrieved from fujixweekly.com: https://fujixweekly.com/2021/04/05/two-fujifilm-x-trans-iv-film-simulation-recipes-kodachrome-ii/

Roesch, R. (2020, November 18). *How To Add Film Simulation Recipes To Your Fujifilm Camera*. Retrieved from fujixweekly.com: https://fujixweekly.com/2020/11/18/how-to-add-film-simulation-recipes-to-your-fujifilm-camera/

Mullins, K. (2020, October 4). *My Fujifilm JPEG Settings*. Retrieved from kevinmullinsphotography.co.uk: https://www.kevinmullinsphotography.co.uk/blog/best-fujifilm-jpeg-settings

Peltier, J. (2020, March 18). *My Fujifilm Settings for Travel Photography – And Why*. Retrieved from jmpeltier.com: https://jmpeltier.com/fujifilm-settings-travel-photography/

Gallagher, W. (2024, February 2). *How to clean your new Apple Vision Pro*. Retrieved from appleinsider.com: https://appleinsider.com/inside/apple-vision-pro/tips/how-to-clean-your-new-apple-vision-pro

Cooke, A. (2024, March 6). *A Photographer's Review of the New Fujifilm X100VI*. Retrieved from fstoppers.com: https://fstoppers.com/reviews/photographers-review-new-fujifilm-x100vi-660365

FUJIFILM Corporation. (2024). *X100VI*. Retrieved from fujifilm-x.com: https://fujifilm-x.com/en-us/products/cameras/x100vi/

Made in the USA
Monee, IL
14 July 2024

61773907R00216